Praise for *Difficult Men*

"Following what the journalist Brett Martin identifies as a first burst of literary energy in the 1950s (when the medium was young) and a second in the 1980s (when the forward-thinking television executive Grant Tinker's MGM Enterprises begat the groundbreaking *Hill Street Blues*), this moment of ascendancy has become television's 'Third Golden Age.' And in *Difficult Men*, Martin maps a wonderfully smart, lively, and culturally astute survey of this recent revelation—starting with a great title that does double duty.... Martin writes with a psychological insight that enhances his nimble reporting."
—Lisa Schwartzbaum, *The New York Times Book Review*

"Martin is a thorough reporter and artful storyteller, clearly entranced with, though not deluded by, his subjects.... In between the delicious bits of insider trading, the book makes a strong ... argument for the creative process."
—*Los Angeles Times*

"[A] smart, fascinating read on the serpentine histories of some of this generation's most celebrated TV dramas."
—*San Francisco Chronicle*

"Martin offers sharp analysis of the advances in technology and storytelling that helped TV become the twenty-first century's predominant art form. But his best material comes from interviews with writers, directors, and others who dish about Weiner's egomania, Milch's battles with substance abuse, and Chase's weirdest acid trip ever."
—*Entertainment Weekly*

"Keenly observed ... offers readers a rare glimpse inside the writers' rooms."
—*Salon*

"I read *Difficult Men* with the bingelike intensity of discovering *Deadwood* on DVD—in three days, to the neglect of other responsibilities.... I've been waiting for years for someone to write an *Easy Riders, Raging Bulls* for the HBO era.... Martin does all that, with dry wit and a flair for juicy detail.... An authoritative and downright riveting account of the stories behind these shows."
—*The Huffington Post*

"Enjoyable, wildly readable."
—*The Boston Globe*

"Martin operates with an enviable fearlessness, painting warts-and-all portraits of autocratic showrunners such as David Milch (*Deadwood*), David Simon (*The Wire*), and Matthew Weiner (*Mad Men*).... Anyone interested in television should read this book, no matter how much or how little they know about the shows it chronicles."
—*Newsday*

"Martin's analysis is intelligent and his culture commentary will be of interest to fans of many of today's better-written shows." —*The Christian Science Monitor*

"This book taught me a thing or two about how a few weird executives enabled a handful of weirder writers to make shows I still can't believe were on TV. But what I found more interesting—and disturbing—is how it helped me understand why an otherwise lily-livered, civic-minded nice girl like me wants to curl up with a bunch of commandment-breaking, Constitution-trampling psychos—and that's just the cops."

> —Sarah Vowell, *New York Times* bestselling author of *Unfamiliar Fishes*, *The Wordy Shipmates*, and *Assassination Vacation*

"Aptly titled, and written with verve, humor, and constant energy, *Difficult Men* is as gripping as an episode of *The Sopranos* or *Homeland*. Any addict of the new 'golden' television (or extended narratives on premium cable) will love this book. Along the way, it is also one of the smartest books about American television ever written. So don't be surprised if that great creator, David Chase (of *The Sopranos*), comes out as a mix of Rodney Dangerfield and Hamlet."

> —David Thompson, author of *The Big Screen* and *The New Biographical Dictionary of Film*

"Brett Martin has accomplished something extraordinary: he has corralled a disparate group of flawed creative geniuses, extracted their tales of struggle and triumph, and melded those stories into a seamless narrative that reads like a nonfiction novel. With characters as rich as these, you can't help but reach the obvious conclusion—*Difficult Men* would itself make one heck of a TV series."

> —Mark Adams, *New York Times* bestselling author of *Turn Left at Machu Picchu*

"The new golden age of television drama—addictive, dark, suspenseful, complex, morally murky—finally gets the insanely readable chronicle it deserves in Brett Martin's *Difficult Men*. This group portrait of the guys who made *The Sopranos*, *Six Feet Under*, *The Wire*, *Deadwood*, *Mad Men*, and *Breaking Bad* is a deeply reported, tough-minded, revelatory account of what goes on not just in the writers' room but in the writer's head—the thousand decisions fueled by genius, ego, instinct, and anger that lead to the making of a great TV show. Here, at last, is the real story, and it's a lot more exciting than the version that gets told in Emmy acceptance speeches."

> —Mark Harris, *New York Times* bestselling author of *Pictures at a Revolution: Five Movies and the Birth of the New Hollywood*

"Sometime in the recent past the conversation changed. My friends were no longer talking about what movie they'd been to see, but what television show was their latest obsession. Brett Martin's smart and entertaining book illuminates why and how this happened—while treating fans to the inside scoop on the brilliant head cases who transformed a low-brow medium into a purveyor of art."

> —Julie Salamon, *New York Times* Bestselling author of *The Devil's Candy* and *Wendy and the Lost Boys*

ABOUT THE AUTHOR

Brett Martin is a correspondent for *GQ* and a 2012 James Beard Journalism Award winner. His work has appeared in *Vanity Fair, Gourmet, Bon Appétit, The New York Times, The New Yorker, Food & Wine,* and multiple anthologies. He is a frequent contributor to *This American Life.* He lives in New Orleans.

DIFFICULT MEN

BEHIND THE SCENES OF A CREATIVE REVOLUTION:

From *The Sopranos* and *The Wire*
to *Mad Men* and *Breaking Bad*

Brett Martin

PENGUIN BOOKS

PENGUIN BOOKS
Published by the Penguin Group
Penguin Group (USA) LLC
375 Hudson Street
New York, New York 10014

USA | Canada | UK | Ireland | Australia | New Zealand | India | South Africa | China
penguin.com
A Penguin Random House Company

First published in the United States of America by The Penguin Press,
a member of Penguin Group (USA) Inc., 2013
Published in Penguin Books 2014

Grateful acknowledgment is made for permission to reprint excerpts from the
following copyrighted works:
"The Beast in Me" by Nick Lowe. © 1994 Planget Visions Music Limited.
Used by permission of Planget Visions Music.
"I'm the Slime" words and music by Frank Zappa. © 1973 Munchkin Music.
Reprinted by permission of the Zappa Family Trust.
All rights reserved.

THE LIBRARY OF CONGRESS HAS CATALOGED THE HARDCOVER EDITION AS FOLLOWS:
Martin, Brett, date.
Difficult men : behind the scenes of a creative revolution: from The Sopranos and The wire
to Mad men and Breaking bad / Brett Martin.
pages   cm
Includes bibliographical references.
ISBN 978-1-59420-419-7 (hc.)
ISBN 978-0-14-312569-3 (pbk.)
1. Television series—United States.   2. Television broadcasting—Social aspects—United
States.   3. Television program genres—United States.   4. Television actors and actresses—
United States—Interviews.   5. Cable television—United States—History.   I. Title.
PN1992.8.S4M2655 2013
791.450973'09049—dc23   2012047001

Printed in the United States of America
1   3   5   7   9   10   8   6   4   2

DESIGNED BY AMANDA DEWEY
TIMELINES BY MGMT DESIGN

For Barry and Barbara Martin

Contents

Prologue 1

PART ONE

Previously On

One. IN THIS MALIGNED MEDIUM *21*

Two. WHICH FILMS? *34*

Three. A GREAT NOTION *47*

Four. SHOULD WE DO THIS? *CAN* WE DO THIS? *59*

PART TWO

The Beast in He

Five. DIFFICULT MEN *83*

Six. THE ARGUER *108*

Seven. THE MAGIC HUBIG'S *133*

Eight. BEING THE BOSS *154*

Nine. A BIG PIECE OF EQUIPMENT *171*

Ten. HAVE A TAKE. TRY NOT TO SUCK *191*

PART THREE

The Inheritors

Eleven. SHOOTING THE DOG *211*

Twelve. SEE YOU AT THE EMMYS *239*

Thirteen. THE HAPPIEST ROOM IN HOLLYWOOD *264*

Epilogue *278*

Acknowledgments *291*

Notes on Sources *293*

Index *297*

DIFFICULT
MEN

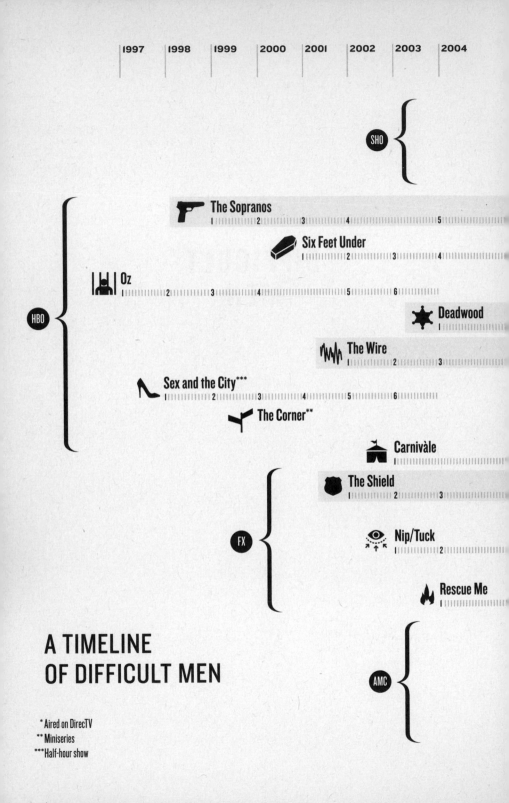

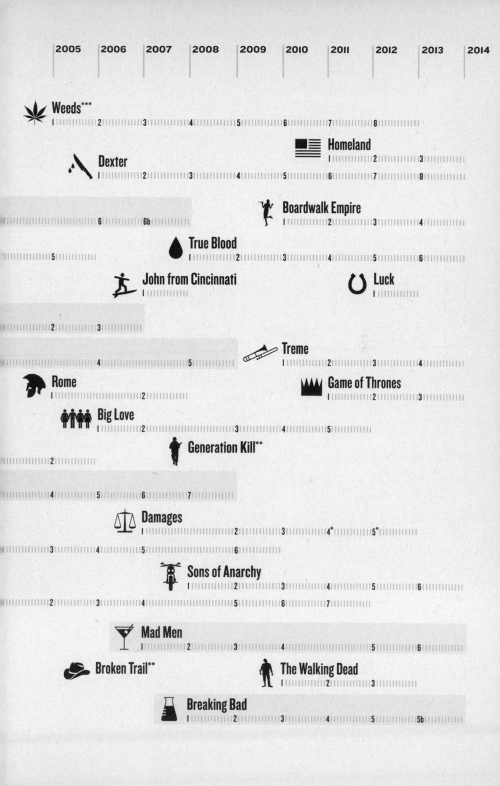

SPOILER ALERT:
IN THE FOLLOWING PAGES, I DISCUSS A GREAT MANY
PLOT POINTS OF A GREAT MANY TV SHOWS.

Prologue

You think it's easy being the boss?

TONY SOPRANO

O ne cold winter's evening in January 2002, Tony Soprano went missing and a small portion of the universe ground to a halt.

It did not come completely out of the blue. Ever since *The Sopranos* had debuted in 1999, turning Tony—anxiety-prone dad, New Jersey mobster, suburban seeker of meaning—into a millennial pop culture icon, the character's frustration, volatility, and anger had often been indistinguishable from those qualities of James Gandolfini, the actor who brought them to life. The role was a punishing one, requiring not only vast amounts of nightly memorization and long days under hot lights, but also a daily descent into Tony's psyche—at the best of times a worrisome place to dwell; at the worst, ugly, violent, and sociopathic.

Some actors—notably Edie Falco, who played Tony's wife, Carmela Soprano—are capable of plumbing such depths without getting in over their heads. Blessed with a near photographic memory, Falco could show up for work, memorize her lines, play the most emotionally devastating of scenes, and then return happily to her trailer to join her regular companion, Marley, a gentle yellow Lab mix.

Not so Gandolfini, for whom playing Tony Soprano would always require to some extent *being* Tony Soprano. Crew members grew accustomed to hearing grunts and curses coming from his trailer as he worked up to the emotional pitch of a scene by, say, destroying a boom box radio. An intelligent and intuitive actor, Gandolfini understood this dynamic and sometimes used it to his advantage; the heavy bathrobe that became Tony's signature, transforming him into a kind of domesticated bear, was murder under the lights in midsummer, but Gandolfini insisted on wearing it between takes. Other times, though, simulated misery became indistinguishable from the real thing—on set and off. In papers related to a divorce filing at the end of 2002, Gandolfini's wife described increasingly serious issues with drugs and alcohol, as well as arguments during which the actor would repeatedly punch himself in the face out of frustration. To anybody who had witnessed the actor's self-directed rage as he struggled to remember lines in front of the camera—he would berate himself in disgust, curse, smack the back of his own head—it was a plausible scenario.

It did not help that the naturally shy Gandolfini was suddenly one of the most recognizable men in America—especially in New York and New Jersey, where the show filmed and where the sight of him walking down the street with, say, a cigar was guaranteed to seed confusion in those already inclined to shout the names of fictional characters at real human beings. Unlike Falco, who could slip off Carmela's French-tipped nails, throw on a baseball cap, and disappear in a crowd, Gandolfini—six feet tall, upward of 250 pounds—had no place to hide.

All of which had long since taken its toll by the winter of 2002. Gandolfini's sudden refusals to work had become a semiregular occurrence. His fits were passive-aggressive: he would claim to be sick, refuse to leave his TriBeCa apartment, or simply not show up. The next day, inevitably, he would feel so wretched about his behavior and the massive logistic disruptions it had caused—akin to turning an aircraft carrier on a dime—that he would treat cast and crew to extravagant gifts. "All of a sudden there'd be a sushi chef at lunch," one crew member remembered. "Or we'd all get massages." It had come to be understood by all involved as part of the price of doing business, the trade-off for getting the remarkably intense, fully inhabited Tony Soprano that Gandolfini offered.

So when the actor failed to show up for a six p.m. call at Westchester County Airport to shoot the final appearance of the character Furio Giunta, a night shoot involving a helicopter, few panicked. "It was an annoyance, but it wasn't cause for concern," said Terence Winter, the writer-producer on set that night. "You know, 'It's just money.' I mean, it was *a ton* of money—we shut down a fucking airport. Nobody was particularly sad to go home at nine thirty on a Friday night."

Over the next twelve hours, it would become clear that this time was different. This time, Gandolfini was just *gone*.

The operation that came to a halt that evening was a massive one. *The Sopranos* had spread out to occupy most of two floors of Silvercup Studios, a steel-and-brick onetime bread factory at the foot of the Queensboro Bridge in Long Island City, Queens. Downstairs, the production filmed on four of Silvercup's huge stages, including the ominously named Stage X, on which sat an endlessly reconfigurable, almost life-size model of the Soprano family's New Jersey McMansion. The famous view of the family's backyard—brick patio and swimming pool, practically synonymous with suburban ennui—lay rolled up on an enormous translucent polyurethane curtain that could be wheeled behind the ersatz kitchen windows and backlit when needed.

A small army, in excess of two hundred people, was employed in fabricating such details, which added up to as rich and fleshed out a universe as had ever existed on TV: carpenters, electricians, painters, seamstresses, drivers, accountants, cameramen, location scouts, caterers, writers, makeup artists, audio engineers, prop masters, set dressers, scenic designers, production assistants of every stripe. Out in Los Angeles, a whole other team of postproduction crew—editors, mixers, color correctionists, music supervisors—was stationed. Dailies were shuttled back and forth between the coasts under a fake company name—Big Box Productions—to foil spies anxious to spoil feverishly anticipated plot points. What had started three years earlier as an oddball, what-do-we-have-to-lose experiment for a network still best known for rerunning Hollywood movies had become a huge bureaucratic institution.

More than that, to be at Silvercup at that moment was to stand at the center of a television revolution. Although the change had its roots in a wave of quality network TV begun two decades before, it had started in earnest five years earlier, when the pay subscription network HBO began turning its attention to producing original, hour-long dramas. By the start of 2002, with Gandolfini at large, the medium had been transformed.

Soon the dial would begin to fill with Tony Sopranos. Within three months, a bald, stocky, flawed, but charismatic boss—this time of a band of rogue cops instead of mafiosi—would make his first appearance, on FX's *The Shield*. Mere months after that, on *The Wire*, viewers would be introduced to a collection of Baltimore citizens that included an alcoholic, narcissistic police officer, a ruthless drug lord, and a gay, homicidal stickup boy. HBO had already followed the success of *The Sopranos* with *Six Feet Under*, a series about a family-run funeral home filled with characters that were perhaps less sociopathic than these other cable denizens but could be equally unlikable. In the wings lurked such creatures as *Deadwood*'s Al Swearengen, as cretinous a character as would ever appear on television, much less in the role of protagonist, and *Rescue Me*'s Tommy Gavin, an alcoholic, self-destructive firefighter grappling poorly with the ghosts of 9/11. Andrew Schneider, who wrote for *The Sopranos* in its final season, had cut his teeth writing for TV's version of *The Incredible Hulk*, in which each episode, by rule, featured at least two instances of mild-mannered, regretful David Banner "hulking out" and morphing into a giant, senseless green id. This would turn out to be good preparation for writing a serialized cable drama twenty years later.

These were characters whom, conventional wisdom had once insisted, Americans would never allow into their living rooms: unhappy, morally compromised, complicated, deeply human. They played a seductive game with the viewer, daring them to emotionally invest in, even root for, even love, a gamut of criminals whose offenses would come to include everything from adultery and polygamy (*Mad Men* and *Big Love*) to vampirism and serial murder (*True*

Blood and *Dexter*). From the time Tony Soprano waded into his pool to welcome his flock of wayward ducks, it had been clear that viewers were willing to be seduced.

They were so, in part, because these were also men in recognizable struggle. They belonged to a species you might call Man Beset or Man Harried—badgered and bothered and thwarted by the modern world. If there was a signature prop of the era, it was the cell phone, always ringing, rarely at an opportune time and even more rarely with good news. Tony Soprano's jaunty ring tone still provokes a visceral response in anyone who watched the show. When the period prohibited the literal use of cell phone technology, you could see it nonetheless—in the German butler trailing an old-fashioned phone after the gangster boss in *Boardwalk Empire*, or in the poor lackeys charged with delivering news to Al Swearengen, these unfortunate human proxies often bearing the consequences of the same violent wishes Tony seemed to direct to his ever-bleating phone.

Female characters, too, although most often relegated to supporting roles, were beneficiaries of the new rules of TV: suddenly allowed lives beyond merely being either obstacles or facilitators to the male hero's progress. Instead, they were free to be venal, ruthless, misguided, and sometimes even heroic human beings in their own right—the housewife weighing her creature comforts against the crimes she knows her husband commits to provide them, in *The Sopranos* and *Breaking Bad*; the prostitute insisting on her dignity by becoming a pimp herself, in *Deadwood*; the secretary from Bay Ridge battling her way through the testosterone-fueled battlefield of advertising in the 1960s, in *Mad Men*.

In keeping with their protagonists, this new generation of shows would feature stories far more ambiguous and complicated than anything that television, always concerned with pleasing the widest possible audience and group of advertisers, had ever seen. They would be narratively ruthless: brooking no quarter for which might be the audience's favorite characters, offering little in the way of catharsis or the easy resolution in which television had traditionally traded.

It would no longer be safe to assume that everything on your favorite television show would turn out all right—or even that the worst wouldn't happen. The sudden death of regular characters, once unthinkable, became such a trope that it launched a kind of morbid parlor game, speculating on who would be next to go. I remember watching, sometime toward the end of the decade, an episode of *Dexter*—a show that took the antihero principle to an all but absurd length by featuring a serial killer as its protagonist—in which a poor victim had been strapped to a gurney, sedated, and ritually amputated limb by limb. The thing a viewer feared most, the image that could make one's stomach crawl up his or her rib cage, was that the victim would wake up, realize his plight, and start screaming. Ten years earlier, I would have felt protected from such a sight by the rules and conventions of television; it simply would not happen, because it *could not* happen. It was a sickening, utterly thrilling sensation to realize that there was no longer any such protection.

N ot only were these new kinds of stories, they were being told with a new kind of formal structure. That cable shows had shorter seasons than those on traditional network television—twelve or thirteen episodes compared with twenty-two—was only the beginning, though by no means unimportant. Thirteen episodes meant more time and care devoted to the writing of each. It meant tighter, more focused serial stories. It meant less financial risk on the part of the network, which translated to more creative risk on-screen.

The result was a storytelling architecture you could picture as a colonnade—each episode a brick with its own solid, satisfying shape, but also part of a season-long arc that, in turn, would stand linked to other seasons to form a coherent, freestanding work of art. (The traditional networks, meanwhile, were rediscovering their love of the exact opposite—procedural franchises such as *CSI* and *Law & Order,* which featured stand-alone episodes that could be easily rearranged and sold into syndication.) The new structure allowed huge creative freedom: to develop characters over long stretches of time, to tell stories over the course of fifty hours or more, the equivalent of countless movies.

Indeed, TV has always been reflexively compared with film, but this form of ongoing, open-ended storytelling was, as an oft-used comparison had it, closer to another explosion of high art in a vulgar pop medium: the Victorian serialized novel. That revolution also had been facilitated by upheavals in how stories were created, produced, distributed, and consumed: higher literacy, cheaper printing methods, the rise of a consumer class. Like the new TV, the best of the serials—by Dickens, Trollope, George Eliot—created suspense through expansive characterization rather than mere cliff-hangers. And like it, too, the new literary form invested in the writer both enormous power (since he or she alone could deliver the coal to keep the narrative train running) and enormous pressure: "In writing, or rather publishing periodically, the author has no time to be idle; he must always be lively, pathetic, amusing, or instructive; his pen must never flag—his imagination never tire," wrote one contemporary critic in the London *Morning Herald*. Or as Dickens put it, in journals and letters to friends: "I MUST write!"

The result, according to one scholar writing of Dickens's *The Pickwick Papers*, the first hugely successful serial, certainly sounds familiar: "At a single stroke . . . something permanent and novel-like was created out of something ephemeral and episodic." Moreover, like the Victorian serialists, the creators of this new television found that the inherent features of their form—a vast canvas, intertwining story lines, twists and turns and backtracks in characters' progress—happened to be singularly equipped not only to fulfill commercial demands, but also to address the big issues of a decadent empire: violence, sexuality, addiction, family, class. These issues became the defining tropes of cable drama. And just like the Victorian writers, TV's auteurs embraced the irony of critiquing a society overwhelmed by industrial consumerism by using precisely that society's most industrialized, consumerist media invention. In many ways, this was TV *about* what TV had wrought.

Certainly this was the view of the only man on the fourth floor of Silvercup Studios more crucial to *The Sopranos'* success than its missing star. For all of the show's accomplishments, its creator and executive producer,

David Chase, was at best ambivalent about his career in television, at worst as tormented as Gandolfini. Chase had grown up worshipping Film with a capital "F." His heroes were the auteurs of the European New Wave and the 1970s American filmmakers inspired by them. These men were mavericks, artists who sacrificed the easy path to realize their vision on-screen. Television was for sellouts and hacks.

Yet any of the directors Chase idolized would have killed for a fraction of the godlike powers over an ever-expanding universe that he exercised from his office overlooking the Queensboro's off-ramp. Every decision—from story direction to casting to the color of seemingly insignificant characters' shirts—passed through that office. In the halls of Silvercup, his name and its power were so often invoked, usually in whispers, that he came to seem like an unseen, all-knowing deity.

This, too, was part and parcel of the wave washing over television: the ascendancy of the all-powerful writer-showrunner. It had long been a truism that "in TV, the writer is king," accustomed to power and influence unheard of in the director-dominated film industry. Now, that power would be wedded to the creative freedom that the new rules of TV afforded. And the men who seized that role—again, they were almost all men: Chase, David Simon, Alan Ball, David Milch, Shawn Ryan and, later, Matthew Weiner, Vince Gilligan, and others—would prove to be characters almost as vivid as the fictional men anchoring their shows.

It was not an especially heroic-looking bunch—not a barrel-chested Balzac or Mailer-like wrestler of words among them. Generally speaking, they conformed to the unwritten television rule that the more power you have, the more aggressively terribly you dress. A similar working-class ethic—part affectation, part genuine (it is, after all, a business dominated by teamsters)—combined with a fatalistic sense of any show's provisional life span, prevailed in showrunners' offices. Some of the most powerful men in television worked in digs that would draw a labor grievance from assistant editors at lesser Condé Nast magazines.

And being writers, they were not necessarily men to whom you would have automatically thought it prudent to hand near total control of a multimillion-dollar corporate operation. Indeed, this story is in many respects one of writers asked to act in very unwriterly ways: to become collaborators, managers, businessmen, celebrities in their own right, all in exchange for the opportunity to take advantage of a unique historical moment.

If that occasionally led to behavior that was imperious, idiosyncratic, domineering, or just plain strange, it could perhaps be understood. "The thing you've got to remember is there's a lot of pressure to deal with when you're running one of these shows," said Henry Bromell, a longtime TV writer and sometime showrunner himself. "You'd probably be better off with a Harvard jock CEO-type guy. But that's not what you got. You got writers. So they react to pressure the way most people do; they internalize it or they subvert it. They lash out."

Or as another television veteran put it, "This isn't like publishing some lunatic's novel or letting him direct a movie. This is handing a lunatic a division of General Motors."

What all the showrunners shared—and shared with the directors whom Chase held in such esteem—was the seemingly limitless ambition of men given the chance to make art in a once vilified commercial medium. And since the Hollywood film industry had long been in a competitive deep-sea dive toward the lowest common denominator, chumming the multiplexes with overblown action "events" and Oscar-hopeful trash, Alan Ball, the showrunner of *Six Feet Under*, was entirely justified in his response to hearing Chase's stubborn assertion that he should have spent *The Sopranos* years making films.

"Really?" said Ball. "Go ask him, '*Which* films?'"

W hat all this added up to was a new Golden Age—by most counts the third in television's short lifetime, the first being the flowering of creation during the earliest days of the medium, the second a brief period of unusual network excellence during the 1980s. This isn't bad for a medium with a reputation somewhere beneath comic strips and just above religious pamphlets.

It might be more precise to call it "the First Wave of the Third Golden

Age," since whether the age is indeed over remains an open question. At the time of this publication, two of the six or seven major shows on which it focuses were still in production; all the major players were still actively working. Several of the conditions that sparked the revolution—primarily a proliferation of channels (both broadcast and Internet), all with a fierce hunger for content—were still in place. At the same time, there can be no replicating the creative fecundity that comes with a genuine business and technological upheaval—from people not knowing what the hell to do and thus being willing to try anything. That is what distinguished the generation of cable drama that lasted roughly from 1999 through 2013.

I was able to enjoy most of the Third Golden Age as a lay viewer. I have never been a television critic or someone inclined toward rabid fandom. I remember taking a VHS advance copy of *The Sopranos* out of the free bin at the magazine where I was working in the late 1990s. I watched about half before dismissing it as a carbon copy of a Harold Ramis film being advertised at the same time: *Analyze This*, starring Robert De Niro and Billy Crystal as a mobster and his shrink. In retrospect, the knee-jerk comparison (in favor of *Analyze This*) was based solely on the fact that one was a film and the other merely TV.

Then, in 2007, I was hired by HBO to write an official behind-the-scenes companion to *The Sopranos*, then preparing for the second half of its final season. By that point, I'd long since recanted and become a fan of the show, which, with or without my endorsement, had been accepted by the outside world as a canonical accomplishment in the history of television. A representative from the Smithsonian Institution visited the set one day when I was there, to discuss which iconic props they might seize after the final wrap.

I hung around—on set, around the makeup trailers, in meetings—chatting with everyone from actors to parking supervisors. (A singular exception was Gandolfini, who did not acknowledge my presence for weeks and sat for a half-hour interview only on my very last day in the building.) I found myself entranced by the world into which I'd parachuted. It was, first of all, exciting to suddenly be at the white-hot center of the pop culture universe, to have intoxicating access to rooms into which the rest of the world feverishly wanted to peer.

More than that fascinated me, though: I have spent my working life in magazines—a place, like television, in which the demands of art and commerce are in constant, sometimes tense, negotiation. In that wider war, this was a battlefield on which art had seized the upper hand. After eight years, there was plenty of fatigue among the show's staff and crew, along with the complaining you'd find in any huge organization, but there was also a universal understanding that everyone from writers to set designers to sound editors was being allowed to do perhaps the best work of their professional lives. The satisfaction was palpable and heightened only by a truth that *Breaking Bad* showrunner Vince Gilligan later confirmed for me: "The worst TV show you've ever seen was miserably hard to make." It was entirely possible, even likely, to have a long, highly successful career in television without ever working on a show one felt truly proud of; here, at least for a brief time, the product was undeniably worthy of the talent and effort.

I left the world of *The Sopranos* convinced that something new and important was going on. The feeling deepened as I continued to watch David Simon's *The Wire*, HBO's other masterpiece, and a new show from one of the writers of *The Sopranos*, Matthew Weiner's *Mad Men*. The ambition and achievement of these shows went beyond the simple notion of "television getting good." The open-ended, twelve- or thirteen-episode serialized drama was maturing into its own, distinct art form. What's more, it had become the signature American art form of the first decade of the twenty-first century, the equivalent of what the films of Scorsese, Altman, Coppola, and others had been to the 1970s or the novels of Updike, Roth, and Mailer had been to the 1960s. This is a book about how and why it happened.

A ttempting to keep up with the flow of great and good programs to come out of the Third Golden Age often felt like trying to get one's arms around a rushing torrent of water. For the purposes of this book, I needed to set parameters: The shows on which I concentrate are all an hour long and appear in short seasons of between ten and thirteen episodes. All are categorized as "dramatic" (though I can't think of any that don't incorporate a strong dose of humor). All appear on cable, as opposed to traditional network TV.

More subtly, all employ an open-ended, ongoing mode of storytelling that distinguishes them from either of their closest precedents: the largely episodic "quality" network dramas of the 1980s and early 1990s (*Hill Street Blues, thirtysomething, St. Elsewhere*, and so on) and the closed-ended high-production-value miniseries of the BBC.

These rules eliminate, at least from a starring role, not only a handful of noteworthy network shows of the same period (*Friday Night Lights* foremost among them), but also several fine cable shows that are very much the product of the TV revolution but are essentially structured as season-long mysteries that are solved, or at least put temporarily to bed, at the end of each cycle, rather than remaining deliriously, riskily unresolved. I'm thinking in particular of the early seasons of *Dexter* and of *Damages*, shows I'm sad not to spend more time on.

It also more or less segregates a parallel generation of half-hour-long comedies that did nearly as much to define the era and the networks on which they appeared. At least one of these, *Sex and the City*, helped to pave the way for the revolution by establishing HBO as a destination for distinctive original programming. Many would, like their dramatic counterparts, push the definition of what had previously been thought possible on the medium— even if those boundaries had, by the nature of comedy, been easier to push. (*Married . . . with Children*'s Al Bundy pioneered awful fathering on network TV long before Tony Soprano made it a staple of cable.) These shows—*Curb Your Enthusiasm, It's Always Sunny in Philadelphia*, and *Louie*, to name a few— shared many of the themes of the dramas, including that of the deeply flawed, usually male protagonist; but on the whole, they did not partake of the formal innovations of the dramas on which I focus. Moreover, comedy was the one area in which the traditional networks actually kept some sort of pace with cable, albeit sometimes seemingly against their will, with smart, multilayered, and provocative shows like *The Office, Arrested Development, Community*, and *30 Rock*.

Another kind of half-hour program emerged during this time, and that was the cable show (not necessarily a sitcom) that centered on women rather than men. It was comic itself, this chauvinism of the clock: a male suburbanite turned drug dealer was worth sixty minutes (*Breaking Bad*), while his female counterpart (*Weeds*) warranted thirty. Only with the advent of *Damages* did a female-centric show break through this new glass ceiling.

This is only one reason for a plain fact: Though a handful of women play hugely influential roles in this narrative—as writers, actors, producers, and executives—there aren't enough of them. Not only were the most important shows of the era run by men, they were also largely *about* manhood—in particular the contours of male power and the infinite varieties of male combat.

Why that was had something to do with a cultural landscape still awash in postfeminist dislocation and confusion about exactly what being a man meant. It may also have had something to do with the swaggering zeitgeist of the decade. Under George W. Bush, matters of politics had a way of becoming referenda on the nation's masculinity: were we a nation of men (decisive, single-minded, unafraid to use force and to dominate) or girls (deliberative, empathetic, given to compromise)?

Or the answer could be much simpler. Peter Liguori—the executive who developed the first wave of FX programming and, later, *House M.D.*, a Fox network show that mimicked the kinds of heroes suddenly successful on cable— was candid enough to look inward. He had turned forty in 2000. "At one point," he said, "I was looking at the body of shows I was associated with and I realized, 'Oh, my God, Vic Mackey: forty-year-old guy, flawed. Screwed up. The two guys from *Nip/Tuck*, same descriptor. *Rescue Me*, same thing. Dr. House, same thing.' It was like I was looking at Sybil."

In other words, middle-aged men predominated because middle-aged men had the power to create them. And certainly the autocratic power of the showrunner-auteur scratches a peculiarly masculine itch. The auteur theory, Pauline Kael wrote in one of her attacks on that orthodoxy, "is an attempt by adult males to justify staying inside the small range of experience of their boyhood and adolescence—that period when masculinity looked so great and important..."

Or as Barbara Hall, herself a showrunner, said of her male counterparts: "Big money, big toys, and a kind of warfare. What's not to like?"

Truthfully, I'd hoped to avoid the cliché "Golden Age," redolent as it is of fusty "Greatest Generation" nostalgia for the playhouse dramas and vaudeville comedies that dominated the medium's earliest years. (There was plenty of garbage on television in 1950 and would undoubtedly have been much more had there been twenty-four hours and five hundred channels to fill.) However, no other term adequately expresses the sense of bounty, the constant, pleasurable surprise, that being a TV watcher during this period entailed. The shows came one after the other, with startlingly consistent quality: first HBO's astonishing run, with *Oz, The Sopranos, Six Feet Under, The Wire*, and *Deadwood*; and then the migration to other pay channels and basic cable, with *The Shield, Rescue Me, Damages, Dexter, Mad Men, Breaking Bad*, and more. Even if not all of these were to your liking, none could be dismissed as anything but new and challenging in the television universe. Sunday night, when the majority aired, became something akin to a national, communal holiday.

And the revolution in what we watched was inseparable from a revolution in *how* we watched. DVDs were barely in use when *The Sopranos* debuted. By the time it ended, not only had DVDs represented a significant extra revenue stream for HBO, but—along with TiVo and other digital video recorders, online streaming, on-demand cable, Netflix, file sharing, YouTube, Hulu, and more—they had introduced a new mode of television viewing. Now you could watch an entire series in two or three multihour, compulsive orgies of consumption—marathon sessions during which you might try to break away, only to have the opening credits work their Pavlovian magic, driving you forward into yet another hour. Or for those who resisted the binge method and watched in real time, there was its opposite: the unusual sensation of actual suspense, delayed pleasure, in a world of instant gratification.

About those credits—or, to use the industry term that better hints at their epic quality, those "main titles": These were no minimalist flashes of music and graphics. (Think *Seinfeld*'s rippling bass line.) Nor were they the melancholic credit sequences of the 1970s and 1980s (*Taxi, The Rockford Files, WKRP in Cincinnati, Welcome Back, Kotter*) that promised more depth than their shows ever delivered. They were expansive little movies in their own right, guides to the vocabulary and palette of the show to come.

Here, as in so much else, *The Sopranos* set the template. Arriving in an era of *Friends* frolicking dumbly in a fountain, it began with a characteristic David Chase joke—Good news: There's a light at the end of the tunnel. Bad news: It's New Jersey!—and went on to present, in Tony's drive home, nothing less than a minute-and-a-half-long representation of Italian American progress in New Jersey: from the working-class apartments of Newark's old North Ward, up Bloomfield Avenue into starter homes in the Oranges, Glen Ridge, Verona, and finally to the Promised Land of the Caldwells. By the time Tony crankily slammed the car door in his driveway, it was clear that he was not a character who would be there for you when the rain started to fall, or any other time, for that matter.

As for the TVs themselves, perhaps every new generation of televisual technology sounds like science fiction when it's introduced, but, good God: liquid crystals, 3D plasma, Blu-ray. This is the stuff of dreams. The sets themselves became objects of beauty, downright sensual delights to watch. And TV's directors and cinematographers, suddenly freed from the restrictions imposed by the old grainy square box—establishing shot, close-up, close-up, establishing shot, close-up, close-up, camera always on whoever was speaking, everything flooded with light—seized on the possibilities. Now they could work with shadows and darkness; hypnotic depth of field; beautiful, endless wide shots; handheld pyrotechnics—the entire toolbox once seen only on the big screen. While shooting the pilot of *Breaking Bad* in Albuquerque, New Mexico, cinematographer John Toll gave a bewildered local Circuit City employee an outraged lecture on the correct picture settings for the flat-screens in his showroom. "Do you realize how long I spend lighting these things?" he said. The "small screen" had gone big, only without the indignities of modern moviegoing: extortionary prices, cell-phone-chatting strangers, and, in an ironic switch, relentless advertisements.

All of this conspired to create a remarkable new intimacy between show and viewer. Even the most inveterate gorger on season-long blocks of a show might find him- or herself slowing down as the number of remaining episodes dwindled, hesitant to say good-bye, a victim of something very much like separation anxiety. After all, by that point he would have spent at least as much sustained time with those fictional characters as with his own friends or family.

With the simultaneous rise of the Internet, a new breed of fan-cum-critic was born. Once, a TV critic might review the pilot episode of a new series and then never revisit it. Now, just as TV evolved into a true serial form—making it necessary to watch an entire season, or even multiple seasons, before assessing the work as a whole—it became paradoxically common to review each and every episode as soon as it aired or even, via live blogging and live tweeting, in real time. It became common to watch TV with a so-called second screen, a smartphone or tablet, open and at the ready. Deep into the night and the wee hours of Monday morning, the keyboards would click, turning out heroic rafts of prose, parsing each nuance, pouncing on each inconsistency, speculating on what might come next. After one episode of the FX comedy *Louie*, one fan-critic tellingly tweeted: "Let's have a sleepover right now only instead of going to each other's houses we just sit here and tweetconverse about #Louie till sunrise."

The most diehard, or smitten, took to the strange practice of "recapping"—which became the dominant way of talking about these shows on the Internet. Recaps were precise, moment-by-moment retellings of an episode just aired. They may have been an opportunity for editorializing and snarkiness, but they also smacked of ritual reenactment—not unlike a young writer fastidiously typing out a favorite short story, word for word, in an attempt to commune with its author.

Through all this, an unusual bond was formed, not only between viewer and show, but between viewer and *network*. A new drama on HBO or AMC was deemed all but automatically worthy of the recap treatment and of hopeful goodwill—a level of brand loyalty and affection never granted, say, CBS or Paramount Pictures.

If it had once been axiomatic that audiences might tolerate difficult characters at the safe remove of the movie theater, but not in their own bedrooms, it turned out that the result was nothing less than a kind of overwhelming, seismic love. Is it any wonder James Gandolfini might have felt just the tiniest bit of pressure?

U nderstandable or not, Gandolfini's absence was becoming increasingly worrisome at Silvercup. The production team had already performed all the acrobatics it could—switching the schedule around to shoot those few scenes that could be done without its star. The whole operation had been nervously treading water for days; many began to expect the worst. Terence Winter, driving into work, heard a newscaster report, "Sad news from Hollywood today . . . ," and his heart stopped. "It was some drummer for a band," Winter said. "But I thought, 'Holy shit! He's dead.'" Sooner or later, the press, hungry for *The Sopranos* gossip at the best of times, would get hold of the story, and the upper echelon of producers at Silvercup and at HBO began to prepare a damage control strategy.

Then, on day four, the main number in the show's production office rang. It was Gandolfini calling, from a beauty salon in Brooklyn. To the surprise of the owner, the actor had wandered in off the street, with no money and no identification, asking to use the phone. He called the only number he could remember, and he asked the production assistant who answered to put someone on who could send a car to take him home.

The Sopranos would go on. And so would the world it had created.

PART I

Previously On

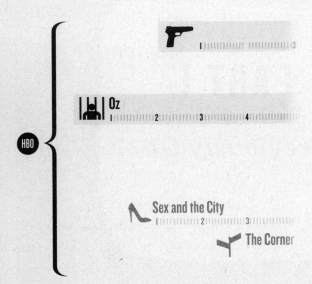

HBO

1 |||||||||||||| |||||||||||||| 3

Oz
1 ||||||||||||| 2 ||||||||||| 3 ||||||||||| 4 |||||||||||||

Sex and the City
1 |||||||||||||| 2 |||||||||| 3 |||||||||||

The Corner

1996-2001

One

In This Maligned Medium

In the beginning, there was the Vast Wasteland. And it was bad.

Already this is easy to forget: that for the overwhelming majority of its existence, the idea that television was an artistic dead zone would have been self-evident. The very term *quality television,* used by academics to denote anything that rose above the level of brain-dead muck, betrayed the very lowest of expectations. But to understand just how revolutionary the notion of *good* television was—and how voraciously those who had a chance to make it on cable between the late 1990s and the early 2010s attacked the opportunity—it's useful to revisit the utter depths in the public's perception from which the medium had to rise. And it's worth looking at a prior generation of producers and writers who were given a brief window in which they, too, could do good work and wound up paving the way, in many cases directly, for the Third Golden Age.

There had, of course, been the so-called *First* Golden Age, that brief, early period in the 1950s of televised Shakespeare and opera and brilliant, original anthologized drama. But in retrospect, that was just a technology finding its legs. In those early days, quality was a default, born of technological limitation (clunky, immovable cameras and limited recording capability made broadcasting live theater a natural starting place) and low stakes: in 1950, a television set cost several weeks' worth of an average salary and could be found in only a fraction of generally affluent, well-educated homes. Television was, of all things—if only for the briefest moment—an elitist technology.

By 1954, however, 56 percent of American households had TV sets. And from the moment TV became a mass medium, it was a reviled medium. Federal Communications Commission chairman Newton Minow coined the phrase *vast wasteland* in a 1961 speech to the National Association of Broadcasters, but policy types were hardly the only ones with disdain for TV. Perhaps intuiting its power, other artists took every opportunity possible to slag the new medium. In the same way that novelists thank God for short-story writers, short-story writers thank God for poets, poets for more experimental poets—all for making their own career choices seem like models of sober-minded life management—TV might have been invented by moviemakers for the express purpose of allowing them to point to any commercial art form more degraded than their own.

Most striking, though, is the degree to which TV's own practitioners have joined in the hate fest. No other medium contains such a matter-of-fact strain of self-loathing. HBO, indisputably a television network, made its bones declaring it was "not TV."

The criticism, furthermore, has always transcended mere snobbery and included something more primitive and superstitious—as though these boxes of pulsing light and sound had dropped out of the sky into our pristine forest clearing. The exposure to artificial light, it's been said, inhibits cognitive development; the flickering images replicate hypnotism. Television has been accused of being addictive, corrupting, responsible for driving otherwise perfect, well-behaved children to violence and depravity.

Which is to say that TV's crimes have never been merely aesthetic, but also moral, even metaphysical. The set, with its sinister, alien antennae, its ubiquity, became the very symbol of American vacuity and anomie, pouring an unstoppable sludge of false reassurance and pernicious advertising into suburban homes. At best, it was the "glass teat" dispensing anesthesia to the conformist masses; at worst, it was a sinister conspiracy of the capitalist Mind Control Machine, designed to keep us fat, sleepy, and spending. The rhetoric could become nothing short of apocalyptic: Ray Bradbury branded TV "that insidious beast, that Medusa which freezes a billion people to stone every night, staring fixedly, that Siren which called and sang and promised so much and gave, after all, so little." E. B. White prophesied, "We shall stand or fall by television—of that I am quite sure," while, rounding out this unlikely troika, Frank Zappa sang (from the point of view of TV itself):

> *You will obey me while I lead you*
> *And eat the garbage that I feed you*
> *Until the day that we don't need you*
> *Don't go for help . . . no one will heed you*
> *Your mind is totally controlled*
> *It has been stuffed into my mold*
> *And you will do as you are told*
> *Until the rights to you are sold*

Of course, such awestruck hate could only have its source in a kind of love. Orson Welles, as good a man as any to address the nexus of commerce and art, might have had the last word: "I hate television. I hate it as much as peanuts. But I can't stop eating peanuts."

Or as Steven Bochco said: "It's always been fashionable to say at cocktail parties, 'I never watch TV.' That's nonsense. *Everybody* watches TV."

The existential fear and loathing of television may have reached its apex with the 1978 publication of a volume titled *Four Arguments for the Elimination of Television*, written by an ex–advertising executive by the apparently real name of Jerry Mander. Mander described his career at a high-powered San Francisco firm, "commuting coast to coast weekly, taking five-day vacations in Tahiti, eating *only* in French restaurants, jetting to Europe for a few days' skiing." This Master of the Universe idyll was interrupted by a scales-falling-from-his-eyes moment in 1968, experienced while sailing through the Dalmatian Straits, amid craggy cliffs and azure seas: "Leaning on the deck rail, it struck me that there was a film between me and all of that. I could 'see' the spectacular views. I knew they were spectacular. But the experience stopped at my eyes. I couldn't let it inside me. I felt nothing. Something had gone wrong with me." That something, he came to believe, was the same something that afflicted the rest of the modern world: television.

Having awoken from the machine's hypnotic spell, Mander urged the rest of us to follow suit, laying out his indictment in such chapters as "War to Control the Unity Machine" and "How Television Dims the Mind" and "How We Turn into Our Images." In one chapter he listed thirty-three "Inherent Biases of Television." Among them: "War is better television than peace." "Lust is better television than satisfaction." "The one is easier than the many." "The singular is more understandable than the eclectic." "Any facts work better than any poetry." "Superficiality is easier than depth."

"This cannot be changed. The bias is inherent in the technology," Mander asserted with the absolute confidence of a zealot. The notion of television redeeming itself was "as absurd as speaking of the reform of a technology such as guns."

As it happens, almost simultaneous with the publication of *Four Arguments for the Elimination of Television*, an event took place that would begin to challenge Mander's ironclad assumptions. In early 1978, Steven Bochco went to work for Grant Tinker.

T he veteran TV writer and showrunner Henry Bromell once sketched a family history of quality TV. After starting at the bottom with *The Sopranos*, *The Wire*, and *Mad Men* and a handful of other recent shows, he quickly moved upward, along a spreading spiderweb of connections that filled the page. At the top, alone, he wrote one name in capital letters: Grant Tinker.

Four decades after he left an executive position at 20th Century Fox Television to form MTM Enterprises—named for his second wife, Mary Tyler Moore, and created to produce her eponymous sitcom—Tinker remains that rare, if not unique, creature: a television executive revered by television writers. If you know anything about the species, you may be able to guess that writers loved Tinker because Tinker believed in the importance of writers.

This has by no means ever been a given in Hollywood. Certainly not in the movie business, which had long granted power and prestige to directors while regarding writers as, at best, regrettably necessary inconveniences: in the immortal words of Jack Warner, "schmucks with Underwoods." From the beginning, the ongoing nature of television programming—the medium's merciless hunger for a constant flow of new material—made writers a more valuable commodity than they had ever been. Still, by and large, producers remained in charge of TV through the sixties and seventies, with writers either working freelance or saddled with the peculiarly diminished title of "story editor."*

There's a condition, common among executives and other TV "suits," that involves the secret conviction that—if only they were less damnably good at making money and more willing to spend their time mooning about, wearing rags, and making up stories—they could write and create at least as well as any of their writers.

"Mike Post [the prolific TV-theme composer] used to say, 'Everybody is an expert on two things: their jobs and music.' The same is true of television," said Stephen J. Cannell, one of the most successful writer-producers of the seventies and eighties. "Why? Because we've all watched so damned

---

* The term *producer* used throughout this book is a devilish one, meaning different things in different contexts: *The Sopranos*, for instance, had five credited "executive producers" for its final episodes: Chase, as creator and head writer; Brad Grey, as one of the original developers; Ilene Landress, who was in charge of budgets, scheduling, and all other physical, nonwriting matters; and then Terence Winter and Matthew Weiner as the most senior writers, also responsible for overseeing production on episodes they wrote. In addition, there were seven other "producers," ranging from associate to co-executive, with duties as varied as writing episodes, overseeing postproduction, and acting as Landress's assistant. To further confound matters, the Writers Guild mandates specific "producer" credits for its writers, tied to their pay level and seniority. Here, anyway, I mean a more old-fashioned definition of executive, noncreative types.

much of it. It's like saying, 'I fly first class all the time. I think I could land this thing.'"

Crucially, Tinker appears to have been immune to this particular disease. By the time he started MTM in 1969, he'd already spent two decades working for NBC, Radio Free Europe, Universal, Fox, and the ad agencies McCann Erickson and Benton & Bowles. Along the way, he'd developed a faith in creative talent that could easily pass for common sense. "From my earliest days around and about television," he wrote in his memoir, *Tinker in Television*, "it's been clear to me that good shows could only be made by good writers."

He became known as an indefatigable advocate for his writers and a tireless defender of their work against meddlesome networks. Both John Falsey and Joshua Brand—who would create *St. Elsewhere* at MTM—remember sitting in Tinker's office, listening to one side of a phone conversation with NBC Entertainment president Brandon Tartikoff, who was apparently unhappy with the ratings performance of a particular show. "But is it *good*, Brandon?" Tinker said over and over. "Is it *good*?"

Of course Tinker, for all his genuine appreciation for and support of writers, wasn't running a nonprofit artists collective. He believed that his approach was not only good for art, but good for business. This was the era of "Fin-Syn," the Financial Interest and Syndication Rules, enacted in 1970, that among other things prohibited the big three TV networks from producing and owning their own programming. Until their repeal in the 1990s, the Fin-Syn Rules bestowed enormous power and profit on independent producers, who maintained ownership over their programs and syndication rights. Not only would happy writers produce profitable programs, Tinker believed, they would also attract a steady stream of *more* good writers. He proposed a show business axiom—"The best creative people love to work with other best creative people"—and described the ensuing "magnet effect" that made recruiting talent surprisingly easy.

In this, Tinker's studio provided a blueprint for what HBO would become in the late 1990s and early 2000s. MTM's offices in Studio City became the place writers wanted to be—not necessarily because it was where they'd get the most money, but because they'd have the freedom to do good work. Said Tinker's son Mark, who began his own career as a director and producer at MTM, "It was *the* gig in town."

Several dramas to come out of MTM had direct bearing on the generation of TV to follow. The studio's second drama, *The White Shadow,* about a white ex–NBA player coaching at an inner-city high school, turned out to be one of those strange intersections in television history at which a disproportionate amount of talent ends up working on a show that doesn't necessarily reflect that talent. By the nature of the business, people working on good TV shows almost always got there by working on bad—or at least less good—ones; at one point, the list of past credits assembled in the writers' room of *The Sopranos* included *The Incredible Hulk, The New Adventures of Flipper,* and *Xena: Warrior Princess.* "*All* TV credit sheets look terrible," said HBO Entertainment president Sue Naegle.

No show or producer, however, would have the impact of the studio's fourth dramatic series, *Hill Street Blues*—in terms of both what was on the screen and how it got there.

Steven Bochco was thirty-four when Tinker hired him, a veteran of the Universal Television script mill, where he had specialized in churning out scripts for cop shows but had failed to break through with a real hit. Bochco arrived at MTM with no small amount of self-confidence but little interest in doing another police series—even less so when his first effort for the studio, *Paris,* starring James Earl Jones as a detective, flopped after a single season on CBS.

Nevertheless, even at MTM the customer had some power, and what the customer—in this case NBC president Fred Silverman—had set his mind to in early 1980 was a police drama. Silverman dispatched Brandon Tartikoff to pitch the idea to Bochco and Michael Kozoll, a fellow Universal alum, at a meeting at La Scala in Beverly Hills. The pair were reluctant. "It was late in the cycle and they were desperate. So we had some real negotiating leverage," Bochco remembers. He and Kozoll agreed to write a police pilot if Tar-tikoff would grant them autonomy. And Tartikoff, on behalf of NBC, agreed.

What he and Kozoll delivered, ten days later, was nearly the Platonic ideal of a form that would define quality television well into the Third Golden Age: the Trojan horse. That is, a show that by nominally fulfilling a network's (or viewer's) commercial demands allowed its creators the freedom to sneakily achieve something far richer.

In this case, NBC got its police show but also something quite different. The pilot, then called *Hill Street Station*, in many ways owed more to MTM sitcoms than to the cop genre. It portrayed the workplace as surrogate family. It married comedy and drama. Its multiple, character-driven story lines took on social and political issues. (The unglamorous look of its station house was inspired by another sitcom: *Barney Miller*.) Meanwhile, the show's visual style—gritty and hyperrealistic, with a restless camera and overlapping sound track—showed the marks of the decade of new American filmmaking that had just passed.

Even now, the first moments of the *Hill Street* pilot, which aired January 15, 1981, feel shockingly modern. As would be the convention for much of its run, the show opened as the cops of Hill Street station, located in an unnamed city that resembled New York, gathered for morning roll call. The handheld camera roved over a vast assemblage of characters, with no conventional cues as to which deserved more of the viewer's attention than the others. It was an unkempt, sleepy-eyed group, black and white, male and female. The muddy din of dialogue could have been lifted from a Robert Altman film. Finally, the duty sergeant, played by Michael Conrad, calls the gathering to order with a rundown of the previous night's news and today's advisories. The mood see-saws giddily from hoots (over a drag queen purse snatcher) to grave silence (news of two gang killings and probable reprisals). Finally, Conrad announces a new dictate from district command, barring the carrying of "bizarre and unauthorized weapons by the officers of this precinct." With much grum-bling, the cops shuffle forward to surrender their arsenal—switchblades, clubs, nunchucks, and guns of every possible variety—until it becomes a sight gag worthy of the Marx Brothers.

"Okay, let's roll," says Conrad, setting up the show's most famous recurring line: "Hey, let's be careful out there." Whereupon the cops matter-of-factly collect their weapons and begin their day.

Little in the scene would seem out of place on an episode of *The Wire* or *The Shield.* Likewise the rest of the episode, which includes the *Mad Men*–like coy reveal of the police captain's ongoing affair with the public defender and the possibly fatal shooting of two cops who, until that moment, have appeared to be around primarily for comic relief.

Unsurprisingly, NBC was perturbed. An internal memo from May 1980 provided a neat accounting of their concerns. It cited focus group testing: "The most prevalent audience reaction indicated that the program was depressing, violent and confusing. . . ." "Too much was crammed into this story. . . ." "The main characters were perceived as being not capable and having flawed personalities. Professionally, they were never completely successful in doing their jobs and personally their lives were in a mess. . . ." "Audiences found the ending unsatisfying. There are too many loose ends. . . ."

In other words, it was an entirely unwitting blueprint not only for what made *Hill Street Blues* such a historic program, but for all the shows that make up the Third Golden Age.

B ochco was never shy about invoking his autonomy, often threatening to walk rather than follow a network note. That the creation of a television show is largely a state of outright scorched-earth warfare with the very people paying for said creation was an item of faith for Bochco, and he pursued it with the zest of Sun Tzu.

"I probably did come off as an arrogant asshole," he said. "But you *had* to be. We were bucking a system. And the reason I slept fine at night, despite having all these terrible wars and knowing how resentful they must have been, was that it was in the show's best interest and, ultimately, the network's best interest. I always felt that part of my job was protecting them from themselves."

That position wasn't the only legacy Bochco left for the next generation of showrunners. He and his team wound up producing thirty-eight hour-long episodes in *Hill Street*'s first year and a half. That breakneck pace might have been common for shows with contained episodes, but this show's sprawling canvas demanded the invention of new systems.

Traditionally, TV dramas had been either written by a small group of producer-writers or farmed out to a network of freelancers. The idea of a writers' room was mostly a comedy phenomenon. *Hill Street*'s ongoing story lines necessitated an institutional memory, so Bochco assembled a full-time staff that included Jeffrey Lewis, Michael Wagner, and, for season three, an old Yale roommate of Lewis's, David Milch. (Kozoll left the show after its second season.) Together, steeped in the world of the show, they became responsible for a sprawling saga.

Since he was spending so much time with the writers, Bochco deputized an executive producer whose job it was to oversee shooting on set and all other production issues, leaving him free to concentrate on scripts. And since no director popping in to direct a single episode could be expected to know the full backstory, or what might be important three or four or more episodes down the line, he instituted what would later come to be known as "tone meetings." These are conferences at which the writers, director, and production staff all come together to pore over the complexities of each script in fastidious detail. The meetings are also, implicitly, displays of obeisance on the part of the rest of the production staff to the writer. Bit by bit, Bochco was institutionalizing the role of the autocratic writer-showrunner.

I t wasn't just Tinker's support or the quality of *Hill Street*'s writing that made this possible. For starters, NBC was in terrible shape. The network had but one show in the Nielsen ratings top ten (the seventh season of *Little House on the Prairie*, tied for ninth place) and was the object of much ridicule for a prime-time lineup that included both *B.J. and the Bear*, about a trucker and his chimpanzee, and its spin-off, *The Misadventures of Sheriff Lobo*. Fred Silverman had a hopeless man's incentive to run in the opposite direction and take a risk. In this case, that meant sticking with *Hill Street Blues* even after it debuted to dismal ratings. "If NBC had been flush," said Bochco, "I don't think we would have seen the light of day."

The television business was also changing. By 1980, nearly a fifth of American homes were hooked up to cable TV, a growing portion of those paying even more for premium stations such as the newly born HBO. Cable not only cannibalized network viewers' time and attention, it trained them to seek out different kinds of programming on different parts of the dial—sports on ESPN, news on CNN, and so on. Television was becoming a kind of food court—made up of many kiosks selling individual cuisines—rather than a one-size-fits-all cafeteria pumping out a slurry of least objectionable grub. "Quality," it seemed, could be another niche.

Meanwhile, the explosive rise of VCRs—from 1.1 percent of TV households in 1980 to 20 percent in 1985—encouraged viewers to accept more serialized stories, since they could now catch up at their leisure. It also began the process of importing film, and the expectation of filmic production values, onto the blocky screen in the living room. And it sliced the number of viewers any one show could expect ever thinner.

As a result, the numbers that had defined success in a three-network world were being drastically reduced downward; a show could succeed with many fewer eyeballs. More important, networks were becoming ever more sophisticated at measuring the *quality* of those eyeballs rather than simply their quantity. Instead of aiming to attract one-third of all viewers (which was becoming increasingly impossible in any event), networks now targeted specific demographics—rich, young, educated, male, and so on. The fragmentation of the American audience had begun. And, as it would again twenty years later, that meant good things for quality TV.

To be young, talented, and well compensated at MTM in those years was a beautiful thing. It became even more so when Bruce Paltrow began producing *St. Elsewhere*, which transplanted much of the *Hill Street* formula to a

Boston teaching hospital. The show's offices were one floor below *Hill Street*'s. "There was great excitement," said Milch. "It was as if everyone felt as if he or she had been caught doing something wrong."

"We were just a group of guys, all in our mid- to late thirties, and suddenly, because of the power Grant had given us, we were changing the business. We were *becoming* the business," Bochco said. "It was very, very thrilling. To suddenly have the sense that you could be proud of what you were doing, that you could begin to use the word *art*. We began to tentatively say, 'We're artists.' In this maligned medium."

Across Hollywood and New York, TV writers stood up and took notice. As important, so did those in MFA programs, theater workshops, journalism programs, and elsewhere. "Look at what else was on the air that season," said Andrew Schneider, who was a producer on the *The Incredible Hulk* at the time. "Go watch an episode of *Simon & Simon*. We were toiling along on shows like that, and then *Hill Street* came out and said, 'This is possible.' I remember coming to work the day after the pilot aired and everybody was like, 'We're going to get to do stuff like this!'"

And yet, the window that MTM had thrown open would remain so only briefly. Grant Tinker would leave the studio in 1981 to become head of NBC. Bochco was fired from his own show by MTM's new regime, for chronic cost overruns. He'd continue his career with *LA Law, NYPD Blue,* and a host of variously successful shows at 20th Century Fox Television. The regulations and incentives of Fin-Syn would be eroded in the early 1990s and finally abolished in 1995, drastically sliding power away from independent producers and toward the networks while at the same time spurring the proliferation of new, smaller networks like the WB and UPN. Cable would march inexorably forward, along with video games, the Internet, and more, exploding the audience into ever smaller fragments. Network TV, on the whole, would remain a dismal landscape. Indeed, the networks would run in the other direction from the new writer monarchy the first moment they had the chance, seizing instead on programming that dispensed with writers altogether in favor of "reality."

Yet before long, strikingly similar circumstances would conspire to continue what Tinker and his writers had started: new, disruptive technology, an anxious, shifting industry, a network with little to lose, and men who had labored long and hard in the Wasteland, sniffing the air hungrily for the chance to call themselves "artists."

Two

Which Films?

David Chase never liked *Hill Street Blues*. Or *St. Elsewhere*. The rest of the world may have been thinking that television was rising from the muck, but not him. "I thought it was getting worse," he said. "It was just more cops and doctors."

But then, David Chase liked almost nothing about television—not even the paychecks, each one of which reminded him that he was a sellout, too weak and compromised, he imagined, to follow the path of the renegade filmmakers he'd come of age idolizing. If ever a man who spent his entire career in television could claim intellectual, emotional kinship with Jerry Mander and his campaign to eliminate the medium itself, Chase was that man.

"Look, I do not care about television. I don't care about where television is going or anything else about it," he said three years after the finale of *The Sopranos* became one of the signal cultural events of the decade. "I'm a man who wanted to make movies. Period." Even the title *showrunner* annoyed him: "It sounds like some kind of Jet-Ski," he said.

In a generally triumphant story, this is one of the small tragedies: that the Reluctant Moses of the Third Golden Age, the man who, by example, opened the door for so many writers, directors, actors, and producers to work in television gloriously free of shame, was unable himself to enter the Promised Land.

G loom, pessimism, anxiety, paranoia, grudge holding, misanthropy— such were the highlights of most David Chase stories, including those he told about himself. Which is why it was so flummoxing to hear his own self-assessment, so difficult to tell whether he was being coy, oblivious, or simply pugnacious in yet another iteration.

"Maybe I come off as a depressed, morose guy," he said, complaining about a 2007 *Vanity Fair* cover profile that quoted a constellation of colleagues and acquaintances on his negativity. Despite calling *The Sopranos* "one of the masterpieces of American popular culture, on a par with the first two *Godfather*s, *Mean Streets*, and *GoodFellas* . . . or even European epics such as Luchino Visconti's *The Leopard*," the piece continued to irk Chase. "Maybe people find me that negative. I just don't see it," he said. "Because the truth is, in my experience, when I'm in a room, I hear a lot of laughter."

As a child, he dreamed of nuclear apocalypse under the suburban stars of Passaic and Morris and Essex counties. Perhaps this was reasonable for someone born August 22, 1945, sixteen days after Hiroshima, a charter baby boomer. He was the only child of second-generation Italians—family name DeCesare—who had more or less made the journey he would later replicate in *The Sopranos*' opening credits. His father, Henry, owned a store, Wright Hardware, in Verona. His mother, Norma, well, you've met her: insecure, passive-aggressive, fearful, domineering. As embodied by the actress Nancy Marchand, she would become one of the more idiosyncratically terrifying and funny characters to ever appear in American living rooms: Livia Soprano.

Norma was one of ten daughters of an Italian leftist who, family lore had it, once jumped out a window at a Eugene Debs rally when the cops busted in. Henry came from a line of Italian religious reformists called the Waldensians. The Chases were secular Protestants in the land of Catholics. Having escaped

Newark, they had WASPy ambitions. They played tennis and golf, vacationed in the Poconos. The wiseguys and *guidos* from down Bloomfield Avenue were referred to around the dinner table as *cafoni*—peasants. "My mother aspired to a kind of genteel life, I think," says Chase. "Although her home life was not genteel at all."

Norma, who had left high school after her freshman year, had the almost absurdist job of proofreading the New Jersey Bell phone book. She ruled the house by threat of filibuster: you did what she wanted because it was easier than hearing her complain. "The tyranny of the weak," Chase called it. This played into Henry's sense of thwarted ambition. He radiated frustration in a way that would later find expression in Tony Soprano.

"He was a disappointed man. A frustrated man," Chase said. "He would make her out to be the heavy. If something couldn't happen, for whatever reason, he would blame it on her: 'Look what I have to deal with.' But he was the one who had picked her. He got what he wanted."

It was a cramped, suffocating home, with both parents intimately involved in their only child's comings and goings. Chase suffered adolescent bouts of anxiety and depression that a generation later would likely have been identified as clinical. Outside, he and his friends engaged in the kind of petty vandalism that makes obedient sons feel rebellious: knocking over mailboxes, breaking into the local country club and throwing furniture into the pool. "It was a time when you could just run wild," he said. "Outside the home, it was really an idyllic American boyhood." Chase developed a fierce love of rock and roll and took up the drums. And he began learning the trick of alchemizing family psychodrama into mordant humor. Long before Livia came to life in America's living rooms, stories about Norma would entertain a generation of procrastinating writers' rooms.

Senior year, he fell in love with Denise Kelly, whose reserved French Irish family was everything the Chases were not. Still, for college Chase fled to Wake Forest in Winston-Salem, North Carolina. He was an ROTC student and thought seriously about the prospect of staying in the army after graduation— the brewing conflict in faraway Vietnam perhaps seeming preferable to a return to the Chase household.

Northern Jersey to Winston-Salem constituted about as large a cultural leap as it was possible to make in 1964 America. "There were cross burnings still going on in North Carolina. You had to go to chapel twice a week, and if it was before a big football game, they'd play 'Dixie' and everybody had to stand," Chase said. "It was awful. Really terrible. Not only were you not allowed to drink on campus, you weren't allowed to dance or play cards."

There was, however, against all odds, a Friday night European film series, part of the great flowering of film appreciation on campuses and in downtowns across the country. "I wasn't hip enough to know that I was seeing new film techniques in a film like *Breathless*," Chase said. "But it sure *seemed* different. Godard said all you need to make a movie is a girl and a gun. I certainly got that part of it. I was into it."

In particular, he fell for Fellini—starting with the director's contribution to *Boccaccio '70*, a lurid anthology of shorts inspired by the Renaissance poet. Fellini's segment featured a woman afflicted by visions of saints. "It was my first glimpse of Italy," Chase remembered. "I thought, 'This is the kind of nonsense that goes on in my house. The melodrama and the self-pity and the obsessiveness and the craziness: This is my DNA.'"

Soon he began dabbling in photography, taking still pictures of *8½* and Stanley Kubrick films on his television. After two years, he transferred to NYU to be closer to Denise and to immerse himself in Greenwich Village's film scene. As they would for scores of others, the art films of that period presented Chase with a new creative model. Leaving a screening of Roman Polanski's *Cul-de-Sac* in 1966, he had a revelation. "Before, I thought films just arrived from the factory, like they were Chevys or Fords. Leaving that theater, I remember thinking, 'These films are personal, they're made by a *person*.' It crystallized for me that it was something one could do."

After college, Chase and Denise married and the couple headed west, ending up at Stanford University, where Chase took film classes. There, Chase became close friends with a fellow student and teaching assistant, John Patterson. He was dashing: ruddy, bearded, an ex-navigator for the Strategic Air Command that had spent twenty-four-hour shifts airborne during the Cuban missile crisis. On the surface, Patterson, who would go on to be the most prolific director of *The Sopranos'* early seasons, couldn't have been more different from Chase, who had left Norma behind, but not her legacies of fearfulness and depression. But the men bonded over film and drugs and rock and roll. On one memorable night, the Chases and Patterson and his girlfriend dropped acid and headed into San Francisco to see *2001: A Space Odyssey.* "It was the best time of my life," Chase recalled. Unfortunately, he made the mistake of trying to go back to the well—tripping once again for a Palo Alto screening of Fellini's *Satyricon,* a disturbing grotesquerie under even the most sober of circumstances. The trip turned bad.

"I was sitting in the theater thinking, 'I don't feel so good . . . I feel pretty bad. I wish I was dead. I'm going to die,'" he remembered. At some point, he began to believe that the Zodiac serial killer, then at large in the Bay Area, was out to get him. "The more I thought about it, the more my brain waves would attract his attention. So I needed to stop thinking about it, which of course made me think about it more," he said. "It was a long twelve hours."

That passage, from joy to despair, became characteristic of Chase's work, in which characters—Tony tripping on mescaline in the Nevada desert, Carmela Soprano musing on the "cold stones" of Paris, Paulie "Walnuts" Gualtieri seeing the Virgin Mary in the back of the Bada Bing! strip club—are constantly glimpsing various kinds of transcendence, only to feel them slip away.

"I would always go like that, in a circle: 'Oh, this is so cool, this is amazing, this is really threatening, oh God, oh God . . . ,'" said Chase. "Experiences like that trip showed me the pattern very concisely: 'This is the way you are. You get all excited, and then *too* excited, and then you start to worry and go into this slew of despond until something else distracts you and you go back up.'"

After Stanford, the Chases relocated to Los Angeles. The city entranced David. "L.A. was kind of cool then. It was all happening: *Easy Rider,* the Byrds, Jim Morrison—even though I was never a big Morrison fan. There was a whole bohemian thing, a lot of drugs around. And I loved all the old studios, the Raymond Chandler aspects of them at night, the fog. I was crazy about that shit," he said. "It was weird, but I liked it."

Chase set out to become a screenwriter, laboring over film scripts while Denise worked. Throughout the next twenty years, he would always have at least one screenplay going. They would come to varying states of near success before collapsing. One, titled *Fly Me*, was about stewardesses. Another, *Female Suspects*, written in 1981, concerned a sociologist in New Jersey who gets caught up in the lives of the violent women she is studying. That script flirted with getting produced for ten years and was even briefly revived at Sony Pictures, following the debut of *The Sopranos*. "Now, it would probably be on the Black List," Chase said, referring to the yearly index of "best unproduced scripts" that began being compiled in 2005. Time after time, however, his film dreams ended in frustration. He said, "The word was, I was 'too dark.'"

Back in L.A., his career was prematurely stalled. He and Patterson took the Directors Guild trainee exam; Patterson passed, but Chase didn't. He picked up odd jobs such as assistant director on soft-core porn films and stayed home, smoking a lot of pot and working on scripts. Then came a break: Toward the end of film school, Chase and a friend had written a spec script for Roy Huggins, a television producer most famous for creating the western *Maverick*, starring James Garner. "It was terrible. Just some Godardian half-assed gangster thing," he said. But it was good enough that Huggins gave him a freelance script assignment for a new show about lawyers he was producing at Universal. Chase figured he'd made it: "I joined the guild, I got paid $2,300, which I couldn't believe, and I was in the industry."

In fact, it was the last paid writing he'd do for two years. Given his lack of union-aided employment, he was indignant when the Writers Guild ordered him to the picket lines during its 1973 strike. It proved fortuitous. Marching dutifully outside the main gate of Paramount Studios, Chase was introduced to Paul Playdon, a writer and story editor with a reputation as a kind of storytelling wunderkind for his work on *Mission: Impossible*. The two hit it off, and Playdon gave Chase his first staff writing positions—first on the back-nine episodes of a show called *The Magician*, starring future Hulk Bill Bixby, and then on *Kolchak: The Night Stalker*, an influential proto–*X-Files* featuring Darren McGavin as a Chicago newspaper reporter who seemed to constantly stumble upon stories of the supernatural.

Thus began David Chase's long, unfortunate slide upward into success. *Kolchak* was produced at Universal Studios, which at the time was churning out some seventeen hours of prime-time television per week. To be on the lot was as close to experiencing the heyday of the Hollywood studio system as television production ever got. "The commissary was filled. You'd see extras walking around dressed like Martians. There was a huge costume department. A giant wood shop that made all the sets. It was really like 1942," Chase recalled.

The show was a crash education in TV storytelling, both on the page and on set. Such incidentals as plot had never been of much interest to Chase before. "'Story' was cheap Hollywood crap," said the Fellini fan. "For me it was all about dialogue and character." That began to change under Playdon's tutelage, as they pumped out script after script, often less than twelve hours ahead of that episode's shooting schedule. Chase discovered he had not only a gift for driving a story forward in television's familiar four- or five-act structure (separated by commercial breaks), but also a taste for the process of bringing those stories to life on-screen, detail by arduous detail.

"I remember my first production meeting, at Paramount, on *The Magician*. All the department heads were going through the script: 'Okay: The police uniform. Long-sleeve or short-sleeve? Let's see, it's October, so short-sleeve.' So you settle that and then you go on. This was fascinating to me," Chase said.

As important, he was being trained in TV's eternal, intimate dance between story (which is to say, creativity) and time (which is to say, money). "Like, you have a scene in a funeral home, but the locations person says you can't afford to shoot a funeral home. So you need to change it to an exterior, where you see people leaving and getting into their cars. It was real fundamentals. Paul Playdon taught me all that. And then later, of course, Stephen Cannell."

Nobody (or at least no boy) growing up between the late 1970s and early 1990s could fail to know the prodigious body of work Stephen J. Cannell produced throughout that era—a collection of character-based, humor-laced, action-packed shows that included *Riptide, The Greatest American Hero, Wiseguy, 21 Jump Street, The Commish, Baretta, Hunter, Hardcastle and McCormick,* and more. (TV has always had a taste for last names as titles, particularly if the names are fortuitously punny and evocative.) As far as popular success went, there was, above all others, *The A-Team,* a perfectly calibrated piece of Reagan-era juvenile junk featuring a team of vigilante ex–Special Forces soldiers back from Vietnam and intervening on behalf of the little guy, preferably one running a wood mill, trucking company, or other suitably blue-collar operation.

What's more surprising is that the same boys, who would have been of an age not accustomed to considering, much less caring, how their entertainment was made, would probably also know *who* Cannell was—even if they knew no other television producer or even that such a thing existed. This was thanks largely to Cannell's signature "bumper," a snippet of video that ran after the credits of each of his shows. It depicted the man himself, bearded, impressively coiffed, and usually puffing on a pipe, at his typewriter at the final moments of finishing a script. He would pound out a final few characters—no doubt a last-minute plot twist or crucial piece of character nuance—and then confidently rip the page from its carriage and fling it across the room, whereupon it morphed into animation, fluttered onto the top of a manuscript, and settled into a royal, curved "C."

It was a classic piece of narcissism, to be sure; the video logo was periodically updated, and each iteration made sure to include more conspicuously displayed awards in the writer's office. But it was also something more important: Regardless of what you thought of the quality of Cannell's output (and it ranged wildly from awful to underappreciated), he was making a claim of television auteurship. What's more, though he was a savvy, in some ways revolutionary, businessman, making a fortune by essentially starting his own studio and thus owning all his shows, Cannell's bumper specifically insisted on his role, first and foremost, as a *writer.*

As he told an interviewer in 2004: "Somewhere in the early part of the eighties, I was starting to be referred to as a 'television mogul.' And I just kind of hated that. Because to me a mogul was a guy in a green suit who tried to score actresses. I kept saying, 'I'm not a mogul, I'm a writer. I write every day for five hours. If that doesn't make me a writer, what does?'"

Neither that figure nor Cannell's pride in it, heightened by the fact that he had grown up dyslexic, ever wavered—though in later years he applied it to the writing of mystery novels rather than TV shows. Lunching at the Beverly Hilton several months before he would die of melanoma, at the age of sixty-nine, he was magnificent: bull-chested, hair swept back, wearing a thin, ribbed black turtleneck tucked into the tightest of tan pants and a corduroy jacket. He ordered tuna on white and used an entire room-service mini-jar of extra mayonnaise.

And though he could justly claim credit for kicking off the careers of such stars as Johnny Depp, Kevin Spacey, Jeff Goldblum, Michael Chiklis, and many others, he seemed most proud of hiring David Chase as a staff writer for *The Rockford Files*.

Years later, Chase described what he learned writing for *Rockford*, which ran from 1974 to 1980, was later revived as a series of occasional TV movies, and stands as Cannell's most accomplished creation. "Cannell taught me that your hero can do a lot of bad things, he can make all kinds of mistakes, can be lazy and look like a fool, as long as he's the smartest guy in the room and he's good at his job. That's what we ask of our heroes." Jim Rockford, in other words, was an early shade of Tony Soprano.

Played by James Garner, Rockford was a semi-deadbeat private eye who lived in a beachside trailer in Malibu. He had an astonishing collection of plaid jackets that he wore with equally astonishing aplomb. He didn't like guns, or to work very much, and beyond a grudging sense of decency, he embraced no lofty cause of justice. "With Rockford it was always about '$200 a day, plus expenses,' that's all," Chase said, giving the PI's oft-mentioned terms of employment.

If *The A-Team*'s cigar-chomping, leeringly macho colonel John "Hanni-bal" Smith was the perfect incarnation of 1980s triumphalism, Rockford was equally in tune with his times, a post-Watergate, post-Vietnam wiseass, the closest that TV could get to Elliott Gould's shambling, scruffy take on Philip Marlowe in Robert Altman's 1973 version of *The Long Goodbye*. The show was underscored with just a whiff of melancholy, an intimation of resignation and loneliness discernible in the harmonica break of Mike Post's theme music, if you were inclined to hear it.

Even allowing for retrospective clairvoyance, it's hard not to see Chase's fingerprints all over "The Oracle Wore a Cashmere Suit," his first credited episode of *Rockford*. This is less true in the main action—a characteristically convoluted double murder into which Rockford is reluctantly drawn—than in the details stuffed in around the edges: the rock-and-roll references, the malapropisms, the happy coincidence of Rockford making an appearance, shuffling, Tony-like, out to the beach in his bathrobe. The "oracle" of the episode's title is a celebrity psychic with the Sopranoesque name Roman Clementi, whom Chase seems to have taken gleeful pleasure in writing as an oily, unrepentant charlatan. Clementi has precisely the blend of qualities most likely to draw out the sharpest point of Chase's pen: vanity, fatuity, pretension, physical cowardice. To see the psychic flinch from a drug dealer who hits him in the face is to immediately flash on Assemblyman Ronald Zellman cowering as Tony Soprano beats him with a belt for the crime of falling in love with the mobster's old mistress.

An even clearer indication of Chase's creative temperament came with *Off the Minnesota Strip*, which aired in May 1980 on the *ABC Monday Night Movie*. It is hard to imagine a film of its bleak tenor appearing in a modern movie theater, much less on prime-time network TV, interrupted by sunny ads for detergent. It was the story of Michele, nicknamed Micki and played by Mare Winningham. Micki is a teenage runaway who returns home to suburban Minnesota after spending time as a prostitute in New York. Again, premonitions of *The Sopranos* abound: Micki's mom is harsh and remote, her father an impotent milquetoast. Micki herself is no reformed angel with a heart of gold: she's a narcissist, a sexual manipulator, and a pain in the ass. There is a brutal scene in which the dad, played by Hal Holbrook, is forced to sit and listen to a frank account of his daughter's sexual exploits. (There is also wicked wit: "Anyway, I guess it feels good to hit the old bed again," Holbrook says by way of good night.) "Just My Imagination" and other rock-and-roll hits are on the sound track.

Above all, *Minnesota Strip* showcases Chase's gift for granting complicated psychologies to characters who are themselves incapable of examining, much less expressing, what's going on in their heads. This is the primary distinction between Chase and two fellow showrunners whose work he loathed: David Milch and Aaron Sorkin, both given to investing all of their characters with an eloquence suspiciously close to that of their creators. (Chase never understood how somebody could like both *The Sopranos* and, say, *The West Wing*. "It's like when I was in high school: if you liked the Supremes, you couldn't like the Marvelettes. If you liked Dylan, you couldn't like Donovan." He left little doubt as to which show was which.)

Off the Minnesota Strip ends as untidily as can be, with Micki and a boyfriend lighting out for the Sunset Strip and stopping just short, the question of what they're looking for and whether they'll get it left dangling and unanswered. In *The New York Times*, John J. O'Connor called it "the champion downer of the year."

"In the end, *Off the Minnesota Strip* is little more than a homily on the futility of it all," O'Connor wrote. "For Michele, for her parents, presumably for the rest of us, the message seems to be 'turn off the set and start slashing your wrists.'"

Nearly thirty years later, after a similarly ambiguous ending, *The Sopranos* fans would be debating whether the message of that series amounted to the same thing.

C hase won his first writing Emmy for the script of *Off the Minnesota Strip*. To his consternation, it made him that much more sought after by television companies. Of the many development deals he was offered by studios such as Warner Brothers, he chose to spend two years with an obscure company called Comworld Pictures.

"I thought, 'These cocksuckers will never get anything on the air and I'll be able to do nothing and write my movies.' Which is what I did," he said.

The convoluted strategies didn't end there: Chase dreamed of selling a TV idea that was good enough to get a pilot made but not so good that it would ever go to series. That way, he reasoned, he could ask the studio, having already invested in an hour-long pilot, to cut its losses by putting up a relatively small amount to finish the story as a stand-alone movie. One idea he pursued on his deal at Universal seemed perfect. It was the story of a dissolving marriage, set in the present but told heavily through flashbacks to happier times in the 1960s. "I thought, 'Most pilots don't get bought, so I'll shoot this, cut it together, and I'll be in the movie business.'"

Not for the last time, Chase's plan backfired. CBS, enchanted by the success of two ABC shows about baby boomers, *thirtysomething* and *The Wonder Years*, picked up Chase's series, now called *Almost Grown*. Chase called his agent, who naturally expected that his client would be elated. "I said, 'Listen, you've got to get me out of this.' He said, 'What are you talking about?' I told him, 'I want to kill myself! I don't want to do a series.'"

Almost Grown debuted in November 1988. The central couple was played by Eve Gordon and Tim Daly, who would later appear in a recurring guest role on *The Sopranos*. On the writing staff was Robin Green, a former magazine writer and alum of the Iowa Writers' Workshop, whose career, along with that of her future husband, Mitchell Burgess, would be intimately entwined with Chase's for the next two decades.

"I don't know how he managed to get it on the air," said Henry Bromell. "It was a show about failure. And that's not a surprise, something you realize in season five: it *starts* with a marriage having failed. Only David would have written that show."

Though well reviewed by critics, *Almost Grown* proved too grim, and with a little help from CBS's decision to air it opposite *Monday Night Football*, the show was canceled after only eight episodes had been broadcast. Chase was left with his worst opinions of TV confirmed and the growing conviction—given the lack of positive response to any of his feature screenplays—that he'd made a fatal karmic error.

"I began to think that I was not going to succeed in movies because I wasn't sacrificing enough. I wasn't willing to quit, to get off that nipple, the weekly salary, the nice house in Santa Monica. I wasn't willing to do the artistic thing, cut myself off and live the freelance life," he said.

The outside world, meanwhile, saw someone with a growing reputation for outsize but wasted potential, a kind of human version of a Black List script: the most talented failure in television. When John Falsey called to enlist Chase as a writer for a new show set in the South during the civil rights movement, Falsey recalled, "The truth is, I don't think anybody else wanted him."

Three

A Great Notion

The industrial coal country of eastern Pennsylvania is an unlikely place to find the seed of an electronic media revolution, much less a cultural one. Yet in this story it provides two.

The first came in 1948, when an enterprising appliance salesman in Mahanoy City, a town nestled in the picturesque but receptionless hills one hundred miles outside of Philadelphia, planted an antenna atop a nearby mountain, ran a literal cable into town, and began offering a new service. He charged $100 for installation and $2 per year thenceforth for the privilege of watching TV without the vagaries of wireless transmission.

The second occurred twenty-four years later, on November 8, 1972, and a mere forty miles away, in Wilkes-Barre. That was when, despite weather problems that forced a technician to stand on top of a roof, physically holding a microwave-receiving dish in place, HBO debuted to a tiny group of subscribers.

The idea for premium cable had been dreamed up by Charles Dolan, who had recently sold a large chunk of his Manhattan cable company, Sterling Communications, to Time Life Inc. and was casting about for a way to make it profitable. The answer—dreamed up, according to company lore, on a family vacation aboard the *Queen Elizabeth II*—was a subscription service focused on sports and movies. He called it "the Green Channel." The name was quickly replaced with a placeholder: Home Box Office.

From the time of that first broadcast—of the film *Sometimes a Great Notion*, based on the Ken Kesey novel—much of both the problems and the promise that would drive HBO for the next four decades was already in place. The primary question, of course, was how to make people pay for something they either already paid for or, worse, got for free. In 1972, the answer was relatively easy: In those pre-VCR days, there were few options to see Hollywood movies outside of the theater, or even *in* the theater, since cinemas had yet to catch up with demographics by shifting from urban downtowns to suburban multiplexes. (The TV writer and essayist Rob Long has argued persuasively that this, as much as any particular upswell of artistic sensibility, was responsible for the New Cinema of the early 1970s and, once the suburbs got screens, its death at the hands of blockbusters such as *Jaws* and *Star Wars*.)

Live sports broadcasts, largely controlled by local networks and afflicted by blackouts, were an equally rare commodity in 1972. In its first decade, a significant chunk of HBO's programming included out-of-market NHL, NBA, and New York Yankees games, in addition to boxing, which would remain an important franchise for years to come. Any honest HBO executive past or present would also allow that two other programming elements made possible by its premium status did as much as anything else to distinguish the network's identity: breasts and curse words.

The mix worked. By 1981, HBO was carried on one thousand local cable systems across the country and boasted some four million subscribers. (Dolan had quickly departed the company and would go on to create Cablevision, which owned Madison Square Garden, the New York Knicks and Rangers, Radio City Music Hall, and AMC Networks.) In the ensuing decade, under the stewardship of Jerry Levin and Michael Fuchs, who took over as chairman and CEO in 1984, that number would grow fivefold. At the same time, certain fundamental problems marked those years, chief among them the difficulty of finding enough content to fill the 168 hours per week that a full-time network demanded. HBO's constant repetition of its stable of movies became a well-known joke. ("Show me a Home Box Office patron, and I'll show you someone who has seen *The Great Santini* fifteen times," Jack Curry wrote in the *Daily News*.) The more subscribers felt they had seen all HBO had to offer, the more vulnerable the network was to the scourge of pay TV: so-called *churning*, in which consumers repeatedly pick up and then drop cable services.

The all-consuming thirst for content also made HBO, for as long as it was primarily a movie station, dangerously dependent on Hollywood studios. These had started out dubious of the network and grown increasingly hostile. In 1980, it took a federal antitrust case to prevent 20th Century Fox, Universal, Columbia, and Paramount from banding together to start their own pay network, called Premiere, as a direct challenge. With the rise of VCRs and competition from networks like Showtime and The Movie Channel, all strategic roads began to lead toward the same destination: original programming.

M ovie and TV production wasn't totally alien to HBO. In 1982, the network had joined with CBS and Columbia Studios to form Tri-Star Pictures, which produced such films as *The Natural* and *Birdy*. (HBO left the partnership in 1987.) In 1986, the first *Comic Relief* concert was aired, a fundraiser that would eventually have eleven installments. The network also had varying degrees of success with sketch comedy (*Kids in the Hall, Not Necessarily the News*), miniseries (Robert Altman's *Tanner '88*), and oddball children's programming like Jim Henson's *Fraggle Rock*. Meanwhile, as the nineties dawned, its documentary division, under the direction of Sheila Nevins, began developing a strong reputation with films ranging from Emmy-winning investigations such as *Real Sports with Bryant Gumbel* to the titillations of *Real Sex* and *Taxicab Confessions*.

For the most part, though, the network had declined to challenge the networks with ongoing scripted series. There were a few exceptions: *1st & Ten* was a football sitcom costarring O. J. Simpson. *Arli$$* chronicled the adventures of a big-time sports agent. To the extent that these shows drew on HBO's nascent brand, they were primarily the easiest, and crudest, expressions of what it could do and most networks couldn't. Nearly every episode of the sitcom

Dream On, from David Crane and Marta Kauffman, who would later birth
Friends, featured at least one sex scene so outrageously gratuitous that it almost felt like an inside joke on the nature of pay TV.

Which is not to say that self-reflexive irony, if indeed there was any on
Dream On, did anything to diminish the appeal to teenage boys, especially in
those pre-Internet days. In that way, an otherwise forgettable show intimated
a canny strategy that continued to work for HBO long after it moved on to
more upmarket fare. Rare is the episode of any HBO show that doesn't take
advantage of the opportunity to remind you that "adult entertainment"
means more than sophisticated storytelling. And if one watched *The Sopranos*
more for the Bada Bing! and the blood than for the existential musings, well,
who was to know? Any more than it could be proven that you *weren't* reading
Playboy for the articles.

The most important premonition of what HBO would soon become came
in 1992, with the debut of *The Larry Sanders Show.* Just as *The Sopranos* would
be nearly as funny as it was dramatic, *The Larry Sanders Show* was a half-hour
comedy as cruelly dark as anything TV had seen before. A behind-the-scenes
look at the making of a late-night talk show, it starred Garry Shandling as
Larry, the neurotic, narcissistic host. If Shandling and his supporting cast, including Rip Torn and Jeffrey Tambor, weren't exactly playing mobsters or
murderers, they were a good deal less likable than any characters you could
find on network TV—much less on a sitcom. That went equally for the celebrities who soon lined up to play exaggerated, usually ugly versions of themselves. To appear on *Larry Sanders* was to show yourself as not only a good
sport, but savvy enough to lampoon Hollywood while participating in it. And
the audience was flattered by its knowing inclusion in that world, the same
way it later felt intimately connected to the jargon of Baltimore homicide cops
on *The Wire* or the economics of running a funeral home on *Six Feet Under.*
The pleasure came less from the putative glimpse into how a late-night talk
show worked than from imagining how one could convince Michael Bolton to
appear as himself in an episode in which he was described as "a pair of lungs
with a dick."

In raw numbers, not all that many people watched. "I used to get the numbers every week, and *Def Comedy Jam*"—the African American comedy showcase that debuted the same year—"had like four times the ratings of *Larry Sanders*," said Kevin Reilly, then the head of television at Brillstein-Grey, the influential management company that produced both shows and would later develop *The Sopranos*. But volume of viewers really didn't matter. Buzz did: among critics, among loyal, chattering viewers on the coasts, and among other Hollywood creatives.

"*The Larry Sanders Show* manifestly revealed to everyone that you could do something totally original, get noticed for it, and that it could have a cultural impact," said Richard Plepler, who later became HBO's CEO. "And I believe that that show opened up the imagination of a lot of creative people who said, 'You know what, you go over there, you can do some interesting stuff.'"

B y most normal standards, David Chase was doing interesting stuff himself in the early 1990s—working for a pair of young writer-producers who would likely have found themselves working on cable had they started ten years later. Josh Brand and John Falsey had been barely thirty when they created *St. Elsewhere* for MTM. They departed the show soon after its debut, thanks to an ugly struggle for control between Brand and executive producer Bruce Paltrow. At Universal, they had created a miniseries called *A Year in the Life* for NBC, which was then picked up for one critically acclaimed season. They then struck improbable gold, or at least fairy dust, with an eight-episode summer replacement called *Northern Exposure*, about a neurotic New York doctor stranded in an eccentric Alaskan town. With its blend of comedy, soap opera, and a kind of hip, literary sensibility (Falsey and several of the writers he recruited had studied fiction at the University of Iowa), the show was an immediate hit with critics.

"They were very conscious of wanting to do something that was not like television," staffer Barbara Hall remembered. "There were constant references to short-story writers and playwrights, not TV episodes." Robin Green, also a writer for the show, was sent home the first week with a collection of John Updike stories to study. Surprisingly, the show was also a ratings hit, which bought Brand and Falsey something approaching a free pass on whatever they wanted to do next.

"Back then, before HBO and cable were players, the networks would set aside an hour or two a week for a show that wasn't going to be a ratings winner but that they could be proud of," said Falsey. "With *Northern*, Josh and I had reached that niche."

What they filled it with was *I'll Fly Away*. Set in the late 1950s and early 1960s, the show centered around Sam Waterston as a southern district attorney navigating the moral and legal displacements of the civil rights movement, and on Regina Taylor as his African American maid, Lilly, caught in the same currents. Brand said the show's inspiration was a scene in *To Kill a Mockingbird*, in which Atticus Finch asks his black housekeeper to stay at his house while he attends to business: "I thought, 'Gee, wouldn't it be interesting to see it from her point of view.'"

Brand had admired *Almost Grown*, so when James Garner sang David Chase's praises one day over lunch at the Hotel Bel-Air, he and Falsey brought him in for a meeting.

"He was David," Brand said. "You know, not the most cheery person you can meet. When he left, we looked at each other and one of us said, 'He's an odd duck, man. But he's a really talented writer.' So we hired him. Frankly, we didn't give a shit about his personality."

Henry Bromell and Hall rounded out the small writing staff, though Chase emerged as the star. "I remember we each went off to write our first scripts and then passed them around," said Bromell. "Mine was pretty good. I remember reading Barbara's and thinking it was really good. But David's . . . David's was like Chekhov."

In "The Hat," which became the second episode of *I'll Fly Away*'s first season, Lilly retrieves and fixes a cowboy hat that her young white charge, John Morgan, has lost out a car window. Before she can return it, though, Lilly's daughter falls in love with the hat, forcing Lilly to pry it away from her to give it back. In the final scene, as Chase wrote it, John Morgan cavalierly discards the hat again.

"It said everything," said Bromell. "About the two families. About money. About power. About how Lilly couldn't say 'Fuck you' to her boss. I said, 'David, that's really good. In any medium.' And he said, 'Eh. I don't know.'"

Brand said, "If you came to see David in his office, he'd kind of look at you like you were trying to pick his pocket. You'd say, 'David, it's nothing! I'm just trying to have a conversation!' He'd be, 'What? What?' Just very suspicious. But I really liked him. I thought he was funny, because he was so intense." Brand paused and smiled. "Though, you know, I always thought Richard Nixon was hysterically funny, too."

Chase was proud of his work on *I'll Fly Away*, but that hardly meant he was happy. His battles with enemies both internal and external continued— the latter camp represented largely by the powers at NBC, on which the series aired. Network commercials for the show featured Louis Armstrong singing "What a Wonderful World." The spots drove Chase crazy.

"If I'd had a gun, I would've killed somebody," he said, as worked up about it in 2010 as he was in 1992. "What fucking wonderful world? Ku Klux Klan, Mississippi civil rights workers being murdered, housewives from Detroit being gunned down in their car, black kids being lynched? They were trying to sell a series about human pain as a cute story about some cute little boy and his nanny. And it fucking made me want to puke."

Hall remembered Chase bringing a woman in the network's standards and practices office to tears over the number of times the word *nigger* would be allowed in an episode. ("What kind of person does your job?" he asked her over and over.) Another time, a young staffer gushed about how important their work was. "It's not TV, it's art," she said. Chase fixed her with his hooded eyes: "You're here for two things: selling Buicks and making Americans feel cozy. That's your job."

Some of Chase's worst opprobrium was reserved for the show being produced right across the hall. "The people who worked on *Northern Exposure* thought they were curing cancer and reinventing drama," he said. "The premise of the show, as I found out later, was that it was a, quote, 'nonjudgmental universe.' Huh? That's something I couldn't understand. To me it was so precious, so self-congratulatory. It strained so hard for its whimsy. We'd go to the Emmys every year and they'd get these awards and we'd get nothing. It wasn't that we really wanted the Emmys, but that show was being celebrated to the hilt and I felt it was a fraud at its core."

By the end of 1993, Chase had taken over *Northern Exposure* as show-runner.

T hat bizarre turn of events had been immediately precipitated by the cancellation of *I'll Fly Away* after just two seasons. PBS subsequently rebroadcast the series, along with a ninety-minute coda, *I'll Fly Away: Then and Now*—an early intimation of how alternatives to the traditional networks might be better suited for serious storytelling.

After their meteoric rise, Brand and Falsey's partnership was faltering. Brand had stayed in day-to-day control of *Northern Exposure* while Falsey concentrated mainly on *I'll Fly Away*. While both shows were on the air, Falsey had pushed Brand to start yet another, *Going to Extremes*, a somewhat transparent copy of *Northern Exposure*'s fish-out-of-water formula, this time about med students on a tropical island. Falsey's dream was to be the first producer with three shows nominated for an Emmy in the same category, but shortly after the show launched, in September 1992, he began to fall apart. Soon, he would withdraw completely into a decades-long battle with alcoholism, during which he and Brand had no contact for nearly twenty years. Brand, burned out by his partner's life dramas as well as increasing conflicts with *Northern Exposure* star Rob Morrow over his contract, decided to leave the show after its fourth season.

Universal handed the reins to Chase along with husband-and-wife writing partners Andrew Schneider and Diane Frolov. Predictably, given Chase's feelings and the odd three-headed showrunner structure, things didn't go well. *Northern Exposure* left the air two seasons later.

"The studio asked me, 'Who can run this thing? David?' I said, 'Well, I'm sure he *could*. He's a great writer. But I don't see David having any affinity for this stuff whatsoever,'" said Brand. "Only he would have the answer to why he said yes."

Indeed, Chase did. "I did it for the money," he said. "The only time I ever did that."

M eanwhile, at HBO there had been a changing of the guard. Michael Fuchs had been fired and Jeff Bewkes, previously the CFO and president, became CEO. With his ascendancy came that of his head of programming, an executive who would have as much influence over the Third Golden Age as any writer or producer: Chris Albrecht.

In the early 1990s, the comedy troupe the State performed a sketch on MTV called "Doug & Dad." Michael Showalter played Doug, a teenager intent on rebellion despite being afflicted with a cool father. (Sample dialogue: "I'm Doug. And I'm not going to stop having sex in the parking lot behind the supermarket just 'cause you said that I can do it in my own bed!") Similarly, the showrunners of the Third Golden Age ritually railed and fumed against the destructive influence of network "suits" in a way that suggested mere habit or a kind of Kabuki ritual, since they generally enjoyed the most simpatico talent-executive relationships in the history of the medium. Albrecht, himself as big a personality as the artists he empowered, would eventually prove to have serious problems and idiosyncrasies of his own. But he, along with his right-hand woman, Carolyn Strauss, set the template for the generation's enlightened executives.

The Queens-born Albrecht had started as an aspiring comic. He quickly ended up employing them instead. In 1975, he became manager and eventually part owner of the Improv, New York's premier comedy club, where he developed a reputation as a smart spotter of talent and a hard partyer with the likes of Robin Williams. Albrecht's comedy pedigree, like that of Bernie Brillstein of Brillstein-Grey, seems important to his eventual role in the TV revolution. If there is any true, pure auteur art form, rising and falling entirely on the voice of one performer alone onstage, it's stand-up. The value of those voices could not have been lost on anyone spending night after night in a comedy club, nor could the recognition of how the new, genuine, and unexpected could affect a crowd.

"The way I learned it in the clubs," said Albrecht, "was that the highest form of stand-up was someone who had a point of view. Having a point of view was a necessary element of original voices."

In 1980, Albrecht became an agent at International Creative Management (ICM), representing Billy Crystal, Jim Carrey, Whoopi Goldberg, and Eddie Murphy, among others. In 1985, he joined HBO as the West Coast senior vice president for original programming.

At that time, HBO's center of gravity was still very much its New York City headquarters—and it would remain so as long as Fuchs, a volcanic figure in his own right (*Esquire* once dubbed him "the most potent, feared and hated man in Hollywood"), was in power. "I think there was an ingrained suspicion from a lot of the New York folks to the people in L.A.: 'Those *Hollywood* people,'" said Albrecht, who spent the first half of the 1990s developing projects that HBO produced for other outlets, Ray Romano's sitcom *Everybody Loves Raymond* the most successful among them.

It was frustrating, too, to those in the network's fledgling original series department, which Albrecht oversaw. "You were always struggling to make the case that this was the way to keep subscribers," said Susie Fitzgerald, who worked there at the time. "In order to eke out money, we were saying, 'We need continuing characters for the audience to fall in love with, so when they move or something, they don't just disconnect.'"

Bewkes, who took over from Fuchs in 1995, was a different kind of manager, more willing to delegate and more committed to the idea that HBO's future lay in original series. Crucially, satellite TV had been revolutionized by the introduction of light, easily mountable Ku-band receivers, which did away with the requirement for giant dishes seemingly more appropriate for searching the heavens for alien life. Through services like DirecTV and the Dish Network, this provided a new stream of revenue for Bewkes to play with. To the consternation of some in New York, the balance of power began to shift west toward Albrecht.

Strauss, too, had started at HBO in the mid-1980s, as a temp, and cut her teeth producing comedy specials. In style and temperament, she was Albrecht's polar opposite: shy to the point of seeming aloof, concerned with the kinds of details in a script or pitch that Albrecht found boring, herself allergic to his brand of charismatic glad-handing. Yet the two were equally sure of what they believed constituted the HBO brand.

"I'm not the kind of guy who's going to sit down and write four pages of notes," said Albrecht. "I'm going to say, 'Big picture: Here's what I thought.' So Carolyn and I had skills that fit well together. The great thing is that we didn't necessarily agree on everything, but we always saw the same thing. I never looked at a show and went, 'That's red,' and have Carolyn go, 'No, that's orange.'"

Ironically, given the increasing power of the California office, the first two successful series of the Albrecht/Strauss regime were about as New York as it was possible to get. First came *Oz*. Set behind the walls of an open-floor prison and shot entirely indoors, the show had the feel of eighties downtown experimental theater, down to a dreadlocked, wheelchair-bound Nuyorican-style poet in fingerless gloves acting as chorus. The cast—stocked with actors who would populate later HBO shows—functioned like such a theater company, often decamping from the one-floor soundstage over the Chelsea Market on Manhattan's West Side to La Nonna, a West Village restaurant of which showrunner Tom Fontana was part owner.

"Tom is from Buffalo, but he likes to think he grew up in Little Italy," said Seth Gilliam, who played an unstable corrections officer for seventeen episodes of *Oz* and later Sergeant Ellis Carver on *The Wire*. "He curses profusely. More than anything, he likes to make fun of you and invite you to make fun of him."

Fontana had a policy of helping out his cash-strapped cast members with drinks and food at the restaurant, sometimes to the consternation of his chef and partner. He also supported his actors' outside theater ventures, but instead of going to see them, he would make donations to the theater company. It was, he said, "worth $1,000 not to have to see a play."

Oz ran for six seasons, well into the *The Sopranos* era, and it's hard to imagine that *The Sopranos* could have existed without it. Aggressively artsy, filled with shocking violence, homoerotic sex, and a charismatic main character who happened also to be a gay, neo-Nazi psychopath, it expanded the definition of HBO's brand in crucial ways.

It remained, though, to prove that original series could create widespread buzz—and increased subscribers. That task fell to Strauss and Albrecht's next show, *Sex and the City*, which premiered June 6, 1998. For women (and plenty of men) across the country, the show, based on Candace Bushnell's frank columns for the *New York Observer*, which had themselves been turned into a book, was an aspirational fairy tale about friendship and glamour in New York. It might as well have been a tourism campaign for a post–Rudolph Giuliani, de-ethnicized Gotham awash in money. Its characters were types as familiar as those in *The Golden Girls*: the Slut, the Prude, the Career Woman, the Heroine. But they talked more explicitly, certainly about their bodies, but also about their desires and discontents outside the bedroom, than women on TV ever had before.

As it had been at MTM a generation prior, it was an exciting time to be at HBO. To be there was to feel suffused with a sense of mission, being outside the Hollywood mainstream ("in the ivory tower," as Fitzgerald put it) and, increasingly, having an impact on it.

"We took our jobs seriously, but we didn't take *ourselves* too seriously. We didn't put a lot of pressure on ourselves, because we hadn't had some measure of success to hold ourselves up against," Albrecht said. "I say to Jeff, 'Hey, here's this thing. What do you think about this?' He'd go, 'Looks pretty good, can you make it?'"

Strauss said, "It was loose. It was fun. We were still very much in the shadows. The fear doesn't creep in until you start winning Emmys."

All of which is to say that landing at HBO no longer seemed completely insane when Lloyd Braun, a former lawyer turned manager and executive at Brillstein-Grey, caught up with David Chase at the company's elevator bank and asked, "Have you ever thought about doing *The Godfather* for TV?"

Four

Should We Do This?
Can We Do This?

Every great TV show tells its whole story in its pilot. Often in just one line.

Think of *The Wire*, in which a young black man explains why his group of friends would repeatedly let a serial (now dead) thief named Snot Boogie enter their crap game. "You got to," the boy said, in a line borrowed from a real-life Baltimore homicide detective's tale. "It's America, man."

Or *Mad Men*, in which Don Draper and a potential conquest have this exchange:

> **Don:** The reason you haven't felt [love] is because it doesn't exist. What you call "love" was invented by guys like me to sell nylons. . . . You're born alone and you die alone, and this world just drops a bunch of rules on top of you to make you forget those facts. But I never forget. I'm living like there's no tomorrow, because there isn't one.
>
> **Rachel:** I don't think I realized it until this moment, but it must be hard being a man, too.

Or, shorter and sweeter, *Six Feet Under*: "No one escapes."

Or *The Shield*, shorter and not at all sweet: "Good cop and bad cop left for the day. I'm a different kind of cop."

A pilot is a strange beast. It must accomplish several things simultaneously. Foremost, of course, it must pack enough entertainment punch in its own right to convince, first, network executives that an entire season is worth making and, later, viewers that they should keep watching. At the same time, it must acquit itself of a hefty amount of scene-setting business—essentially calling a world into being—without becoming bogged down in exposition. (Given only a half hour to accomplish this, sitcom pilots have notoriously erred on the side of too much "sit," not enough "com.")

The pilot for an ongoing serialized drama has yet another imperative. Through some combination of deliberate craft and something less easily defined, it must imply a future often not yet imagined even by its creators. Almost alone among the narrative arts, these shows are composed with no ending—indeed, with the hope that it will stay that way indefinitely. And, of course, there is no ability on the part of the author to go back and adjust once the story begins rolling. It is a unique and uniquely terrifying trapeze act, in which the creator goes swinging out into a narrative abyss, with the conviction that the story will continue to come. The leap of faith continues throughout the process; often, once a season gets rolling and the writers' room, inevitably, falls behind, scripts are written, shot, and broadcast before the events of two or three episodes hence are even set in stone. Again, the serialized novel is the closest analogue, and Dickens didn't have an army of bloggers and recappers waiting to pounce when a character suddenly disappeared or changed names midstory.

Nor did he face the added task of investing an executive with enough faith to spend millions of shareholder dollars, employ hundreds of people, put his or her reputation on the line, and essentially open a corporate division based on an hour of story.

For all these reasons, a good pilot must engage in what's known in network jargon as "universe building." "You have to lay in enough DNA," said James Manos Jr., a *Sopranos* veteran who went on to write the pilot for *Dexter*.

"You have to give it legs so you can say, 'Wow, I can see where that character may go over the next five years. I understand what that wink means, what that one line means.' You're not figuring out what's going to happen in episode 309, but you're putting enough in the Petri dish so that character can *be* there in 309."

By the same measure, every pilot that doesn't either get made or get carried to series—which is to say, the vast, vast majority of them—is like a universe blinking out, along with its entire potential future. Occasionally, that world can miraculously spring back to life, at a different network or after a shift in regime. But in a business ruled by fear of risk and the eagerness to find easy reasons to say "no"—not to mention the mortal terror of seeing something you passed on succeed elsewhere—dead universes tend to stay dead.

For a writer with a good reputation and a handful of awards—as David Chase was by the 1990s—writing failed pilots is a viable career path, even an upwardly mobile one. But even to someone who purports to disdain TV and shrinks from success in it, all those dead and discarded universes start to weigh on the mind. Since *Almost Grown* and his stints with Brand and Falsey, Chase had moved from one lucrative development deal to the next, without getting his own show on the air.

"He'd come into my office, very pale, sit on my couch, and say, 'I've got nothing,'" said Susie Fitzgerald, then in development at Brillstein-Grey, where Chase had signed a two-year deal in 1995. "I'd say, 'Well, come on! Let's talk about some ideas.'"

One abortive effort from those years was an idea about a Miami Mob wife, to be played by Marg Helgenberger, who enters the witness protection program and moves back to New Jersey. It featured a character named Big Pussy— a fact that could scarcely have helped its chances at CBS.

Another potential gig was unintentionally funny: ABC briefly considered handing Chase the reins of the sitcom *The Wonder Years*, hoping to add a little edge to the show's gauzy nostalgic glow as its main character, Kevin, matured into high school age. In what must surely be considered one of the great lost scripts of history (or a *Saturday Night Live* sketch), Chase brought his usual sensibility to a trial run, having Kevin discover *The Catcher in the Rye* and start smoking cigarettes, drinking coffee, and conversing with the shade of Holden Caulfield. The powers that be quickly decided that perhaps they didn't need quite so much edge.

All of this, said Kevin Reilly, then of Brillstein-Grey, had the effect of hardening, rather than softening, Chase's resistance to outside interference. "You could say to him, 'I love everything you've done here. But you know how the character, at the end, lets the bad guy get away? And he's really depressed? Can we just get the sense that he's going to continue tirelessly, that he's not going to give up? Even if the bad guy gets away?' And David would say, 'No. I just can't see it that way.' And sometimes you'd say, 'Can we just move this comma over here?' And he'd say, 'I thought about it and I just can't do it.'"

Rejections, like punches, eventually start to hurt whether you respect the person giving them or not. "Some creative people are very volatile: up today, down tomorrow. David was down today, *more* down tomorrow," Reilly said. "After CBS passed on that Helgenberger thing, he called me at home probably every Sunday. He wanted to know why. 'But why? Why? *Why?*' I was like, 'David, I don't know. It was a year ago. Let it go.'"

"I had done five, six, seven of these things and I started to think, 'What the fuck?'" Chase said. "They always raved about the writing, but, 'It's too dark.' 'Oh, it's too complicated.' Every time, I'd think, 'Thank God I don't have to do that fucking series.' But after a while, you get . . . dejected."

Driving home after that brief meeting with Lloyd Braun at the Brillstein-Grey elevators in 1995, Chase quickly dismissed the notion of a TV *The Godfather*. But an idea began turning over in his head. The world of the Mafia certainly interested him; as a child, he had watched countless late-night movie re-airings of such James Cagney movies as *The Public Enemy* and *Angels with Dirty Faces*. Later, he'd been fascinated by the New Jersey *cafoni* from which his family had worked so hard to distinguish itself. New Jersey itself—its layers of trash and aspiration, its voices—had always acted as a kind of muse for Chase, even when he was writing about, say, the lost girl of *Off the Minnesota*

Strip. "I could never really get the fucking thing until I imagined her back in Caldwell, New Jersey," he said. "Then I felt more secure."

Francis Ford Coppola and Martin Scorsese, his heroes of America's New Cinema, had long since claimed the gritty world of organized crime as a subject worthy of high art. "The pantheon," as Chase described *The Godfather, Mean Streets, GoodFellas,* and others, had posited the Mob as the quintessential American story, a way to talk about both the aspirations and the rot at the nation's core.

Meanwhile, a legion of colleagues and friends had by now been treated to his mordant, hilarious stories about growing up with Norma. He'd been exploring the same material on and off with a series of therapists since his midthirties, when a family trip to Rome finally made him seek help. Alone for the day, he had been sitting in a café on the Piazza della Rotonda, across from the Pantheon, drinking a glass of champagne.

"I found myself thinking, 'What is it with this city? It's just thousands of years of death. The center of Western civilization and there's this feeling of death, violence, decay.' It just made me feel horrible. Then I thought to myself, 'Here you are, you have a healthy child, you have a happy marriage, you're sitting in front of the Pantheon, holding a glass of fucking champagne, and you're thinking this way. You need help.'" Recently, he had worked with a talented, patient female analyst named Lorraine Kauffman, who became the model for Jennifer Melfi.

Perhaps most important, Norma had died in 1992, freeing her son to tell his stories to a wider audience. As he drove west from Brillstein-Grey's Beverly Hills office toward home in Santa Monica, he recalled a conversation he had had with Robin Green, in which she'd encouraged him to write about his mother. He had gone home and jotted a short note in a computer file he called "Themes File": "Mafia Mother and Son—The father dies. Junior is in charge. His only rival is his mom. The old victim becomes the ballbuster/killer she always was. She must kill him or vice versa. (Or maybe he should put her in a nursing home.)"

At the time, he had imagined the project as a comedy. But now, turning it over in his head, he began to see deeper possibilities.

"Really early on, David started talking thematically, about America," said Kevin Reilly. "I remember a very early conversation in which he said, 'Look at what's going on in this country. This used to be a place where people would join a company and they knew the company would take care of them forever. Now, nobody's taken care of. And marriage is the same thing: You go to work and everybody's selling you out and you get home and your wife's busting your balls."

Thus the line in *The Sopranos* pilot that foretold so much staring into the cultural and spiritual void that was to come: "Lately I'm getting the feeling that I came in at the end. The best is over."

If the pilot was a culmination of David Chase's career and life experience, it started out acting just like a regular, doomed pilot. Chase and his agents went first with a pitch to CBS. President and chief executive Leslie Moonves, perhaps vying for the Executive Cliché of the Year Award, said he loved the idea but asked whether Tommy Soprano, as he was then known, had to be in therapy.

Next up was Fox, then still enjoying the role of insurgent network based on the strength of unconventional programs such as *The Simpsons* and *Married . . . with Children*. Bob Greenblatt, who then headed prime-time programming at the network, bought Chase's pitch in the rooms, making a $300,000 commitment for a pilot script. Chase was excited but characteristically pessimistic.

"As I started to write, I began to think, 'How is this going to work?' You know, with the language: 'Fuck this' and 'Fucking that.' I thought it was probably going to be a case of diverging expectations, that both me and the network were going to wind up hugely disappointed," he said.

"Strangely, I'd say the challenges of the show working on broadcast TV had more to do with narrative than with language," said Reilly. "Granted, you wouldn't have had as authentic an experience if you couldn't say 'Fuck you.' But the real problem was the story." As in the eventual pilot for HBO, this involved Tony's friend Artie Bucco, who is worried about the fate of his restaurant, Vesuvio. In impeccable Mob logic, Tony's solution is to blow the place up. "What he doesn't realize is that he's ruining his friend's dream. And at the end, he's sort of adrift," said Reilly. "That's not a network story."

Neither man was wrong. After many weeks of silence, word came that Fox would pass. Years later, at the height of his success, Chase delighted bitterly in naming the executive who had neglected to call and deliver the news; he would relate a chance meeting at a Television Critics Association event at which the poor fellow (who surely suffered more than his share of sleepless nights) came up to him to say, "Well, it all worked out for the best!"

The pilot now made the rounds—to NBC, to ABC, back to CBS. Everywhere, the answer was no. The universe of Dr. Melfi and Paulie Walnuts and Vesuvio and the Bada Bing! seemed destined to vanish in the usual atrophic way. Tired and dispirited, with his contract at Brillstein-Grey a few days from its expiration, Chase was preparing to sign yet another development deal, at Fox, that would include running *Millennium*, a spin-off of Chris Carter's *The X-Files*. That's when Braun called. "Listen," he said. "We sent the script over to HBO. There've been some changes over there and they may have some needs in this department."

The Sopranos couldn't have arrived at HBO at a more propitious time, but Albrecht and team weren't completely immune to the same worries that afflicted the networks. "Could we have a show with a criminal as a protagonist? It seems like a quaint little argument now, but at the time it was huge," said Carolyn Strauss. "I remember sitting in a room with Jeff [Bewkes] and Chris and hashing through it: 'Should we do this? We should do this! *Can* we do this?'"

Another sticking point was Chase's desire to direct the pilot. Albrecht was set against the idea. Chase had directed the *Almost Grown* pilot, two episodes of *I'll Fly Away*, and a *Rockford Files* TV movie, but he was hardly an experienced hand. Plus, on principle, Albrecht was hesitant to give one person so much control. Brad Grey called and asked that the HBO chief meet with Chase to hear him out: "That way, you'll say no but he'll at least feel like he got heard." Chase came in and put on a virtuoso performance.

"He talked about his vision: about how New Jersey was a character, the tone of it all. He was able to talk about it as a visual execution, not just a written execution," Albrecht said. "By the time he was finished talking, I thought, 'Wow. I might find somebody who's a "better director" than David, but I'll never find somebody who's a better director of *this*.'"

On the same day that Chase was required to make a final decision on his Fox deal by two p.m., he was summoned to a meeting at HBO at noon. Albrecht gave him the green light. And the search for the Man Who Would Be Tony began.

C hase's first, quixotic choice was a non-actor: As a good New Jerseyan, he of course knew Steven Van Zandt from Van Zandt's long-standing role as guitarist in Bruce Springsteen's E Street Band. Early in the band's career, in addition to what would become his trademark head scarves, the musician would occasionally wear a porkpie hat that Chase always thought made him look like an old-fashioned mobster. "He looked like a Jersey guy," he said.

"We had that gangster kind of Jersey thing going on," Van Zandt agreed. "Like the Rat Pack translated through some bizarre rock 'n' roll prism. Bruce was like Sinatra. I was like the fun Dean Martin character. And Clarence was Sammy Davis on steroids."

In 1996, Van Zandt had long since left the gang. He'd mostly stopped touring with Springsteen and given up his own solo career. In fact, he had given up almost everything beyond walking his dog around the West Village, where he lived, and passing his days in a state of nonproductive, though not entirely unpleasant, lassitude. "I did nothing. I literally walked my dog for seven years. I did not work. I just was sort of meditating and reflecting on my crazy world and my life and how I got to the point where I'd gotten to," he said.

One obsession did remain: advocating for the inclusion of the blue-eyed soul band the Rascals, pride of Garfield, New Jersey, in the Rock and Roll Hall of Fame. When that effort finally succeeded, Van Zandt was tapped to make the induction speech. And so it was that Chase, in bed one night and flipping through channels, suddenly saw that gangster face pop up on his TV screen.

It quickly became apparent that it was not the face of Tony Soprano. HBO was not prepared to bank its evolution on a musician with zero acting experience, no matter what he looked like in what kind of hat. The most serious candidate early in the process was Michael Rispoli, who would eventually take the smaller role of Jackie Aprile. As a consolation, Chase asked Van Zandt if he wanted to play any other role. Despite a nagging conscience about taking a job from a real actor, Van Zandt mentioned a treatment he'd once written for a film about a onetime hit man turned club owner. The main character's name was Silvio Dante.

But before the birth of *The Sopranos'* Silvio—he of the immaculate pompadour and chartreuse suits—Van Zandt did fly out to Los Angeles to do a screen test for Tony, alongside Rispoli and one other candidate. Leaving his audition, he passed this third actor in the waiting room and recognized him as a character actor he'd seen in the films *True Romance* and *Get Shorty.* "I didn't know his name, but I thought, 'That guy's great. He's got a kind of greatness about him. *He's* the one who should get the part,'" he said.

James Gandolfini was another Jersey boy, an alumnus of Park Ridge High School and Rutgers University. He had as little experience playing leading men as Van Zandt did. And he was far more unknown. Large, balding, and older looking than his thirty-five years, he was nobody's idea of a conventional movie star—though many women would come to find him startlingly sexy (not, in most cases, without some degree of internal conflict). What he brought with him was an almost instantaneous facility for inhabiting and deepening the role of Tony. His charisma, his petulance, his capacity for violence, his vulnerability—all of it bubbled and seethed beneath the surface as Gandolfini read at the audition.

"I felt this gut thing, that it was him, but David took some convincing. He loved Stevie Van Zandt," said Fitzgerald, who became Gandolfini's fiercest advocate. Gandolfini met with Chase in Los Angeles for three hours one Friday, and Fitzgerald called excitedly Saturday morning. "Is it him?" she asked breathlessly. "He said, 'I don't know. . . .' 'No, seriously, is it him?' 'He's a pain in the ass on set.' 'I don't care about that,'" said Fitzgerald. "'*Is it him?*'"

Chase came around, but he now faced Albrecht's worries about such an unusual leading man. "Rispoli had done a fantastic job, and his was a much more accessible Tony," Albrecht said. "David said, 'Look, in the real world it would be Jimmy.' And it was like, 'Yeah, you're right.' It wasn't a long conversation." (Gandolfini, for his part, understood the reservations: "This was an incredible leap of faith. I mean, it wasn't four pretty women in Manhattan [as in *Sex and the City*]. This was a bunch of fat guys from Jersey.")

The rest of the cast fell eclectically into place. With an unknown in the lead, Lorraine Bracco, as Tony's therapist, Jennifer Melfi, was the closest thing to a star; she and others would often say later that she had originally been called to play Carmela Soprano, but that casting was never likely, if only because it would have too closely aped her role in *GoodFellas*. From that movie, too, came an intense downtown New York theater actor and screenwriter, Michael Imperioli, to play Christopher Moltisanti. "He was already in the pantheon," Chase explained. John Ventimiglia read for nearly every male role in the script before landing the part of Artie Bucco.

For Paulie "Walnuts" Gualtieri, the team uncovered a rare and rough gem: Tony Sirico had played mobsters previously, notably for Woody Allen and James Toback, and he lent the cast a frisson of mobster street cred, having served time himself for some long-ago offense. As Paulie, his performance bordered on the savant; it was difficult to tell where the actor ended and the character began. As his germaphobic, immaculately dressed character might have done, Sirico insisted on preparing his own hair each day, often rising at three a.m. at his home in Bay Ridge, Brooklyn, to coif before reporting for an early shoot. Wherever he went, a fog of Drakkar Noir cologne followed, lingering for days in the clothing of female staffers whom he never missed an opportunity to embrace.

The most difficult role to fill proved to be Carmela. Days before shooting was scheduled to start, the part remained empty. Here, *Oz*, which would provide a pool of talent for many future shows of the Third Golden Age, made its first contribution. Edie Falco had spent three seasons playing single mother and prison guard Diane Whittlesey on that show, about as far from a suburban Mob housewife as it's possible to get. Nevertheless, she said, "Maybe it's because I'm part Italian, or grew up on Long Island, but I read the part and thought, 'I know exactly who this woman is. I can feel her already.'" After watching Falco reading two scenes—one in which Carmela tells Tony he's going to hell as he enters an MRI machine and one in which Tony admits he's started taking Prozac—the producers agreed, and Diane Whittlesey was sent on permanent "vacation."

The Sopranos pilot filmed in New Jersey over two weeks in the summer of 1997. Within days, Chase received powerful confirmation that casting Gandolfini had been the right move. He was directing a scene in which Christopher is complaining to Tony about not receiving enough credit for a job. As written, Tony gives him a quick slap, but instead, "Jim fucking went *nuts*—picked him up and grabbed him by the neck and just about throttled him." Chase had to catch his breath. "I thought, 'Wow. Right! That's exactly right!'" Already, the strange alchemical process by which a character who has resided inside one person's head comes to life outside it had begun. Tony would never again be Chase's alone.

Chase returned to California for postproduction, and cast and crew dispersed. Before leaving, Falco remembered, Chase told them, "You've been great. It's been lots of fun. Unfortunately, nobody is ever going to watch this."

Secretly, as it had upon completing *Almost Grown*, a part of Chase hoped the pilot would fail. If HBO declined to bring the show to series, he reasoned, the network might be willing to cut their losses by giving him an additional $750,000 to finish the story as a feature film. Even in the midst of filming, he would ask producer Ilene Landress if she thought HBO would prefer to release it that way. "Actually, no," Landress told him. "They're a *television network*. They're in the business of putting things on TV."

The finished pilot was submitted to HBO at the end of October. The Brillstein-Grey team arranged a screening for Albrecht. "The lights came up, and Chris, I'm not exaggerating, just sat there, with his head in his hands, rubbing his eyes. It felt like an eternity," said Reilly. "I think that on some level he was just trying to get his bearings. Just trying to screw his courage to the sticking place to say, 'Okay. I guess we're doing this kind of thing now.'"

Finally, Albrecht lifted his head and said, slowly, "It's really good."

Still, HBO, which had until December 20 to deliver a verdict, stalled on giving the official green light. One month passed. Chase was proud enough of the finished product to pay for his own screening for friends and family, catered with pasta and sausage and peppers. The response from those who'd spent their lives in TV was at once overwhelmingly positive and reflexively pessimistic.

"I just remember feeling, 'I cannot believe I'm looking at this. This is the greatest thing I've ever seen. If it fails, it won't be the fault of the project,'" said Barbara Hall, Chase's friend and former colleague on *I'll Fly Away*.

"It was the first time I thought, 'Okay. Really good shit doesn't get picked up,'" said Mitchell Burgess.

Three more weeks ticked by. HBO was silent. Chase fretted. "David," recalled Fitzgerald, deadpan, "is not a good waiter."

Finally, on the next to last day, the call came. Chase's feelings were mixed, as usual. "I thought, 'Here we go. It's going to be a tremendous amount of work.'" At the same time, he had the conviction of a condemned man given one more chance: "I didn't give a fuck about failing. I had nothing to lose. Once I had the go-ahead, I thought, 'You know what? We're just going to go for it.'"

C hase knew the main arc of the first season, where it began and where it ended, from Tony's initial panic attacks to his dawning realization that his mother tried to have him killed. That story would have constituted the feature he'd once dreamed of making. Now, though, he had to figure out how to get from point A to point B while filling twelve additional hours of television. That meant bringing in other writers.

No other art form—certainly none that putatively bears the imprint of an auteur—is created as collaboratively as the television drama. True, the Fellinis and Altmans of the world relied on the talent and creativity of dozens of other artists—from actors to lighting designers to hairdressers. What they didn't do was sit down in a room filled with other directors and solicit their input. Yet the very same essential truth about television that elevates the writer to Master of the Universe—the medium's voracious appetite for ever more content, ever more quickly—guarantees that he or she cannot do it alone.

Each showrunner must bend and shape this necessity to serve his or her own method, and there are as many subtle variations of writers' rooms as there are rooms themselves. The only near-absolute is that there will be a quantity and flow of food reminiscent of a cruise ship, as though writing were an athletic feat demanding a constant infusion of calories. (Or, to be cynical, as though writers are so craven and easily manipulated that mere food will keep them loyal and docile. To which it can only be noted that every writer brags about the food in the writers' room. Every single one of them.)

In most rooms, there is a conference table around which the writers gather. In the center will be a pile of snacks and takeout menus, as well as pads, pens, and other implements of creativity. Along the walls, there will be spaces to organize and visualize ideas—usually either whiteboards or bulletin boards covered with index cards. Depending on where in the process the room is, one might contain random ideas, bits of dialogue, stray themes. Another may have the evolving outline of a particular episode, a vertical stack of numbered scenes, or "beats." Along the longest wall, there will likely be a grid divided into twelve or thirteen vertical columns, representing the number of episodes. Running horizontally will be the names of characters and what happens to them in each episode, thus allowing the writers to see each story arc at a single glance. If there's a signature tool of the Third Golden Age, the whiteboard is it.

In one seat around the table, there will be a younger person, the writers' assistant, feverishly transcribing the proceedings into a laptop. He or she will be the only one apparently engaged in what most of the world identifies as "work." Indeed, a functional writers' room must embrace, at least in its early stages, the creative ferment of procrastination, as its members get to know one another, trade stories, and mull over the themes and narrative threads of the show at hand. Most successful showrunners encourage such bullshit sessions. Eventually, the business of the room will turn to actually "breaking" story—that is, creating an outline of specific beats. As the show progresses, the writer assigned to a specific episode will take these often incredibly specific outlines and disappear for a week or two, to write. Later still, there will be rotating absences as writer-producers supervise the shooting of their scripts on set or location.

The ultimate goal, even if it's unstated, is something that goes well beyond some version of screenwriting by committee: a kind of creative communion. Said David Milch, "The best situation of all is to come clean in the writers' room and discover, through your encounter with your fellow writers, the nature and rhythms of the story that you're trying to tell."

But between reality and that lofty goal lie any number of quotidian pitfalls: writers who talk too much, writers who don't talk at all, yes-men, naysayers, egos run amok. In other words, precisely as complicated and intense a set of conditions as one might imagine results from taking a group of artists—each the smartest and funniest in his or her class, each having gotten into the business with the dream of producing his or her own work, most neurotic to one degree or another, and all feeling the pressure of competition—and putting them in a room together for eight hours a day, mostly to face rejection and all in service of another person's vision.

"That's the job. You're there to serve the Creator," said James Manos, who also wrote for Shawn Ryan's *The Shield*. "It's a difficult position because someone like David or Shawn hires you because you have your own, strong voice and then, as soon as you get there, you have to start writing in *their* voice."

Matthew Weiner admitted to being driven crazy by the idea that nobody outside the inner circle of *The Sopranos* would ever know the good writing he did while on the show. But, he said, "I could never live not expressing the fact that I was working *for* David, in David's brain, with David's characters, trying to please David, not operating a Matt Weiner franchise of the *Sopranos* show."

The best analogy might be a draftsman charged with designing one small element—a sconce, say— of an architect's grand cathedral. He may find satisfying ways to express himself, might even get some career-advancing recognition from hard-core sconce aficionados, but ultimately it's all about illuminating the Master's work. That gives the showrunner, who of course knows his own vision better than anybody, immense powers of rejection and benediction. The ultimate dream is to find writers who bring something absolutely new into the universe he's created, who give him exactly what he wants but could never have dreamed of himself. "That's when you get this stupid look on your face," Milch said.

Or as Weiner put it, "It's like falling in love."

It should come as no surprise, then, that writers' rooms are somewhat intense workplaces. (It hardly seems accidental that "the room" is a term also used in analysis and in Alcoholics Anonymous.) They are hotbeds of emotional turmoil and transference.

"I've never been in a writers' room where the writers didn't end up psychologically picking apart the showrunner, down to the finest grain," said Chris Provenzano, a writer for *Mad Men* and other shows. "Writers are already interested in motivations and psyches. They've all been in therapy. They're all messed up and trying to fill some hole. So when the showrunner invariably does something that doesn't square or that they don't like, they start saying, 'He must be at war with his ex-wife. It's got to be something like that.' You become involved in this slow but inexorable dismantling of the person's psyche because that's the brain in charge of all the other brains and you're the appendages of this superorganism."

D avid Chase, devotee of the film auteurs, had predictably complicated feelings about writers' rooms. Early in his career, he had worked at *The Rockford Files* with a staff of just three who would get together and brainstorm stories, letting a tape recorder capture sudden inspiration. Later, grappling with the more complex storytelling of *Almost Grown* and *Northern Exposure*, he'd headed larger rooms. And he'd come to terms with their necessity for generating stories.

"Story construction is the hardest part of the process. It's very difficult not to do things that everybody in America has already seen a thousand times. So, you go in there and you say, 'What do we want to make happen?'"

That, he said, is the fun part, along with the gossip, the eating, the discussing current events, the bullshitting. It's when it came time for what he called the "professional" part of the job that he was more dubious.

"Other people have good ideas. And they're hard to come by. But in another sense, they're a dime a dozen," he said. "Turning an idea into an *episode*—that's the grunt work. The organization can rest for a day or so, secure in the notion that we've got an idea. But eventually the showrunner's the one who has to look at his watch and say, 'How do we fill up forty-two minutes?' We can all sit around and decide we want to make a Louis XIV table, but eventually somebody has to do the carving."

What happens next, he says, is a private epiphany, experienced in public.

Invariably what would happen is I would get up, go off by myself, and they would continue talking. There was a couch and I would lie on that couch and just put my story hat on. And this is not a natural thing for me. I don't like math. I don't like puzzles. At all. Story work to me is that: it's figuring out this puzzle. But I would go on that couch by myself and they'd all be talking. And then I would just sort of like suddenly—this idea, that idea—all of a sudden you get a run. It's like music. I'd see where the peaks and valleys are: "This goes like this, like that, like *this*." And I would get up and go to the board and *bam bam bam*. "And then and then and then." It's very impressionistic. You're running really fast. Sometimes, *boom*: It's done. You have fourteen scenes. I don't know how it works, but it would happen.

To what extent such breakthroughs are facilitated by being surrounded by other writers, or happen in spite of them, appears to be an open mystery even to Chase himself.

"My experience is that the showrunner really has to just do it," he said.

Yet if he had all the time in the world to write every word of every episode of a series? "I would hire a staff. I'd get lonely."

Chase began building *The Sopranos* writers' room by looking to old colleagues. Robin Green and Mitchell Burgess had met at the University of Iowa. Green, who had written for *Rolling Stone* in its San Francisco salad days, was at the Writers' Workshop; Burgess, a tall, deep-voiced native Iowan, had just come out of a stint in the army and was a student in her undergraduate writing class. Eventually, Green landed at Brand and Falsey's *A Year in the Life* and then worked for Chase on *Almost Grown*.

The two bonded over their equally problematic mothers. "We would laugh so hard, we'd cry," Green said. Chase was intrigued by Green's single (albeit tenuous) connection to the world of organized crime: as a teenager growing up in Providence, Rhode Island, she'd double-dated with a son of crime boss Raymond Patriarca.

After *Almost Grown*, both writers returned to the Brand-Falsey camp: Chase to *I'll Fly Away* and Green to *Northern Exposure*. Burgess joined Green as a writing partner, and the two would go on to write nearly a quarter of the show's 110 episodes, including many during Chase's two-year tenure.

David and Denise Chase were creatures of gustatory habit, claiming a restaurant they liked and then returning over and over. In Santa Monica, their spot was an Italian restaurant called Drago, where they often anchored dinner parties. Green and Burgess remained regular attendees after *Northern Exposure* ended, and they followed the progress of *The Sopranos* pilot, which Chase had given them to read when it was still at Fox. If this thing goes, he asked them, will you come write for me? The answer was an enthusiastic yes. In the meantime, they suffered through staff positions in the writers' room of *Party of Five*, which is where they were just a few days before Christmas, breaking yet another story of teen drama, when an assistant came in to say they were wanted on the phone: a Mr. Tommy Soprano was calling.

The Sopranos' writers began meeting in a rented portion of Oliver Stone's production offices in Santa Monica. Chase assembled packages of material on Mob life for his writers to read. Dan Castleman, a Manhattan assistant district attorney who would remain with the show as a consultant throughout its run, came in to talk about his organized crime prosecutions. Another visitor was a former made man, now in the witness protection program, who showed off scars from long-ago bullet wounds and shared his expertise on such matters as how best to break a person's arm and the Mafia's relative views on penetrating stewardesses with broomsticks (pro) and performing cunnilingus (con).

Also in the room was Manos, a chain-smoking semi-agoraphobe who had helped pen an HBO movie called *The Positively True Adventures of the Alleged Texas Cheerleader-Murdering Mom*; two young writers, Mark Saraceni and Jason Cahill; and a colorful chatterbox named Frank Renzulli, the closest thing to an actual wiseguy that *The Sopranos* writing team ever had.

Renzulli, a big man with a Brillo goatee, was the son of first-generation immigrants from Sicily and Naples. He had grown up in the Maverick housing projects on Boston's East Side, in underworld terms a stronghold of the Patriarca crime family. Renzulli's parents were not themselves connected, but their feelings spanned the range of Italian American response to the Mafia. His father looked down on mobsters, though Renzulli suspected that, ironically, his paternal grandfather had migrated to upstate New York during Prohibition for reasons connected to bootlegging. His mother, meanwhile, had grown up in the neighborhood. "One of the wiseguys once told me, 'Thank God your mother wasn't born a man. We'd all be in trouble,'" Renzulli said. "She would have been the happiest woman in the world if I'd become a wiseguy."

She half got her wish. By the time he was nine years old, Renzulli had started hanging out around the local social club. He would run errands for the older guys with shiny Cadillacs and thick bankrolls and entertain them with his precocious antics.

"You're a poor kid in the inner city, and life looks hopeless. People are telling you it's hopeless. Then you see a guy pull up in a fucking Mercedes. Fucking air-conditioned, smelling good, looking good. And he's got his own little social club. They got air-conditioning in there. They got food in there, all this stuff. And one of them says, 'C'mere, you little prick. What's your name? Do me a favor, go to this store, get me this, this, and this.' And then it builds from there."

If that induction sounds as though it could have been ripped from a screenplay, it's worth remembering one of *The Sopranos*' more trenchant insights: that Mob life and pop culture's portrayal of it have been locked in such a long cycle of reference, echo, and imitation that it's often hard to tell which came first.

By his teens, Renzulli had become a fine pool player, an astute observer of Mob mores, and a peripheral, though increasingly involved, participant in the world of petty crime and occasional violence. By his early twenties, he began to think it was time to get out.

"I had an epiphany one night: Everything was either feast or famine. One night I'd have a couple thousand dollars in my pocket, the next I'm looking to borrow money for cigarettes." Going straight wouldn't be easy, especially given the disdain he'd developed for the straight world. "I needed to exorcise those demons that said, 'You're a sucker if you work a legitimate job.' I was always at risk of losing my regular job the minute somebody told me what to do. I was always at risk of saying, 'Go fuck yourself.'"

He headed for New York, to study acting and playwriting. For two years, he worked odd carpentry jobs and lived in the Sixty-third Street YMCA. Eventually, he found work as a doorman in a Hell's Kitchen building filled with the same breed of wiseguys he'd left behind. By now, though, the call of show business was stronger than that of criminality. He landed his first speaking role in Woody Allen's *Broadway Danny Rose*.

In 1987, he went west to Los Angeles in search of more parts. After a few years, he turned to writing. "There's only so many goombahs you can play," he said. By the time he came to Chase's attention, he'd co-created a short-lived show called *The Great Defender*, which starred Michael Rispoli as a blue-collar lawyer; developed one failed pilot set in East Boston that featured future *Shield* star Michael Chiklis; and worked on another with David E. Kelley, for whom he also played a recurring role as a pimp on *The Practice*.

Chase met with him at a coffee shop in Santa Monica, and both men left wary. "I'd read the pilot, and I couldn't figure out what the point of view was. I mean, Why is he writing this?" Renzulli remembered. He had the feeling Chase didn't like him. "I irritated him," he said. "I think he called David Kelley to ask if I always talked so much."

Chase, for his part, reported back to Green and Burgess: "This guy's got the real marinara," meaning Mob knowledge, "but he's crazy as hell."

Still, the two saw eye to eye on at least one important matter, one that would secure Renzulli's participation in building the *Sopranos* universe. "Every wiseguy I saw played on TV made me want to scream," Renzulli said. "He [David] told me, 'It's not bad acting, it's bad *writing*. Those shows are written poorly. We're not going to do that.'"

The first several episodes came together in the office in Santa Monica. Green would write each beat on an index card and tape them together in long strips. After four episodes were written, the crew—minus Renzulli, who, with three children and another on the way, remained in California—packed up to move to New York and begin production. Chase left no question about his ambition. "David was after big fish," Burgess said. "He wanted this to be as good as *The Godfather*. As good as *GoodFellas*." Over dinner at a Japanese restaurant, Chase told Burgess and Green, "This is it for me. If this doesn't work, I'm out of the business."

Meanwhile, back in New Jersey, producers and location scouts had been fanning out across the Garden State, looking for the building blocks of *The Sopranos'* physical universe. The North Caldwell house that had been the family's home in the pilot was reconstructed at Silvercup Studios (it would become ever more expensive to get permission to shoot the handful of necessary exterior scenes at the real house each season). The Bada Bing! remained a strip club called Satin Dolls in Lodi. An empty storefront in a Scottish Irish neighborhood in Kearny became the semipermanent site of the fictional Satriale's Pork Store, as well as production storage.

Because HBO had no real prime-time schedule and nobody was waiting on the show's debut, Chase and team had the luxury of filming, editing, and finalizing all thirteen episodes long before a single one aired. At the conclusion of shooting, in November, Chase was his usual self. "Jim, Edie, all of us were like, 'This was fun. It was an interesting challenge. We enjoyed ourselves.' Which of course meant that we weren't going to be able to continue, because TV is never about enjoying yourself."

As the January premiere approached, there were positive rumblings from critics and a handful of private screenings, but nobody knew what to expect. "We were really living in a bubble: It was a pilot that had been passed on. Cast with unknowns and shooting in New Jersey. For HBO. Who was paying attention?" Fitzgerald said.

On January 10, while a snowstorm rolled up the East Coast, *The Sopranos* made its debut.

And then, as one cast member would later put it, "all hell broke loose."

PART II

The Beast in He

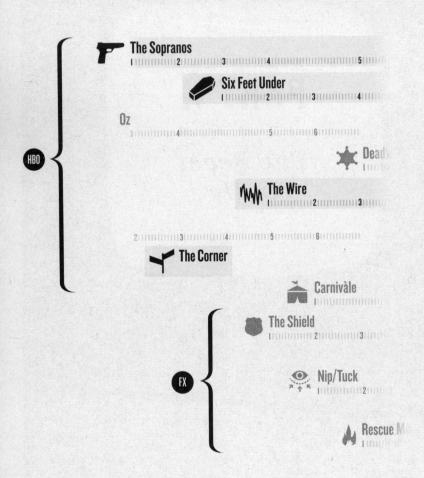

1999 | 2000 | 2001 | 2002 | 2003 | 2004

The Sopranos

Six Feet Under

Oz

Dead

The Wire

The Corner

Carnivàle

The Shield

Nip/Tuck

Rescue M

HBO

FX

1999–2004

Five

Difficult Men

The opening theme of *The Sopranos* was a remix of a 1997 song by a mostly unknown, America-obsessed band from Brixton, London, called Alabama 3—or, in the United States, A3, to avoid legal complications involving the band Alabama. At first listen, it seemed an odd, almost perverse choice for a show so steeped in its particular social world—even less "Italian" and "Jersey" than David Chase's other top choice of song, Elvis Costello's "Complicated Shadows." But Chase, early on, was shy of being too straightforward with his musical choices; it would be a while before he considered Springsteen or Sinatra. And the discordant, driving "Woke Up This Morning" quickly became inseparable from the show, so intrinsic to its effect that it was soon unclear whether it had been the perfect choice all along or had simply been transformed by the material it introduced.

In any event, the most important song in the *Sopranos* pilot played not over the main title, but in the closing credits: Nick Lowe's "The Beast in Me." It could be the theme song for the entire Third Golden Age.

The beast in me
Is caged by frail and fragile bars
Restless by day
And by night, rants and rages at the stars
God help the beast in me

Men alternately setting loose and struggling to cage their wildest natures has always been the great American story, the one found in whatever happens to be the ascendant medium at the time. Our favorite genres—the western; the gangster saga; the lonesome but dogged private eye operating outside the comforts of normal, domestic life; the superhero with his double identities—have all been literalizations of that inner struggle, just as Huckleberry Finn striking out for the territories was, or Ishmael taking to the sea.

It should have been no surprise, then, that the Third Golden Age of TV began by revisiting those genres. The same had been true of sixties and seventies cinema, with its retelling of the flight to the frontier (*Easy Rider*), the detective story (*The Long Goodbye*), the western (*The Wild Bunch, McCabe & Mrs. Miller*), and so on. Above all, no genre suited the baby boomers' dueling impulses of attraction and guilt toward American capitalism as well as the Mob drama. The notion that the American dream might at its core be a criminal enterprise lay at the center of the era's signature works, from *Bonnie and Clyde* and *Chinatown* to *The Godfather* and *Mean Streets*.

The Sopranos yoked that story to one of postwar literature's most potent tropes: horror of the suburbs, which in novels from Richard Yates's *Revolutionary Road* to Joseph Heller's *Something Happened* to John Updike's Rabbit series had come to represent everything crushing and confining to man's essential nature. In his self-absorption, his horniness, his alternating cruelty and regret, his gnawing unease, Tony was, give or take Prozac and one or two murders, a direct descendant of Updike's Rabbit Angstrom. In other words, the American Everyman. (He was also a twisted version of yet another archetype, the "TV dad"; as Chase said, "It was *Father Knows Best* . . . how to kill people.")

Out of the two traditions came a very modern, very relatable hybrid:

an old-school man—blunt, physical, taking whatever he wanted, a seductive if uncomfortable fantasy for men and women alike—in a postfeminist world. *Rescue Me*'s Tommy Gavin and *The Shield*'s Vic Mackey were versions of the same thing: men in the most macho of professions—fireman and policeman—undone by women the moment they stepped off duty. And Don Draper, of course, was swept up, head-on, in the revolution of gender roles and expectations.

"Here's a guy with all that power, yet completely emasculated by his mom and wife," FX executive, and later head of Fox Broadcasting, Peter Liguori said of Tony. "Guys watched and thought, 'I'd like to be the boss, I'd like to have big balls. I'd like to make all the calls and do things according to my rules.' But also, 'Man, he's a lot like me, because even when I am the boss, the second I go home, I'm Hazel.'"

For all that, Tony was also precisely the kind of character that conventional wisdom had long held viewers might embrace in the safety of a movie theater, or in the pages of a book, but would reject if he appeared on-screen in their own homes. If that was ever true, what had changed?

In part, by the late 1990s those traditional boundaries between art consumed outside and inside the home had long since started to blur, thanks to cable, video games, home video, and the nascent Internet. This process would vastly accelerate over the next ten years, until children coming to media consciousness in 2012 would make no meaningful distinction between "movie," "TV," "YouTube," "podcast," and so on.

At the same time, shifting economics revealed that maybe it had always been advertisers, rather than audiences, who were so averse to difficult characters—a throwback to the time when individual advertisers produced and sponsored their own shows and exercised a chilling effect on the shows' content. Generally, that meant rejecting anything that threatened too directly the warm feelings and consumerist status quo that viewers would carry over into the commercial break.

HBO, of course, had no such sponsors to worry about. Its concern was building the sense that a culturally aware person could not afford not to have a subscription, even if he or she watched only an hour per week. And basic

cable was quick to catch up, for reasons more similar than immediately apparent. Advertising, to which ratings matter so much, is only one of two revenue
streams vital to a basic cable network's bottom line. The other comes from
carriage fees, which are what cable operators (Time Warner, Cablevision, Cox)
pay for the right to include the network in its cable packages. Even as operators expanded to thousands of stations, the sheer number of networks fighting for space introduced a fear more pressing than the hoary Grendel of low
ratings—being dropped and disappearing altogether.

John Landgraf, who became president of FX Entertainment in 2004, explained the value of having original shows like *The Shield* and *Rescue Me*:
"There is a group of consumers out there, in the tens of millions"—way more
than watch any individual FX show—"that would really be bothered if they
couldn't get FX. They would either change cable providers or bitch to their
cable provider. I'm not sure that would happen if all we had was *Two and a
Half Men* repeats and a really good lineup of Hollywood movies."

With success also comes leverage, in particular for the ability to "bun-
dle" a media company's other stations alongside a popular one. So, for instance, AMC Networks (pointedly renamed that, from Rainbow Media, after
the success of AMC's original programming) could insist that a carrier take on
IFC, Sundance Channel, and WE tv if it wanted also to show *Mad Men* and
Breaking Bad. And when the satellite provider Dish Network refused, it could
wage a public relations war, appealing directly to subscribers.

At the same time, the era in which Stephen J. Cannell could have a show
canceled while pulling a 32 share—that is, over a third of the entire viewing
audience (*Black Sheep Squadron*, in 1978)—was obviously long gone. In its
place was a collection of niches that could be targeted more directly. In magazines, *The New Yorker* versus *Parade* is a good analogy: the former may have
thirty million fewer subscribers than the latter, but theirs are the readers a
certain type of lucrative advertiser most wants to reach.

Somewhere, of course, the vectors meet; a show needs viewers. But for all
the reasons above, raw ratings ceased to be the most sacred of all TV metrics.
They were replaced by something far less quantifiable: Brand. Buzz. David
Milch, who had created an early version of TV's difficult man in Detective

Andy Sipowicz of *NYPD Blue* and would go on to expand the type in *Deadwood*, saw in this shift nothing less than a radical creative liberation.

"For the first twenty-five years of television, commercials were the church—which is to say, you couldn't offend the sponsor. Therefore, certain values had to be underscored in the subject matter." The new realities of cable, he went on, stripped away that stricture, leaving a world ripe for exploring "the antiversions of all forms," a place where "the Story" was free to "declare itself on its own terms, with no preexisting expectations."

"All the conventions have been hollowed out and revealed as barren," he said. "In fact, the expectations are there to be deconstructed."

A nd so came the antiheroes. Long before David Simon proposed that *The Wire* would document "an America at every level at war with itself" or *The Shield* spent an entire season playing out an L.A. allegory of the Iraq War, it was clear that the cultural climate of the 2000s would be propitious for such characters. America, as *The Sopranos* debuted, was well on its way to becoming a bitterly divided country. Just how divided would become vividly clear in the 2000 presidential election. After it, Americans on the losing side were left groping to come to terms with the Beast lurking in their own body politic and—as the decade rolled on with two wars, secret prisons, torture scandals, and more—with what things it might be doing in their name.

That side happened to track very closely with the viewership of networks like AMC, FX, and HBO: coastal, liberal, educated, "blue state." And what the Third Golden Age brought them was a humanized red state: cops, firemen, Mormons, even Nixon-supporting Don Draper and, crime of all crimes, nonvoting Jimmy McNulty. This was different from previous "working-class" shows, such as *Roseanne,* pitched at attracting a large audience who related to its financially struggling characters, or even *All in the Family,* which invited each side to laugh equally at the other. This was the ascendant Right being presented to the disempowered Left—as if to reassure it that those in charge were still recognizably human.

"A show like *The Sopranos* has a soothing quality because ultimately

there's an unspoken assumption behind it that even the most monstrous people are haunted by the same concerns we're haunted by," said Craig Wright, a
playwright who wrote for *Six Feet Under* and others. Such, he went on, has always been the case during conservative pendulum swings: the Left articulates
a critique through the arts. "But the funny part is that masked by, or nested
within, that critique is a kind of helpless eroticization of the power of the
Right. They're still in love with Big Daddy, even though they hate him."

That was certainly true for the women who made Tony Soprano an unlikely sex symbol—and for the men who found him no less seductive. Wish fulfillment has always been at the queasy heart of the mobster genre, the longing
for a life outside the bounds of convention, mingled with the conflicted desire
to see the perpetrator punished for the same transgression. So it was for the
fictional men of the straight world on *The Sopranos*, who were drawn to
Tony's flame with consistently disastrous results. (Davey Scatino loses his
sporting goods store after joining the gang's poker game; Artie Bucco, the lon-
gest-standing member of the outside-looking-in crowd, suffers a never-ending
series of painful humiliations.) Likewise for viewers, for whom a life of taking,
killing, and sleeping with whomever and whatever one wants had an undeni-
able, if conflict-laden, appeal.

A nd likewise, most importantly, for TV's creators themselves. It should
come as no surprise that the job of showrunner—with its power to sum-
mon worlds to life, move characters around the universe, commit unspeakable
acts, at least by proxy—attracts men not totally unfamiliar with the most
primitive impulses of the characters they create.

Certainly David Chase understood. "When I watch Mob movies, part of
me is like, 'Yeah! Yeah! Kick out the jams, motherfuckers!'" he said, quoting
the proto-punk band MC5.

Or, more to the point, there was the day the writer Todd Kessler found
himself alone with Chase in the Silvercup writers' offices. The showrunner
had been late for a meeting to stitch together the two men's halves of the final

episode of the second season, "Funhouse." Now, he distractedly sat down across from Kessler and announced that he'd had an epiphany.

"'Is it something you want to talk about?' I asked. We were sitting across a table that was probably two and a half feet wide," Kessler said. "He said, 'Well . . . I realized . . . that I'll never be truly happy in life . . . until I kill a man.' And then he leaned across the table and said, 'Not just kill a man'—and he raised his hands right on either side of my head—'but *with my bare hands.'*"

The two sat there silently for a long moment. And then Chase broke the spell. "I'm going to get a coffee," he said, getting up from the table. "You want a coffee?"

I n a sense, of course, Chase had already done exactly what he said he needed to do.

If there was a single moment that signaled the new TV reality, it came only a handful of weeks after *The Sopranos* debuted. By that time, audiences had already begun to feel affection for this new, unusual hero. True, they had seen him involved in beating a man up; plotting insurance fraud, extortion, and arson; and committing adultery. On the other hand, he seemed to come by such behavior honestly, what with the crazy mother. And if you were accustomed to traditional TV narratives, there were signs that this might be a straightforward one about a man reforming himself through therapy and the love of his family. After all, the first episode began with what could have been a saint's conversionary vision of the beauty and vulnerability of the world, contained in a flock of baby ducks. It was plausible, too, given the slightly exaggerated cinematography and design of the first few episodes, not to mention the repartee between Paulie Walnuts, Silvio, and the other gangsters, that the show would ultimately turn out to be a comedy more than anything else. Chase often said, quite seriously, that he was never 100 percent sure that wasn't true.

And then, in week five, Tony strangled a man to death. Right in front of us. In real time. While taking his daughter on a college tour.

"College," as the episode was titled, didn't start out as a bid to change television. Instead the story grew, innocently enough, out of a TV impulse as old as *The Brady Bunch*. "After sitting there for three episodes, I said, 'Oh, I'm so fucking *bored* with this. We gotta get these people out of town,'" said Chase. "'Maybe they take a vacation or something.'" Chase had recently taken his own teenage daughter on a tour of colleges and quickly landed on the idea of sending Tony and Meadow on a similar tour of small liberal arts colleges in Maine.

Chase always maintained that the goal of each episode, regardless of what narrative business was necessary to the show's ongoing story arc, was to create a "minimovie." The premise of "College" was promising on that front even before the introduction of the character that would spur Tony to murder. *The Sopranos* was rarely more acute and unsettling than when it pulled back from the hermetic world of the North Jersey mob to allow a glimpse of the straight world outside. Think of a pair of mobsters' flummoxed attempts to shake down a corporate coffee shop, or A.J. visiting a rich classmate and seeing what real money and power looks like. (*The Wire* would hit similar notes with equal effect, as when two young drug dealers drive out of town and are shocked to learn that radio stations differ from region to region—even more so that theirs is broadcasting *A Prairie Home Companion*.)

Sending a mobster into alien territory, on one of the ultimate rites of passage for bourgeois parents, couldn't have been a better setup. The first shot of "College," directed by Allen Coulter, who would become a signature director of this series and many that followed in its footsteps, finds Tony stranded, like a piece of garish lawn statuary, outside an august stone academic building, bells tolling overhead. (The building, of course, like nearly everything else in *The Sopranos*, was actually located in New Jersey, on the campus of Drew University; as a location scout for the show said, "Everything in the known universe you can find in New Jersey.") His conflicting roles of father and mobster are never as poignant as when Meadow confronts him knowingly, in the car, about what he does for a living. Or later, when the two join in a father-daughter conspiracy to keep her drunken evening a secret from her mother. Meanwhile, Carmela has stayed home with the flu, giving her the opportunity to spend a wine- and Merchant Ivory–soaked evening with oily, flirtatious Father Phil. After several glasses, she tearfully admits to knowing, and conveniently ignoring, the moral cost of her comfortable life—a cathartic moment of self-knowledge that, characteristically, will never be acted on.

All of this would have made for an entertaining, satisfying minimovie that deepened and expanded our knowledge of, and queasy affection for, these characters. But the plot point that would define "College" upped all these stakes dramatically. It came from Frank Renzulli, who suggested, in the writers' room, that Tony run into an ex–Mob member, now in the witness protection program. Chase straightened up and walked out of the room, to his office. The next morning, he arrived with the story's eighteen beats intact: At a gas station somewhere on Tony and Meadow's route, Tony believes he spots Fabian "Febby" Petrulio, a onetime made man who flipped on the Family after being busted for selling heroin—a realistic nod to one of the prime factors in the Mob's diminishing power. In between bonding with Meadow and shepherding her to her Colby College interview, he confirms the snitch's identity, tracks him down, and strangles him.

Within a few years, the idea that a TV protagonist couldn't kill somebody would seem as fusty and dated a convention as earlier generations not being able to share a bed or say the word *pregnant*. What remains shocking in "College" isn't the death itself; it's Tony's unmitigated relish in doing the deed. There is no tortured internal debate—even after his snooping reveals that Petrulio, now masquerading as "Fred Peters," has a new family and small daughter of his own—no qualms even about Meadow's presence, other than the inconvenience it poses. Nor is there any suggestion that Tony stands to earn much in the way of credit or prestige by doing away with a rat; indeed, Christopher (whom we've already seen dismember a body for disposal in the back of Satriale's) begs Tony to allow *him* to fly up and take care of the hit. It is simply a given in Tony's world: a rat needs to be killed. At least in Chase's original story, there are none of the "outs" designed to allow viewers to rationalize and justify what they're about to see—which is Tony grunting, spitting, exultant, crushing Petrulio's windpipe with an improvised garrote of electrical wire, the wire cutting deep into his palms from the effort, Petrullo begging for his life between gasps. The scene lasts an unwavering minute and sixteen seconds.

In *The Sopranos* mythology, one that flatters both its creator's sense of authorship and HBO executives' sense of enlightened patronage, the network delivered only two notes during the show's eight-year run. Although it's hard to believe this is literally true, it does seem that the network challenged Chase only twice on issues of substance. And both times, the showrunner prevailed. The first was over the series title, which HBO found sufficiently confusing ("What, is it a show about opera singers?" Jamie-Lynn Sigler thought when called for her audition) that they assembled a binder of alternatives, mostly variations on Chris Albrecht's preferred name: the ham-fistedly punny *Family Man*. In the end, the title proved once again the lesson of the Beatles, Amazon.com, and others: that the silliest, most obscure name will seem perfect and inevitable the moment it is attached to a cultural phenomenon. Before long, a Google search would return hundreds of results on "Sopranos" the show before any on "sopranos" the centuries-old musical tradition.

The second of the legendary two notes was on "College." In Chase's mind, murdering Petrulio wasn't meant to be a grand narrative statement. Like Tony himself, he believed it was simply how things had to be—the natural outcome in the world his characters lived in. Sending the script in to HBO, he expected that it would occasion some discussion, but when the phone rang from Albrecht's office, he wasn't prepared for the passionate exchange that ensued.

"You've created one of the most compelling characters on television of the last twenty years and you're going to ruin him in the fifth episode!" Albrecht yelled.

"What do you mean?" asked Chase, guileless.

"He kills that guy! We're going to lose the audience!"

"Well, Chris, I have to tell you, I completely disagree," said Chase. "In fact, I think we'd lose the audience if he *didn't* kill that guy." Viewers, he argued, understood what being a rat meant in Tony's world; if he was to let Petrulio live, "what kind of mobster is that? He'd be without portfolio."

The argument went back and forth. Chase suggested they simply shelve the episode and move on to the next. "Jesus fucking Christ!" Albrecht sputtered. "We spent all that money and now we're not going to show the episode? I mean . . . maybe if we knew this guy he killed was a real scumbag . . ."

"He's a *rat!*"

In the end, Chase won the war—dragging Albrecht, who happily admitted he was wrong ever after, and TV history along with him. But it wasn't without a concession that nearly cost him the battle. As an accommodation to HBO's point of view, Chase inserted a scene in which it is revealed that Petrulio not only is dealing drugs in town, but is seen trying to hire a couple of junkies to kill Tony and Meadow. Predictably, the scene feels false and conventionally "TV." It was the last such concession that Chase would make.

"After that we'd talk about money, maybe. Budget stuff. He said some intelligent things," said Chase of his relationship with Albrecht. "I never had conversations like that with an executive. Where you're actually talking about the same things, and he's not saying, 'If he's a gangster, maybe . . . his sister's in a wheelchair or something?' I used to joke that on a network, from day one, Tony would have been helping the Feds fight terrorism on the side. I'd never had conversations in which, nine times out of ten, we had the same goal."

For all that, he said of the drug scene, "I don't think it was a terrible compromise, but it was a compromise. I wish we hadn't done it."

T
he "College" story had a slapstick coda. In a good example of how the collaborative process of the writers' room works, the episode was a group effort: Renzulli had suggested the rat, Chase had outlined the main story, and the room had worked out the beats for the B story, of Carmela and Father Phil. However, luck of the draw gave the official credited writing assignment for the first draft to James Manos. By his own account, Manos was an unusual guy, a chain smoker with a few agoraphobic tendencies. "I probably have an uncommon fear of being trampled to death," he said. This made the Emmys, stressful under any circumstances, particularly excruciating. Adding to the strain was the fact that Manos was married at the time to his second wife, Hilda Stark, who several weeks earlier, in an off-screen ceremony, had won an Emmy for the production design of HBO's movie *The Rat Pack*.

"We had a very competitive relationship," he said. "I knew that if I didn't win, it was going to be ugly at home.

"So there were all these famous people around, and I got very tense," he went on. "I thought I had plenty of time to go out and get some air, smoke a cigarette, calm down. So I left. And then I met somebody, met somebody else, we talked . . . and then I remember my phone ringing and it was my mother, in Brooklyn, watching the show live and asking, 'Where *are* you?'"

"College" had won the Emmy for Outstanding Writing for a Drama Series. Chase, onstage alone, asked, "Where's Manos? He was sitting right next to me."

Despite not making it onstage, the award served Manos well; he went on to write for *The Shield* and create the pilot for *Dexter*, during which he also met his next wife, the actress Lauren Vélez. His main memory of the 1999 Emmys, though, is being yelled at by a producer who wondered where the hell he had been and later standing onstage next to Helen Mirren for a group photo of the night's winners. Looking over, he noticed a trickle of blood running down Mirren's side. She had been stabbed by the Emmy statuette's knife-sharp wings.

"I thought, 'What a great fucking metaphor,'" he said.

Writers don't much like complimenting other writers. This is a simple fact that should not be obscured by the amount of time they spend doing so—in blurbs, introductory speeches at readings, and so on. This may not be any worse among Hollywood writers than others, but in a world where success really can be a zero-sum game—there are only so many pilots that can be picked up in any given season—it's certainly not better. Thus, when a piece of work sparks a frenzy of unequivocal praise among fellow writers, you can assume two things: (1) It's pretty good. (2) It promises something for them.

So it was for *Hill Street Blues* when it debuted, and so it was for *The Sopranos*, particularly after "College" aired. One of the many toiling in network trenches who suddenly sat up and took notice was Alan Ball, a forty-year-old TV series writer-producer turned screenwriter. "I felt like I was watching a movie from the seventies. Where it was like, 'You know those cartoon ideas of good and evil? Well, forget them. We're going to address something that's really real,'" Ball said. "The performances were electric. The writing was spectacular. But it was the moral complexity, the complexity of the characters and their dilemmas, that made it incredibly exciting."

Ball, like David Chase, was a veteran of the traditional television machine. Plucked from a moderately successful New York playwriting career, he had been put to work as a writer for two sitcoms built around female comedians, first *Grace Under Fire*, starring Brett Butler, and then *Cybill*, starring Cybill Shepherd. Like Chase, he was filled with self-loathing at the direction his career had taken—even as he grew more and more successful. Both Butler and Shepherd were outsize, volatile personalities; Shepherd was given to midseason fits in which she would fire half her writing staff, resulting in battlefield promotions for those who remained. Within a year, Ball had risen to the position of head writer. "It was like being a member of the court of a mad queen," he said. "The whole environment was toxic. People were terrified. I remember thinking, 'If I ever get my own show, it will not be this way.'"

Ball poured his disillusionment and yearning into the screenplay for the film *American Beauty*, which starred Kevin Spacey as a frustrated, ennui-soaked writer trapped in a loveless marriage and infatuated with his daughter's cheerleader friend. *American Beauty* was squarely in the suburbs-as-death tradition—some might say too squarely. And it hit a nerve, going on to gross some $130 million for its studio, DreamWorks, and to win Academy Awards for Best Picture, Best Actor, Best Director, Best Cinematography, and, for Ball, Best Screenplay. Shortly after the film was released, Carolyn Strauss called.

A decade later, Strauss denied that she and HBO were feeling anxiety about creating the network's first dramatic series since *The Sopranos* had debuted when she met with Ball in October 1999. "Everyone was saying, 'What's the next *Sopranos*?' but that wasn't it at all for us. It was just another show," she said.

This is hard to take at face value. In one fell swoop, *The Sopranos* had thrust the network from its cozy spot under the radar into the harsh spotlight. The company had also become enormously profitable thanks to increased subscriptions; in 2000, HBO earned nearly as much as the six broadcast networks combined. With HBO's parent company, Time Warner, having just completed its ill-fated merger with AOL, there would be pressure to keep those numbers up.

More important was the fear that success could breed creative complacency. Strauss herself had said, "The fear doesn't creep in until you start winning Emmys." In September 1999, HBO won more than any other company, led by the writing award for "College" and Edie Falco's award for Outstanding Lead Actress in a Drama Series. (*The Sopranos* was bested in the Outstanding Drama Series category by *The Practice*; Gandolfini lost the award for Outstanding Lead Actor in a Drama Series to Dennis Franz of *NYPD Blue*.)

At the same time, it wasn't at all clear that *The Sopranos* would not prove to be a fluke, that what HBO offered—more freedom and artistic integrity but less viewership and money—was enough to draw the kind of talent it needed to succeed. After all, it was still just *television*. Scott Sassa, president of NBC West Coast, may have soon had reason to regret his confident pronouncement to *The New Yorker* that traditional networks would always retain their monopoly on serious talent—"If you're a great writer, you don't want to be the tallest midget on cable"—but many at that point would have agreed with him.

All of this had to be in Strauss's mind when she met with Ball. In the wake of *American Beauty*, he was precisely the kind of writer Sassa was talking about: one who, if he was going to opt against the artistic legitimacy of film, could be expected to shoot for the biggest, broadest bucks possible. On top of everything else, Strauss's idea was hardly an obvious career builder: she had recently watched Terry Southern's 1965 adaptation of *The Loved One*, Evelyn Waugh's ice-cold satire of American culture as seen through its funeral industry, and now she wanted to do a show about death.

Specifically, she imagined a show centered on a family funeral home. "I liked the idea and I knew Alan's writing had the right tone for it," she said. "But, you know, you pitch a million ideas and nothing ever comes of it. Like, *never*." Lunch went well, but she soon put it out of her mind.

Thanks to a perfect alignment of personal and professional circumstances, however, the idea couldn't have found a better host in which to incubate. Ball was still in the midst of a three-year TV development contract with

Bob Greenblatt and David Janollari's production company. "I didn't want to be the guy who's like, 'I have this movie, so now I'm not going to honor my commitment.' I knew I had to do something to justify those paychecks," he said. "But people were calling me up with ideas like 'This lame stand-up comedian and that lame stand-up comedian are twins separated at birth!' Or 'Her husband died, but he came back as her *dog!*' I was like 'Oh, Jesus God. Just shoot me.'"

That month had seen the debut of Ball's own network sitcom, *Oh, Grow Up*, about three men living together and encountering various real-life complications to their postcollege bachelor idyll. The cast of characters included types that would be familiar to watchers of Ball's subsequent HBO series: the guy with a Peter Pan complex, the buttoned-down gay man coming out late in life, the precocious teenage girl. But the process, as Ball told it, had been a virtual parody of thickheaded network interference. We love everything about it, one executive had told him, if only it could be set in the suburbs instead of the city and the gay character could be straight. When Ball dared to offer input on a casting issue, another executive gave him a withering look. "I was like, 'Oh. Okay. This is *not* going to be a dialogue,'" Ball said. The results bore out the difficulty of the creation. *Oh, Grow Up* never found its voice or an audience. In December, ABC canceled it after eleven episodes, leaving two forever unaired.

That Christmas, devastated, Ball retreated to his childhood home in Marietta, Georgia. As it happened, it was a place suffused with death. Ball had grown up the youngest, by many years, of four children. His father, a quality control inspector at the nearby Lockheed aircraft plant and a three-pack-a-day smoker, had died years earlier. But by then grief had already been a longtime tenant in the Ball house. When Alan was thirteen, his sister Mary Ann was driving him to a piano lesson in her Ford Pinto. It was her twenty-second birthday. As they passed through a tricky intersection involving a four-lane road and a highway off-ramp, another car slammed into their driver's-side door, killing Mary Ann and leaving Ball with little more than a bruised leg.

The accident broke the family. Ball's mother entered a depression so severe, she was briefly hospitalized. His father, already remote, withdrew further. The notion of grief counseling or therapy for Alan didn't come up. Instead, "the preacher came over and there was a lot of talk about Jesus," he said. Left alone in the sorrow-stricken house, he came to feel invisible, as though he lived among ghosts.

Decades later, the accident still manifested itself in bouts of post-traumatic stress. It would be triggered by any big changes or experiences of loss, and the cancellation of *Oh, Grow Up* fit the bill perfectly. "Grief. Tremendous grief and anxiety," was how he described it. "Just a general meaninglessness and bleakness and hopelessness. The world suddenly seems alien and unrecognizable. Everything seems really absurd."

That feeling was only magnified by the extra surreality of life as the writer of a hit movie. Ball stumbled through what would have been the best period in most writers' lives in a daze, experiencing success as an almost Felliniesque grotesquerie. "I remember standing next to Brad Pitt at a urinal. I remember being on the red carpet behind Charlize Theron and her turning around and saying, 'Is my gold dust okay?' Seeing Joan Rivers in the flesh—that is frightening. Everybody is suddenly your best friend. Everybody goes nuts. It's all odd enough without reexperiencing the most traumatic experience of your life at the same time." Unlike James Manos, Ball was able to make it through the entire awards ceremony by sticking to chemicals digestible at his seat: he accepted his Oscar with a flask tucked into his tux pocket.

Now he was back in the very house where this traumatic state had its roots, even sleeping in his sister's old bedroom, his own room having been converted into a den. Ball's mind began to fix on Strauss's idea. He read Jessica Mitford's scathing *The American Way of Death* and *The Undertaking: Life Studies from the Dismal Trade*, a collection of essays by the poet and small-town funeral director Thomas Lynch. Quickly, the idea for a series began to take shape.

Given the caprice of the entertainment industry, a writer of his stature would almost never produce a script on spec—that is, without negotiating a contract beforehand. He had no way of knowing if Strauss was even still interested. But Ball was possessed by his idea and pressed on, launching what he called a "preemptive strike." Within a few weeks, he had a pilot script for *Six*

Feet Under. Bob Greenblatt sent it to a surprised Strauss the day after Ball's Academy Award nomination was announced. In contrast with David Chase's torturous waiting period, Albrecht and Strauss offered to buy it several days later. Using his newly acquired leverage, Ball demanded an entire series commitment.

"History was on our side," said Alan Poul, a TV and independent film veteran who was brought in as executive producer to assist Ball, a novice at both hour-long and single-camera drama. "HBO had very deep pockets in the wake of *The Sopranos* and *Sex and the City*, and the normal relationship of bottom-line cost to immediate earnings that you could calculate didn't apply."

In *Six Feet Under*'s version of *The Sopranos*' "two notes" legend, Ball supposedly received only one comment on his pilot: "We love the characters. We love the story. But the whole thing feels a little safe. Can it be more fucked up?" In episode three, Claire steals a severed foot from the morgue to place in the locker of a boy who jilted her. Note addressed.

The series was set in a rambling old house/funeral home belonging to the Fisher family and located in a not very glamorous part of Los Angeles. (The house used for exteriors sat at West Twenty-fifth Street and Arlington Avenue, in the West Adams neighborhood.) Ball had originally imagined that a show about death should take place somewhere windswept and severe in New England, but, like Waugh, he quickly came to see that Los Angeles offered the opportunity for sharper satire and deeper poignancy. The city, he said, was "the capital of the denial of death."

In the opening minutes of the pilot, which takes place over Christmas, the Fisher patriarch, Nathaniel, is killed by a bus that plows into the side of his hearse, much as the car had done to Mary Ann's Pinto. That "death of the week" would become a structural element throughout the show's run, as both a convenient plot engine—bodies moved in and out of Fisher and Sons, along with their stories—and a pointed, often cruel illustration of the series' final message: It can happen—*will* happen—to any of us, at any time.

The surviving Fishers were prodigal Nate, home for the holidays from his job managing a health food store in Seattle; his buttoned-up, closeted younger brother, David; their confused, high school-age sister, Claire, who spends the pilot dealing with her father's death while high on crystal meth; and the matriarch, Ruth, forced suddenly to emerge from years of repressed domesticity. The actor Richard Jenkins, who played Nathaniel, learned the happy lesson that dead doesn't always mean dead in the Third Golden Age, where ghosts and flashbacks are as common as shrinks and cursing.

Six Feet's primary protagonist and audience surrogate was Nate, played by Peter Krause; in the writers' room the character was referred to as "Marilyn Munster," the one normal guy in a house of freaks. If Nate's transgressions were less pyrotechnic than Tony's, *Six Feet Under* was no more in the business of providing tidy morality or conventionally cathartic resolution than *The Sopranos* was. Nate was a seductive protagonist, but a deeply disappointing one—not least to himself. His flaws, his fears, his least likable impulses: All recurred as inexorably as the brain condition that finally killed him. His relationship with Brenda Chenowith, a volatile former prodigy, was "basically a relationship between a narcissist and a borderline personality," said Ball, hardly *Friends'* Ross and Rachel.

Brenda, too, was hard to root for, even before departing on the DSJ—writers' room shorthand for "dark sexual journey"—that defined her later seasons. The actress Rachel Griffiths was at home in Australia when her agent faxed her the script. She stood by the machine, devouring each page as it scrolled out. HBO wasn't going to pay for her to fly first class to Los Angeles for an audition, but Griffiths was so enamored of the role that she proposed a deal: She would pay her way to California, but the show would reimburse her if she got the part. "God bless her, she got on the plane, came in, and nailed it," Poul said.

But most complete story lines belonged to David and Ruth. Their parallel journeys—his toward coming out, hers out of a dazed domesticity—were explored in perfectly paced, microscopic detail. Both were stories near to Ball's own experience; he had not mustered the courage to come out until age thirty-three, and he had watched his own mother blossom after his father's death, while the rest of the family looked on, alarmed. Both, in their subtlety, their complicated psychology, and their clear-eyed empathy, are ideal examples of the kind of storytelling thirteen hours affords.

Ball vividly remembered the open casket at his sister's funeral and his mother being hurried behind a curtain the moment she began to express her grief. Years later, he and a cousin had been traveling in Europe and were on a boat off the coast of Stromboli when they witnessed the delivery of a body back to the deceased's village on shore. "It was met on the beach by all these women in black," he said. "They threw themselves on the casket, screaming and beating their chests and pulling their hair." Both approaches to death made it into *Six Feet Under*'s pilot.

Indeed, repression, in varying degrees, was the show's overriding theme, as palpable in its look as in its plot. Ball instructed the set designer to dress the house as though it were buried under a muted layer of carpeted, upholstered insulation. The presiding palette was the green pallor of the Fishers' kitchen. Poul established guidelines for the rotating cast of directors: very few long shots, no extraneous camera movements. The show's standard-shot angle was just beneath eye level, creating a slightly distorted, detached sensation—and something else: "On a certain level, it's a corpse-eye view," Poul said.

Ball insisted on drawing writers from outside television, particularly playwrights. Unlike most showrunners, he refused to read spec scripts, which in this case refers to a fake script written for a different, existing show as a writing sample. Specs had long been the standard audition for TV writing jobs, but Ball found them unreliable, presaging a shift that would take place throughout TV staffing in the following decade.

"I don't need to know if somebody can write a great *Dexter*. I love *Dexter*, but I'm not going to hire somebody based on a *Dexter* script because maybe they can nail the voice of that show but I don't know if they can nail the voice of *my* show. What I'm looking for is an inherent sensibility: am I surprised by what I'm reading, or does it go where I expect it to go?"

In the course of its run, the *Six Feet Under* writers' room would include *New Yorker* cartoonist Bruce Eric Kaplan; the playwrights Rick Cleveland, Nancy Oliver, and Craig Wright (who had also been a seminarian); and the writer Jill Soloway, whom Ball hired on the strength of a short story entitled

"Courteney Cox's Asshole." Soloway had also worked, with fellow future *Six Feet Under* writer Scott Buck, on a short-lived sitcom starring Nikki Cox as a Vegas showgirl married to a professional wrestler. Hired for *Six Feet Under*'s second season, but before the first had aired, she was sent all thirteen finished episodes and found herself sobbing after watching four—not out of sorrow for the characters, but from relief for herself. "I thought, 'I can't believe this is going to be my life. I'm going to get to do this on TV,'" she said. Then she marched over to the house of a boyfriend who had been treating her badly and broke up with him. "I was like, 'I write for *Six Feet Under* now,'" she said.

While working on sitcoms, Ball had compiled a list of things that would be different once he had control over his own show, and for the most part, he stuck to it. He exhibited few of the autocratic impulses of other showrunners. "He had a very different style from some of these other guys," Soloway said. "He didn't wield the big bat. Alan once described the masculine style of show-running as standing in front of your troops, saying, 'Come on! This is where we're going.' The feminine style is standing behind your troops, pushing them forward so they lead you. Alan did the feminine style. The show exists in the center of the room, and we all come to it with our minds and let it rise up, and it belongs to nobody."

Wright, on his first TV job after a successful career in Minneapolis, was equally taken with the atmosphere: "I had thought Hollywood was just highly competitive and deeply venal, and that everybody was a jerk," he said. "But at *Six Feet Under*, I found exactly the opposite. Everybody was so open and friendly, I never laughed more in my life than I laughed that first day."

Ball maintained final word on all design and production decisions, but he tended to leave such details to his writer-producers. "I understand being passionate about your work, but I'm not a person who wants to control every element. I don't feel like I have to write every word. Nothing makes me happier than watching a show come together in a way that surprises me. Or getting a script where I don't have to do anything to it. I want this to be fun," he said, then added. "Maybe I'm just lazier than most people."

For much of its five-season run, *Six Feet Under*'s writers' room could lay plausible claim to being the happiest in TV—a marked contrast to many of the rooms that produced the Third Golden Age, which at the very least were tense and competitive. For the final three seasons, the membership of the room remained exactly the same, an almost unheard-of distinction.

But if Ball wasn't a despot, he was still the king. And it was possible to get on his bad side. The eleventh episode of *Six Feet Under*'s first season, "The Trip," revolved around the death of an infant, depicted in the usual format in the opening credits. One of the writing staff objected, protesting that you couldn't kill a baby on TV without losing your audience. In its way, it was a "College" moment, one in which the very nature of the show came up against the traditional boundaries of the medium. Ball pressed forward, ignoring the objection. At the end of the season, he fired the writer.

As the show moved into its later seasons, there was also increasing friction between the show's producers and its stars, Krause and Griffiths. It's difficult for actors to live for years on end in the head of any character, much less, as James Gandolfini had amply demonstrated, one who keeps making the same mistakes season after season.

"To be trapped in a role week after week, for multiple years, when you don't know how long it's going to go on . . . it takes its toll. Especially for a committed actor who is emotionally invested, who wants to feel the pain the character is feeling," said Poul. "So, on any long-running show, it's almost a guessing game: Who's going to be the problem?"

In this case, the strains of being on her first series, and so far from her home in Australia, weighed heavily on Griffiths, as did the difficulty of following Brenda on her DSJ. Griffiths began demanding private rehearsals before each of her scenes, while the rest of the production waited on expensive hold. Equally troubling, she would often expend herself emotionally in these run-throughs, nailing the scene in private but leaving little for when the cameras were actually rolling.

Krause had a more common but less forgivable complex. As the years of playing Nate wore on, the lines between him and his character appeared, to many observers, to blur. He complained about Nate's being placed in unflattering situations or appearing unlikable. Sometimes the issue would be petty—like refusing to wear an unflattering hairpiece in a flashback scene—but other times they got to the heart of what distinguished the show. As Ball put it, "Like Nate himself, I think he wanted to be a hero. He wanted to be liked."

N ate has good intentions, but he's an amateur jerk. He's a selfish narcissist. And the tragedy is that he never transcends that. He never grows up," Ball said.

That inability is another defining theme of TV's Golden Age. If man's battle with his inner demons defined *The Sopranos, Six Feet Under,* and their descendants, they also drew a crucial dose of their realism from the tenacity of that battle—the way their characters stubbornly refused to change in any substantive way, despite constantly resolving to do so. As Nick Lowe warned:

> *Sometimes it tries to kid me*
> *That it's just a teddy bear*
> *Or even somehow managed to vanish in the air*
> *And that is when I must beware*
> *Of the beast in me . . .*

It's no coincidence that addiction is one of the major tropes of the Third Golden Age. Likewise psychotherapy, with its looping fits and starts of progress and regression. Recidivism and failure stalked these shows: Tony Soprano searches for something to fill the gnawing void he feels; he fails to find it. Jimmy McNulty swears off the twin compulsions of booze and police work; he goes back to both, while the rest of *The Wire*'s most zealous reformers find themselves corrupted. The specter of Don Draper's past infidelities comes to him in a fever dream, in the person of an old conquest. And though he literally chokes the Beast to death, we, and he, know she will be back.

Here again, what may have been a vague millennial undercurrent when *The Sopranos* debuted was given concrete form in the zeitgeist just a few years later. There have been few pronouncements more widely repeated and less genuinely experienced than "Everything changed" after 9/11.

"'I'm going to be different. I'm so lucky to be alive. I'm going to value things more, do things differently. . . .' That's what it was all about," said Chase of the period immediately following the terrorist attacks. "But then it sort of faded away." Or as Tony Soprano morosely put it, "Every day is a gift. It's just . . . does it have to be a pair of socks?"

That Chase was temperamentally suited to this gloomy view of human progress made him the perfect avatar of the kinds of stories Americans responded to in those years. But the formal and commercial demands of TV itself also had a hand in guaranteeing that it was the medium through which they should be told. After all, the goal of a TV show, unlike that of a movie or novel, no matter how ambiguous, is to *never end*. One way to address that basic economic mandate is to create a world in which there is no forward progress or story arc at all, just a series of discrete, repetitive episodes—in other words, the procedural. But if you're interested in telling an ongoing story while remaining true to your own sense of the world, it helps for that worldview to be of an endless series of variations in which people repeatedly play out the same patterns of behavior, exhibiting only the most incremental signs of real change or progress.

In this regard, the common cocktail party quip "You know, *The Sopranos* [or some other show] is just a *soap opera*" is absolutely correct—if you ignore such incidentals as realism, intelligence, emotional acuity, humor, cinematography, production values, actors who have memorized lines, outdoor locations, and so on.

Rescue Me poked fun at its own soap operatic tendencies in a season four scene in which Denis Leary's Tommy Gavin and his on-again-off-again wife, Janet, decide to visit a marriage counselor. The poor therapist asks for a recent family history:

Janet: So . . . we split up and then he rented the place across the street
from us so he could be near the kids and also to keep an eye on
me to see who I was dating.

Tommy: You should have seen that group of guys—that guy Roger.

Janet: Yeah, who swore you tried to burn his face off on your stove.

Tommy: I don't even cook! So, she takes the kids, the furniture, the money, everything, goes to Ohio. I tracked her down.

Janet: Yes, and I came back and then he decided to start dating the widow of his cousin who died in 9/11. And then she got pregnant.

Tommy: Okay, I didn't decide, it just happened, okay? She either had a miscarriage or an abortion, I don't know which. Anyway, she didn't have the baby, but then *she* got pregnant because she was sleeping with my brother, but I'm pretty sure that's my baby because we were having an affair while she was having an affair with my now dead brother. . . .

Janet: Then our son was killed by a drunk driver. . . .

Tommy: Who my uncle then shot. You might have read about that. It was in the papers and stuff. And then there was the "rape." . . .

Janet: So we've been through a lot. . . .

Tommy: But you know, we feel like there's still some passion left.

Janet: So, what do you think?

What the therapist thinks, of course, is that somebody's playing a prank on him.

But births, deaths, illnesses, fights, betrayals, rapprochements, new jobs, new houses, people falling out of view, new people arriving, small heartaches, small joys, none of them lasting very long before the next thing is suddenly upon us—that's what our lives are actually made of. More so, anyway, than discrete, cathartic episodes with tidy endings.

"Heroes are much better suited for the movies," Alan Ball said. "I'm more interested in real people. And real people are fucked up."

It's worth noting, anyway, that soap opera is also the only TV genre to exist uninterrupted for the entire life of the medium.

. . .

*S*ix Feet Under never had a season as perfectly constructed as its first, but it was an important chapter in the transformation of television. Nobody watching it could fail to see in it a vivid illustration of how much more of human life could be dissected over the course of thirteen or twenty-six or fifty-two open-ended hours, rather than a mere two-hour stretch freighted with the need for easy answers and tidy resolution; indeed, there could be no better counterexample to choose than *American Beauty* itself, which would come to seem facile and reductive next to its younger television sibling. For the next decade, when a particular type of film wanted to signify that it was serious, un-Hollywood, concerned with the quirky, dark corners of family life—*Little Miss Sunshine, Juno, The Descendants,* to name just a few—it would do its level best to look like one thing, and that was *Six Feet Under.*

Ball would go on to become HBO's savior. After a period in which it lost ground to basic cable and a string of unremarkable shows, his next series, *True Blood,* drew some of the network's highest ratings since *The Sopranos.* Based very loosely on a series of novels by Charlaine Harris, the show was a frothy, sexy vampire drama that piled on twists and supernatural beings like sprinkles on a sundae. It was about as far, superficially, from *The Sopranos or Six Feet Under* as one could get. Nevertheless, it featured, in the character of Bill Compton, a particular, familiar type of hero: a man (albeit a dead man) trying to get by in the modern world, negotiating relationships, rivalries, and the demands of an undead bureaucracy as elaborate as the living one. Most of all, he would struggle, with varying degrees of success, to overcome his (very literal) bloodlust.

God help the beast in we.

Six

The Arguer

I t was a cold day in December 2009, and the Baltimore Police Department had staged what appeared to be a full-scale invasion of the 1800 block of Frederick Avenue, on the edge of the Western District. Parked on one end of the street was an enormous mobile stage on which was placed a podium, a row of dignitaries' seats, and a cluster of flags representing the United States, Maryland, Baltimore, and various wings of law enforcement. It was a short block of brick-and-Formstone row houses, two of them vacant, two others painted a bright pink and blue, which, like the ground-floor window displaying a white china pitcher filled with fake flowers, served only to poignantly highlight the barren surroundings.

In the street in front of the stage was arrayed an army of cops of every conceivable stripe: macho SWAT dudes, motorcycle cops in big boots, DEA guys in windbreakers, young traffic officers—a gallery of badges and medals and insignia as varied and esoteric as hats in Jerusalem. A scrawny tabby cat wove its way unnoticed through a forest of blue pant legs and disappeared into one of the vacant buildings.

There was an older group in the crowd, greeting one another with particular affection and catching up. The ones still on the force wore black ribbons over their badges; they ribbed one another about having to squeeze into their dress blues. These were veterans of the hardest days of the war on drugs, and they were here to commemorate one of the Baltimore front's signal casualties. In 1984, Marcellus Ward, known as Marty, was assigned to a DEA task force. The thirty-six-year-old, thirteen-year BPD veteran was working undercover, investigating a twenty-six-year-old heroin dealer named Lascell Simmons. On the night of December 3, he had come to Simmons's headquarters on Frederick Avenue, a third-floor apartment over a front called Kandy Kitchen, to get Simmons to admit to the killing of another dealer. Under his shirt was a wire. After an hour and a half of conversation, Simmons incriminated himself and Ward gave a signal to his partners listening in a van outside. Then, as the officers advanced up the stairs, something went wrong. When the tape was later played in court, Simmons's jury could hear a scuffle, shots fired, and finally Ward's dying breaths. Twenty-five years later, the block was officially being renamed Detective Marty Ward Way.

The killing had had a devastating ripple effect. For many, it was proof of the intractability of the enemy in the War on Drugs and of the battle's unwinnability. More immediately, the killing of a cop threw the BPD into disarray. The powers that be wanted high-profile busts to counteract the negative publicity—"drugs on the table"—and no longer had patience for subtler or more penetrating strategies. That included a year-old innovative wiretapping investigation of the drug lord "Little" Melvin Williams that had been spearheaded by an arrogant young cop named Ed Burns.

Burns was at the memorial service, too, Irish beyond all measure, his once red hair now white, pale face inflamed by the cold. Burns wore a leather jacket and tan pants and stood calmly alone with a small smile on his face, avoided by the other old dogs. Long off the police force and now on hiatus from the television career that had occupied much of his past ten years, he had come in from his home in rural West Virginia.

He spotted a woman who had been a newly minted prosecutor assigned to work on his wiretap. The two embraced warmly.

"I remember showing up for work the first day," she said. "Ed looked at me like, 'What kind of Twinkies are they hiring now?' But he was good. I like people who say what they mean, mean what they say, and do what they say they're going to do. As a prosecutor, that's all you want."

"That and a case," Burns said with a rueful smile.

The actual citizens of Frederick Avenue were notably absent, though some watched silently from house windows. The exception was a skinny black man with a puffy face who stood fidgeting on his stoop alongside a friend in a wheelchair. He was making noise, taunting the policemen and complaining about the inconvenience of the ceremony just getting under way. Whenever a cop would head up the street to shut him up, he'd pop into his house and then pop back out again, cuckoo clock style, as soon as the officer retreated.

Occasionally, the proceedings would be drowned out by passing police sirens. The BPD's head of the Homicide Unit, Terrence McLarney, who had worked closely with Ward, was absent. He was on the scene of Baltimore's 218th murder of the year: a teenage girl who had been bludgeoned to death beside her double amputee mother.

All of this actually happened. In the completely real, flesh-and-blood city of Baltimore. Yet to an outside observer, one who had spent much of the past decade learning about the city and its intricate, interlocking bureaucracies via a fictional HBO show, the details were startlingly, almost giddily, familiar. The confusion was only heightened by some of the names in the crowd: the big detective they called "the Bunk"; another named Jay Landsman, and another named Marvin Sydnor; the *Baltimore Sun* journalist William Zorzi. The whole scene was, in one word, Simonian.

And there, in the crowd, was the man himself: David Simon, forty-nine years old, flown up for the day from New Orleans, where he was in the middle of shooting the first season of his new HBO series, *Treme*. He took a place beside Landsman, who, to make matters more confusing, had lent his name to one character in *The Wire* while playing another, minor character on-screen. This made him one of the army of men and women across the Baltimore area who opened their mailboxes each month to find envelopes containing royalty checks for their work on the show—sometimes a few pennies, sometimes more than a hundred bucks. *The Wire* royalty day had become something of a local civic holiday.

Simon was wearing a baggy black suit over an almost ludicrously ugly purple striped shirt. He stood slightly hunched with his hands grasped rabbinically behind him, chin jutted forward in a gesture of attentive listening. He had covered the Ward killing as a twenty-four-year-old reporter for the *Sun*. Now, the master of ceremonies apologized that the next scheduled speaker, Mayor Sheila Dixon, was unable to attend, and Simon looked up with an expression of majestic bemusement. Two days before, Mayor Dixon had been convicted of an embezzlement scheme involving gift cards.

After the ceremony, Simon mingled, catching up with Burns and the other vets in front of the onetime Kandy Kitchen. "The thing is, remember what a terrible front it was?" he said. "They had like four bags of potato chips on the shelves." He gave no impression of having become a famous showrunner in the intervening years, or a multimillionaire, or someone who, in coming months, would have his commonly used descriptor *genius* given a capital *G* by the imprimatur of a MacArthur Foundation Fellowship.

All of which underscored two things: that *The Wire* and its world took place about as far from Hollywood as it is possible to imagine; and that its story was in many ways about an elaborate, intimate dance between fact and fiction.

There are plenty of points of comparison to be made between the two Davids—Chase and Simon—the two showrunners who defined the potential of the Third Golden Age's early years. Chase came to the possibilities of this new art form as a creature, however unwilling, of television itself—the consummate industry pro. Simon had more than dipped his toe in television by the time of *The Wire*, but it was clear from watching him in Baltimore that he was a genuine outsider. Neither suffered a shortage of ego, but where Chase's could manifest as angry and insecure, Simon was bluff, pugnacious, seemingly without neuroses. Even their faces fit a classic Don Quixote/Sancho Panza, Laurel/Hardy, Bert/Ernie dichotomy: Chase, vertically hawkish and old-world European; Simon, fleshy and horizontal, with the prominent brow and jutting jaw of a brawling Jewish gangster.

Their shows reflected these differences in temperament and background: *The Sopranos*, for all its baroque plot twists and turns, was essentially inward facing—a psychological drama about a man seeking to fill a void he didn't really understand. In the tradition of great post-Freudian literature, it was about the gulf between the inner man and the outer world. *The Wire*, meanwhile, was almost pre-modern in its expansive view outward, its Balzacian ambition to catalog every corner of its world.

For all that, the Davids shared one important quality: Both were men who grew up with a bedrock sense of certainty about what they were supposed to do, and in what form, only to find their ambitions better served by the most unlikely of mediums.

F or Simon, the call was always to journalism. He was another child of the suburbs and another baby boomer—albeit one of the last, born in 1960, instead of one of the first, like Chase. He grew up in Silver Spring, Maryland, in an upper-middle-class Jewish household with three newspaper subscriptions, stacks of books, and great value placed on intellectual dexterity, especially in battle. Political and philosophical argument was the family sport and the dinner table the playing field, with Simon's father, Bernard, the public relations director and speechwriter for B'nai B'rith, acting as de facto referee.

Simon, the youngest by many years of three children (his brother was fourteen years older, his sister ten years), was a quick study. "We learned very early what was a weak move: Fallacies of logic were weak. Ad hominem attacks were weak—though if it was funny, you might get one in. But generally, how well you did in carrying forth a credible argument was looked at with merit," he said.

He remembered 1968 as a particularly loud and contentious year at the Simon table, with the family split between supporting Robert Kennedy, Hubert Humphrey, and Eugene McCarthy for president. ("Nobody was for Nixon, I can tell you that.") The first time Simon's brother brought his future wife to meet the family, she left asking, "Do you guys *hate* each other?"

The taste for a fight, and faith in argument as a creative process, would remain such an intrinsic part of Simon's character that he would express genuine puzzlement when people interpreted his later battles as personal feuds. It was, he thought, simply the way serious, smart people interacted. "David could argue the world flat or round, and have you believing both," said Rafael Alvarez, a colleague and friend at the *Sun* and a writer on *The Wire*.

Liberalism, passionate rhetoric, and muckraking journalism all had good pedigree in nearby Baltimore, home of H. L. Mencken, William Manchester, and others. At the University of Maryland, Simon gravitated to the independent school newspaper, the daily *Diamondback*, to the exclusion of almost everything else. He wore a ponytail and ripped jeans, listened to the Clash, and wrote blisteringly funny columns like a two-parter about students assigned to write campus parking tickets. That one was titled "Eat Flaming Death." By the time David Mills, a year younger, arrived at the paper, Simon had a budding rock star reputation.

"He always had something clever to say or had a great story to tell. He was always involved in some fucked-up adventure—driving figure eights on the quad or something," Mills said. "And he had a fully grown writer's voice at that age. He just produced these artfully profane rivers of language."

The romance and the intensity of the newsroom suited Simon perfectly, as did the spotlight it provided. But these were underpinned by a genuine, idealistic belief in journalism's mission. From the time he ascended to the editorship of the *Diamondback* at age nineteen, he became locked in a battle for autonomy and resources with the paper's adult business manager, Michael Fribush. Once, a blizzard, which normally would have canceled the next day's paper, occurred on the same day as several extraordinary stories, including an airplane crash in the Potomac. Simon couldn't bear the thought of all that news going unreported in the *Diamondback*. He ordered a print run of ten thousand copies, without advertising, just for the UMD dorms. When Fribush confronted him, furious, Simon told him impassively that he'd planned to ask for permission the next morning. If denied, he and the rest of the staff had agreed to take salary cuts to pay for the edition. It was a struggle he could recount, and get worked up over, nearly forty years later, in precise, not to say stultifying, detail, leaving the distinct impression that he would rather talk about it than television, *The Wire*, his family, or anything else that had happened since.

When his term as editor ended, Simon began stringing for the *Sun*—or, more precisely, acting like a stringer for the *Sun*, since he hadn't actually been hired. "I put my final issue of the paper to bed and called in a brief: three paragraphs about the vice president of the university resigning," he said. "I told them, 'I just finished editing the *Diamondback* and I'm ready to be your stringer.' Totally arrogant. They said, 'Well, thanks for the brief, but you have to come in and interview.' Two days later, I called in another story. The guy's like, 'No, really, thanks for the piece. But we really need you to come in.'"

Eventually, Simon was persuaded to put on a suit and submit to an interview. As stringer, he submitted so many stories that the newspaper union took notice. None was bigger than a major scoop involving a gifted UMD Terrapin basketball player named Herman Veal. Veal had been mysteriously held out of the ACC tournament for disciplinary reasons. Using sources on the university's student judicial panel and employing a bit of guile with the administration, Simon confirmed that the player had been accused of sexual misbehavior by a female student. Veal, she said, had carried her upstairs at a party and thrown her roughly onto a bed, though he left when she protested. When Simon tracked the girl down, she told him that Lefty Driesell, the Terrapins' legendary head coach, had been calling her dorm room, berating her for costing him Veal's services in the tournament and threatening to ruin her reputation. One such call had even been witnessed by the head of the judicial panel. (Driesell denied any intimidation.) Simon's story ran over three days in the *Sun* and was picked up by *The Washington Post* and nationwide.

Simon assumed that Driesell would be fired. "We had him dead to rights," he said. Instead, the university investigated for a year, slapped the coach on the wrist, and gave him a new contract, with a raise. "That was the last time I ever believed journalism fixes anything," Simon said.

T he *Baltimore Sun*, when Simon finally joined as a full-time reporter, was still a newspaper fetishist's dream—a haven of hardworking, colorful reprobates, lechers, drunks, and misfits. And Baltimore provided more than enough opportunity for a reporter looking to follow Mencken's favorite dictate to "comfort the afflicted and afflict the comfortable."

Simon joined a group of young writers and editors that included Rafael Alvarez and William Zorzi, both of whom would eventually write for *The Wire*. Zorzi, who would also play a version of himself in the show's fifth season, was a political reporter with a lugubrious, bone-dry wit. Alvarez was a twitchy, voluble hipster with a high-pitched shout of a laugh and a penchant for radical shifts of identity, such as what he mysteriously called "my Elvis phase." They were pranksters in the office: if Zorzi was on the phone with, say, the governor of Maryland, there was a fair chance Simon could be found with a foot up on the desk, thrusting his crotch into the other man's face. Well after Simon had left the paper, Zorzi would come back to his desk and find notes from his old colleague, informing him of the various bodily crevices in which he'd wiped Zorzi's phone receiver.

Simon worked hard and stayed out late. "We were young, devil-may-care, work-around-the-clock, party-till-you-drop, rock 'n' roll reporters," Alvarez said. In the newsroom, Simon was not shy about expressing his opinions, often in what would become for him a kind of secondary art form: the devastatingly eloquent, polemical memo. His editor, Rebecca Corbett, eventually had to demand that any further officewide missives be vetted by her first.

"I felt like, I'm a newspaper reporter. I could be making a lot more money doing something else, but the one thing I do get that most people don't, is that I get to come into my office, put my feet up on the desk, and say what I think," Simon said. When it came to edits, his opinions could be expressed with somewhat less civility: Alvarez recalled at least one instance of Simon kicking a trash can across the office, and Zorzi described seeing him in an editor's office, "literally on the floor, kicking his feet."

Simon was assigned to the police beat, filing daily stories on murders, drug busts, and departmental politics. With the encouragement of Corbett and another editor, Steve Luxenberg, he was also experimenting with longer-form features, though he hadn't become what Zorzi neologized as a "writeur"— a reporter with more flair in his prose than chops in his reporting.

Simon was mindful of George Orwell's diagnosis of why writers write. As he put it, "Because you want to show them you're right and they're wrong. That, 'I've learned something about the world, I'm going to share it with you, and fuck you if you don't agree.'

"Anytime I hear a reporter say, 'I want to make the world right,' or, 'I'm writing for the little guy; I'm about the truth,' I think, 'Okay, you're full of shit,'" he said. "I want to hear from the guy who acknowledges the vanity of the byline. Any reporter I knew who was good, he wanted to come back to the newsroom the day after he filed and have everybody be reading his shit, saying, 'Man, this is a fucking good story. I wish I'd thought of it.'"

Yet Simon had a gift for putting his ego and his sense of justice to the same purpose. "One of David's best skills is that he gets pissed off as a citizen and a journalist sort of simultaneously," said Alvarez. "He's righteous about the truth, and he's good at leveraging people, through his journalistic skills, into getting the best version of the truth available. That makes you a great reporter."

Was he cocky about those skills?

Alvarez lifted an eyebrow. "Look, a tiger knows he's a tiger, right?"

Simon found an immediate affinity for the world of working cops, which mirrored the newsroom in its rough jocularity, its camaraderie, and its sense of purpose, however cynical it might sometimes become. He also, like many journalists, not to mention children of middle-class privilege, was susceptible to a romantic notion of working-class men. Irishmen, always kind of Diony-sian twins for Apollonian Jewish boys, fascinated him. He made a point to drink Jameson. Later, as a showrunner, he went out of his way to dress in a style best described as "Polish dockworker." And while the romance of "common folk" would occasionally come to seem like his only blind spot and threaten to undermine his finest work, it also gave him enormous powers of empathy when it came to reporting on both the police and the people they pursued.

On Christmas Eve 1986, Simon spent the overnight shift with a squad of murder detectives in the hopes that an enlightening, or at least amusing, story would come out of the juxtaposition of holiday and homicide. Toward the end of the shift, while toasting from a bottle of whiskey Simon had snuck into the office, one of the detectives said, "The shit that goes on up here. If someone just wrote down what happens in this place for one year, they'd have a goddamn book."

Two years later, on New Year's Day 1988, Simon officially began a leave of absence from the *Sun* and reported for work as a "police intern." In hand he had a book contract from Houghton Mifflin and an agreement from Police Commissioner Edward Tilghman to allow him complete access to one of the city's two homicide squads. (Several cops later speculated that the fact that Tilghman was dying of a brain tumor at the time contributed to his decision— either because it had driven him mad or he figured he wouldn't be around to see the fallout, which indeed he wasn't.)

For the next calendar year, Simon spent nearly every day with the initially wary detectives of Lieutenant Gary D'Addario's homicide squad. It was a deep embed. His marriage—the first of three—dissolving, Simon worked six or seven days a week, often pulling double shifts alongside the detectives and generally coming as close as was possible to joining their ranks. "Sometimes, coming off midnight, we drank at dawn and I would stagger home to sleep until night. I learned to my amazement that if you forced yourself to drink the morning after a bad drunk, it somehow felt better," he wrote in an afterword to a fifteen-year anniversary edition of the book that grew out of his reporting: *Homicide: A Year on the Killing Streets*. At night he would return to his new bachelor apartment, with its mattress on the floor, and pore over the stacks of notebooks he'd fill. In time, he came to have a more global view of the division's goings-on than many of the detectives themselves and could answer such questions as who was working which case on a given day.

The day before the Marty Ward memorial, Jay Landsman and Terry McLarney, both in their fifties, sat at a Caribbean-themed restaurant near the border of Baltimore, the city, and suburban Baltimore County. On the table was a platter of Old Bay–doused wings and the remnants of more than several beers, though neither man made any move toward the bathroom: cop bladders.

These were the last men still on the job from the squad Simon immortalized in *Homicide*. McLarney had since climbed the BPD ranks to become major and head of the Homicide Unit. Landsman had moved out to the county, where he now worked burglaries, but his youngest son, Joe—one of four Landsman children in law enforcement—was a newly minted murder investigator under McLarney. To the degree that there is a David Simon "voice" evident throughout his work, it was in some ways an amalgam of these two men's style of speech—baroque, vulgar, deadpan, in love with language for its highfalutin ballbusting potential.

Landsman, like most of the cops, had disliked the idea of the book at first. "I didn't want anybody looking over my shoulder all the time. You're working murders in the ghetto. What, are you going to come out looking like a saint?" he said. Simon became the victim first of the cold shoulder and then of weeks of hazing—mostly the overuse of his American Express card at the bar after shifts and a series of ever more imaginative ways to question his sexuality.

"But David is a likable guy," McLarney said. "He was young, he was getting a divorce . . . It was like the Stockholm syndrome. We started to identify with him somehow. It became normal for a call to come in and for David to just jump in the car."

Would Simon have made a good cop?

"If they started admitting pinko liberals, I guess," said Landsman.

"Nah," said McLarney. "He'd never pass the drug test and polygraph."

At the end of the year, Simon sat down with his massive pile of notes, files, and recordings and churned out a manuscript. His editor, John Sterling, returned from lunch to find the stack of typed pages sitting on his desk; Simon had been so anxious to deliver the book that he'd driven from Baltimore to Manhattan, dropped it off, and headed home.

If David Simon had never gone into television, he would still have a claim to greatness as a long-form literary journalist based strictly on *Homicide*, as entertaining, compelling, and journalistically convincing an account of men at work as has been written. To have achieved all that while observing the highest standards of journalistic integrity made it all the more impressive. It's little wonder Simon would later be so hard on journalists he accused of being fabulists; never mind issues of ethics and integrity, he must have thought, why would anybody *need* to make things up?

For an aficionado of *The Wire*—or its predecessor, the TV series *Homicide: Life on the Street*—the book is a treasure trove of familiar details. There are scenes like a tender moment between a deeply inebriated McLarney and another detective in which the future head of homicide thanks the other, because "when it was time for you to fuck me, you were very gentle."

There's lingo like "red ball" (a high-publicity, and thus high-priority, case), "dunker" (an easy-to-solve murder), and "stone whodunit" (the dunker's polar opposite). Simon is never better than when diving into such deep linguistic pools—the secret inside languages of the working world. It's an impulse that reached its natural extremity in *Generation Kill*, Simon and Ed Burns's HBO miniseries about the invasion of Iraq, the point of which seemed in part to be the ways in which the Orwellian jargon of the war machine's bureaucracy both drove and obscured the war itself.

And of course there's "the board," a kind of grimly ironic echo of the writers' room whiteboard, which tells the story of which cases are solved (written in black) and which remain stubbornly in red.

But the most important lesson of *Homicide: A Year on the Killing Streets* for Simon was a narrative one. At the dramatic and emotional core of the book is the murder of eleven-year-old Latonya Kim Wallace and one detective's increasingly obsessive and futile search for her killer. "At the time I remember calling my editor and saying, 'My God, what happens if they don't solve this? My story may not have an ending.' And John, being a better editor at that point than I was a reporter, said, 'Then that's your ending. Maybe that's perfect.' Which: Yeah, of course."

Or as Sterling put it, articulating what might have been a credo for the Third Golden Age's narrative philosophy: "Life is like that: endings are rarely provided. There's an awful lot that's messy and unresolved."

Above all, the book is a work of immense confidence. Simon grew to know his subjects so intimately that he could claim, without hesitation, the right to say what they were thinking and feeling at any moment. This is all the more remarkable since he allowed each detective to read, and request changes to, his portions of the manuscript before publication. Nothing of substance was altered.

Indeed, the men ended up impressed, even touched, by the way Simon had portrayed them. "That motherfucker . . . he was good," said Landsman. "He was inside my mind. He really knew us."

McLarney had an even more astonishing takeaway for the subject of a nonfiction book whose author could walk away comfortable that he had told the uncompromised truth. He said, "David Simon taught me that people can be trusted."

Had they experienced any blowback?

"Nah, he never blew any of us," said Landsman, sipping his beer and slipping easily into what was obviously an old routine.

"Well, there was that one incident. On the couch . . . ," said McLarney.

"Oh, yeah. But we'd never blow him back."

One homicide detective who was not around the office in 1988—he was detailed to a federal investigation—was Ed Burns. Burns was the perfect Simonian character: tough, intellectual, antiauthoritarian, Irish. He grew up just outside Baltimore, the son of a once aspiring newsman who had settled for the job of type-composer at the *News-American*. Punished for chronic misbehavior by the nuns at his Catholic school with confinement in the basement, Ed discovered a walk-in freezer filled with ice cream: an early lesson in the pleasures of bucking the system.

Coming out of college in the early 1960s, Burns went to work as a copy boy at the *News-American*. There, he had the newsroom experience of David Simon's dreams. One of his jobs would be to roust reporters from whatever brothel or bar they'd crawled off to for the afternoon. The paper's stairwells were so filled with discarded airplane bottles of booze, one had to be careful not to sprain an ankle.

As the war in Vietnam escalated, Burns, eminently draftable, made a calculation that he'd be better off running toward trouble than waiting for it to come to him. He enrolled in Officer Candidate School. Not for the last time, he found himself less than impressed by the men in charge. "The dumbest fucking people I could have imagined," he said. "And they were not only sending me to die, but to lead *other* people to die."

Again, he calculated that the best path to survival was a counterintuitive one. He quit the officer track and signed on to language school, which meant he'd be assigned as a companion and translator to a Kit Carson scout—one of the North Vietnamese defectors the army had begun using for their knowledge of local terrain. Though more dangerous, the duty also meant an earlier exit from the service and a measure of control.

"At least I would be with somebody who knew what the fuck he was doing," he said.

Once in country, Burns traveled as light as possible. Alongside ammunition, his rucksack contained a few clothes, canned peaches, a container of Old Bay, and a book. He was sent to the central coast, near My Lai, where Lieutenant William Calley would soon become notorious. It was incredibly dangerous: Burns and the scout he was assigned to, a nineteen-year-old ex–NVA sniper named Ba, walked point for a platoon of men that was constantly being winnowed by casualty. Ba, said Burns, saved his life innumerable times by spotting mines and sniper traps. Once, two North Vietnamese soldiers appeared on the path fifteen feet in front of them and began firing down the

American column. "Ba was like a hunting dog," Burns said. "We went after those guys. We found them. And we killed them. Didn't even stand them up against a tree, we just shot them."

Vietnam provided Burns with further education in institutional idiocy. It was also a powerful lesson in the futility of an occupying army facing an entrenched insurgency—a view he would have ample opportunity to develop further as a participant in America's drug war. In large part, that lesson was about the expendability of soldiers on both sides; after one year, Burns rotated back to the States, while Ba stayed behind. The men never heard from each other again. "I assume he was either killed or reeducated," Burns said.

And, he added, he came away with another important lesson about how to deal with an enemy: "You've got to know 'em."

B ack home, Burns spent 1969 drifting. He bought a Volkswagen and drove around the country—occasionally with companions, but most often alone. The roads, he said, were filled with returning soldiers trying to get reacclimated. "That was how I cured myself of PTSD," he said.

He had no good answer for why, after a year, he decided to join the Baltimore Police Department—another paramilitary organization with a suspect bureaucratic command structure and little chance of lasting success. The job did serve an addiction to adrenaline he'd picked up overseas. He was assigned to the Western District—"the Wild West," it was called—and worked the five p.m. to one a.m. shift. "All the guys were young, except the sergeant, who never came out of the station. We had a good time," he said. "I did the same thing I did walking point in Vietnam: went out with the drug squad, went out with the vice squad."

Burns soon proved especially adept at finding and cultivating informants—even more so when he joined the escape squad, tracking down people who had felony warrants or had escaped from prison. On the street, he was known as "Curlytop."

"I had a reputation: When I got you, I got you. But then I'd go to bat for you," he said. Burns's snitches could often look forward to double paychecks—

one from the BPD and one from the Feds, who frequently piggybacked on Burns's work. Eventually, he took to carrying three beepers to manage all his contacts from the Eastern, the Western, and the Northwestern districts.

Among Burns's most reliable informants was an addict named Bubbles who had an astonishing memory for faces and schemes. Generally, though, he looked for players who worked outside the drug gangs: stickup boys, lone wolves. "Guys outside the pale, who had crafted their own little niche in the world. Omar-type guys," he called them, after the character who would become the most popular figure on *The Wire*.

Arguably Burns got along better with his network of street intelligence than with his fellow cops.

"Let me just say this," said Terry McLarney, summing up the prevailing sentiment. "Ed Burns served his country in Vietnam. He's very smart and a very tough guy. A real man." He took a breath. "That said, Ed Burns could be a flaming asshole."

Burns was not one to socialize down at the Fraternal Order of Police hall, preferring to do his drinking in a second-floor joint in the hood, where you bought your beer in six-packs. Once he transferred to homicide in 1979, he would antagonize Landsman by eating granola and spouting radical ideas.

"He would sit there, eating his birdseed, drinking our booze, and arguing that all cops should have four-year degrees. I'd say, 'But then all of us would be like you! It would be a nightmare,'" Landsman said.

"He would speak to you as though he was speaking down to you. As though you were stupid," said Detective Marvin Sydnor, who worked with Burns as a young narcotics officer. "If you heard, 'I'm going to kick that guy's ass,' you knew Ed was somewhere nearby."

Beyond questions of style, Burns and his partner, Harry Edgerton (a version of whom was played by Andre Braugher on *Homicide: Life on the Street*), had no time for the day-in-day-out, small-bore cases that occupied most of the office. They were after big game, which meant they'd often disappear from the office, working single cases, for long periods. Even those who understood the approach philosophically could feel left holding the bag.

"It's like there's five guys running at you with axes," McLarney said. "Ed takes on one. He beats him to death, but the rest of us are still stuck fighting the other four."

Burns, for his part, accepted such opinions with a wry smile and undiminished scorn for most of his past workmates. "Paper pushers," he called them, dead weight. Of one he said, "If you were lying there dead, looked up, and saw him standing over you, you'd think, 'They're never going to solve this.'"

E d Burns's best detective work involved the combination of a conceptual breakthrough and dogged labor. It was illegal at that time to use wiretaps as part of homicide investigations, but not if investigators could prove that a murder was part of an organized criminal conspiracy. Such investigations were long and arduous—they required finding a cooperative prosecutor and judge—but they aimed to bring down entire drug gangs rather than just individuals. The second case Burns worked in this way, while assigned to the DEA, was Little Melvin Williams, the drug lord, and it's what brought Simon to his door.

It was shortly after Williams's arrest in December 1984, and Burns remembered Simon showing up at the DEA office where he was preparing material to bring Melvin before a grand jury. Simon had somehow made it past security without a badge. "I'm here from the *Sun*," he announced. "I'd like to listen to some of the wiretaps."

"Well," said Burns, "I'd love to let you listen, Mr. Simon, because then I can lock you up for ten years because it's a violation of grand jury confidentiality."

Their next meeting went better. Williams had been indicted, and they met at the Towson Public Library. Burns had just checked out a stack of books that included John Fowles's *The Magus*; *Veil*, Bob Woodward's book about the CIA; and a collection of essays by Hannah Arendt. Simon was impressed. "I'm looking at these, thinking, 'You're a *cop*?'" he said. Burns talked differently, too. "He began to speak very delicately about the department, as though it was separate from him, in a way most cops can't," Simon said. Burns also hinted that the case had been forced to close early, thanks to Marty Ward's death.

Several interviews later, Simon's Little Melvin story had grown into a series that would run on the *Sun*'s front page over five days in January 1987. It
detailed not only the police work involved in the demise of Melvin's empire—
including Burns's inspiration to clone the beepers the organization used to
communicate—but also the context in which it thrived: the desperate economy of the streets and the rise of a new, even more violent generation of drug
dealers waiting to fill any vacuum created by the arrest.

What impressed Burns was that Simon took the time to interview Melvin himself, along with other members of the gang, rather than relying solely
on police accounts. Indeed, even before *Homicide*, Simon's interest was broad-
ening. "David started becoming less interested in cops and more interested
in robbers," said Alvarez. "He began to identify with what *The Wire* would
call the victims of capitalism. His argument was that factored into the axiom
of capitalism is a certain percentage of the population that is simply not
needed. And that as we get further into postindustrial America, that percentage grows."

By 1993, Burns's twenty-year run at the BPD had come to an end and he
was turning to a new career, as a public school teacher. "After five great wiretap cases, he ran out of political capital," said Simon. "They said, 'Man, you're
making us tired. You think too hard, work too hard.' Of course, they didn't say
it that way. They said, 'You're a fucking asshole.'"

Hearing of Burns's retirement, Simon first suggested the *Sun* hire him
as an investigator. Instead, another project presented itself. John Sterling,
Simon's editor on *Homicide*, suggested a follow-up that used the same year-in-
the-life structure to tell the other side of the story, that of the participants
in, and victims of, the drug culture. Simon immediately thought of Burns as
a collaborator, and the two took a trip to a beach house in North Carolina,
ostensibly to brainstorm, but also to feel each other out. Simon gave Burns
assignments: "Let's say you've got a white dope fiend coming to cop drugs.
How would you write it up?"

Burns said Simon was worried that they might not find a story. "But I had
this thing: I know Baltimore's not going to let me down. You put corn in enough
heat, it's going to pop. Baltimore is that kind of pressure cooker."

As if to exhibit that faith in the story-granting universe, the two chose a neighborhood corner more or less at random. For three months, while Simon worked at the newspaper, Burns began heading down to the junction of Fayette and Monroe Streets five days a week, getting the lay of the land. He immediately spotted the local heroin shooting gallery, the once nice home of a man named Blue. He also met two men who would become their main characters: Gary McCullough, a hard-luck addict, and his son DeAndre, who over the course of the year would end up in the drug game himself. The third, vital piece was DeAndre's mother, Fran Boyd, also an addict, who was reluctant to cooperate. Burns spent weeks following her into smoky drug dens and broken-down houses until finally winning her trust. Eventually, Boyd would be one of the many Baltimoreans who looked forward to periodic checks for her work writing and recording background chatter (called "wah-wah") for *The Wire.*

When Simon took his second leave from the *Sun* and began coming to the corner, he brought stacks of copies of *Homicide*, to prove he was really an author and not a cop on an elaborate sting; to this day, signed copies can probably be found amid the debris of West Baltimore vacant houses. Like the detectives in that book, the residents of Fayette and Monroe soon came to take the writers' presence for granted. "These people were desperate. They had no one to talk to. So if you're there, and they're momentarily out of the game, they'll come and they'll talk." Once, a carload of armed gang members showed up, fresh off a heist of some kind, and asked Fat Curt, another regular at Blue's shooting gallery, who the two white dudes were. "Them the writers," Curt said, as though every corner in Baltimore came with a pair.

The Corner: A Year in the Life of an Inner-City Neighborhood was finished three years after the project began. ("Simon was very heavy into fantasy baseball one of the years," Burns said by way of explaining why it took so long to write.) The book is as engrossing as its predecessor, but far more political.

"It had to be," said Simon. "Everybody agreed with the fundamental principle of *Homicide*: If someone is murdered, you should try to solve it. There is no 'other hand.' But whether we should fight the drug war or not, who's complicit in the creation of this world . . . to answer those, you have to address modern American history. Because otherwise, looking at these broken lives ... it's just porn."

Among *The Corner*'s many arguments, one in particular provides the central insight that would inform *The Wire*: "Get it straight. They're not just out here to sling and shoot drugs," Burns and Simon wrote of the denizens of Fayette and Monroe.

That's where it all began, to be sure, but thirty years has transformed the corner into something far more lethal and lasting than a simple marketplace. The men and women who live the corner life are redefining themselves at incredible cost, cultivating meaning in a world that has declared them irrelevant. At Monroe and Fayette, and in drug markets in cities across the nation, lives without any obvious justification are given definition through a simple self-sustaining capitalism. The corner has a place for them, every last soul. Touts, runners, lookouts, mules, stickup boys, stash stealers, enforcers, fiends, burn artists, police snitches. ... Each is to be used, abused, and ultimately devoured with unfailing precision. In this place only, they belong. In this place only, they know what they are, why they are, and what it is that they are supposed to do. Here, they almost matter.

The Corner was a premonition of *The Wire* in more concrete ways, too. By 1993, David Simon already had one foot out of journalism and into the world of television.

Several years earlier, Barry Levinson, another Baltimorean, had read *Homicide: A Year on the Killing Streets* and sold it to NBC as a series. Tom Fontana, a veteran of MTM's *St. Elsewhere* and later the creator of *Oz*, became the showrunner. The writers' room was staffed with playwrights, including Eric Overmyer, who had been producing his work in New York, and James Yoshimura, a Japanese American writer from Chicago who drank and swore like a South Side cop.

Production was centered at the disused City Recreation Pier in Fell's

Point, Baltimore. Simon, along with several of the detectives in the book, signed on as a consultant. It was a job that he took seriously in a multipage memo he sent to Fontana pointing out a litany of technical errors in the first several scripts. Fontana took to calling him "nonfiction boy," and it was a point well taken; thenceforth, when cops grumbled about this or that inaccuracy on the show, Simon would defend it on the grounds of good storytelling.

At the beginning of production, Simon had been asked if he wanted a shot at writing the pilot. "Ridiculously ignorant of the money involved," he later wrote, he declined. He did, however, accept the assignment of writing another episode in the season. Treating the gig as a lark, he enlisted David Mills, his old *Diamondback* colleague and a longtime TV aspirant, to join him. The two got together at Simon's house and wrote as a tag team, taking turns at the computer.

The resulting episode, titled "Bop Gun," followed a mugging gone wrong, in which a white tourist and mother of two wound up dead. It delved into the experience not only of the victim's family, but also of the young black perpetrators. It was remarkable for that, and for a scene Simon wrote in which the grieving husband catches the homicide detectives joking callously about the murder—a well-developed defense mechanism of real cops that had never appeared on the small screen before.

"Bop Gun" was deemed too dark to run during *Homicide*'s first season, but it became the first episode of its second. It helped that Barry Levinson called in a favor to get Robin Williams, with whom he'd worked on *Good Morning, Vietnam*, to play the distraught father. Stephen Gyllenhaal directed the episode, casting his thirteen-year-old son, Jake, as Williams's son. The episode was viewed by 16.3 million people, more than twice as many as would see any episode of *The Wire*. When broadcast, it won a Writers Guild of America Award for Best Screenplay for an Episodic Drama.

What with Williams's involvement (which required scenes chewy enough for an actor of his stature) and the normal process of rewrite, Simon later estimated that about 50 percent of the script he and Mills wrote wound up on-screen. Any TV veteran would recognize that ratio, particularly on one's first try, as a wild victory; on the strength of it, Mills headed to Los

Angeles and continued his TV education under David Milch at *NYPD Blue*. But for a reporter accustomed to complete authorship, the degree to which "Bop Gun" had been rewritten felt like a kind of failure. Simon retreated to journalism.

The *Sun*, however, was feeling less and less like the home he knew. The paper had been bought by the Times Mirror Company, and two out-of-towners, William Marimow and John Carroll, had been installed at its helm. As elsewhere in the newspaper world, the new leadership's primary purpose seemed to be cutting costs; a series of buyouts had led to an exodus of veteran editors and reporters. Worse, from Simon's point of view, was the arrogance of the outsiders and their focus on winning high-profile prizes like Pulitzers. "Carpetbaggers," he called them, who'd cultivated "a carefully crafted mythology in which no one knew how to do their job until the present regime brought tablets down from Sinai."

"By the mid-nineties," he later wrote, "there was enough intellectual fraud and prize lust at the *Sun* for me to realize that whatever I had loved about the *Sun* was disappearing, and that, in the end, the artifice of television drama was, in comparison to the artifice of a crafted Pulitzer campaign, no longer a notable sin."

In 1995, he took a buyout and joined *Homicide* as a staff writer.

That didn't mean he was ready to shed the vanities of rebellious journalism. "He showed up with a goatee, black faded jeans, with his little *Miami Vice* ponytail, like, 'All these fucking Hollywood types are invading my city, they're not doing justice to my book,'" said Yoshimura.

He was quickly immersed in a television education, not only in storytelling (Yoshimura told him to go home and read all of Chekhov), but, under the tutelage of Jim Finnerty, another colorful Irishman he idolized, in the physical realities of TV production. One area that took particular adjustment was actor/writer relations. "There was a constant volleyball game between the actors and the writers. We were a really strong-willed, opinionated, confident cast, and they were the same," said Clark Johnson, who played one of the lead detectives and was known for extensive ad-libbing. "Simon came in like Elvis for a little while. You know, 'The writer is God and we [are] just meat puppets.'" At the same time, he admitted, "I would never have said this at the time, but generally speaking the scripts were so flawlessly and beautifully written, you didn't need to change anything; a lot of times you'd be embarrassed that this white Jewish guy from the suburbs of Baltimore would be getting us black guys current with our own street lingo!"

That dynamic—of a white man confidently writing black voices—and the emotional questions it raised would beat like a background drum throughout Simon's career. Soon, it would be raised in a more contentious way. By the time *The Corner* was published, an idea had begun to grow in Simon's head: using the book and its milieu as the starting point for a fictional series about Baltimore on a grander canvas. He approached HBO, which was then developing its first wave of original series, including *The Sopranos*, but he was quickly shot down; instead the network wanted to make *The Corner* as a miniseries.

It did have a concern, though. HBO had always had an uncommonly large black audience, thanks in part to its long history of broadcasting boxing and to such programs as *Def Comedy Jam*. With *The Corner*, which portrayed such a complicated and unpleasant slice of African American life, the network worried about a backlash, particularly since the show came from two very white writers. At an early meeting, Simon was asked, circumspectly, if he knew any other TV writers. He mentioned Yoshimura and Mills, who was African American, though so light-skinned that he often delighted in catching people dropping racist comments in his presence at cocktail parties. HBO leapt at the name ("What, brown wasn't good enough?" Yoshimura asked), and Ed Burns, by then teaching social studies in the Baltimore school system, was effectively shut out.

"I felt bad about that, but at that point I just wanted to get it made," said Simon. "I would still be doing the Lord's work for Ed and me, selling the book." He told Burns that he saw *The Corner* as a foothold toward returning to the larger, more ambitious project and asked him to start drawing up notes for an ongoing series. "I told Ed, 'All the other stuff that we couldn't use in *The Cor-*

ner? That's the place where we start.' With this inverted form of capitalism that is the drug trade. And the failure to police that. And then from there we start building a city." Burns, Simon later learned, thought he was just being given busywork.

With the script for *The Corner* completed, it fell to Chris Albrecht, then in the process of figuring out just what HBO was going to be, to give the ultimate green light. He found himself on a flight from L.A. to New York with two scripts from the miniseries division: one was an adaptation of *The Children*, David Halberstam's account of the Nashville lunch counter sit-ins of 1960. The other was *The Corner*. Both were serious works that grappled with America's racial divide, but only one would get made.

"I started to read *The Corner*, and it was so dark and so intense, I thought, 'Oh, my God, no one's going to want to watch this.' So I picked up the script to *The Children*, and I read a couple of pages and thought, 'I wonder what's happening in that *Corner* script?' Literally I did that about three times," Albrecht said. "By the time I got to New York, I had read two or three hours of *The Corner*. What I realized was, anybody could do *The Children*, but only HBO could do *The Corner*."

As further insulation against charges of exploitation, HBO hired Charles "Roc" Dutton to direct the miniseries. Dutton was a Baltimorean himself and had grown up in *The Corner*'s world, with both a brother and a sister addicted to drugs. He had gone to prison at age seventeen, serving almost ten years over two different stints for manslaughter and weapons possession. While there, he had discovered the works of Douglas Turner Ward, August Wilson, and other black playwrights, and he'd emerged with a new mission in life.

The matter of African Americans' exclusion in Hollywood, particularly on projects like *The Corner*, was a passionate one for Dutton, and he made no secret of his displeasure with how things went. When his mostly white crew of department heads showed up for the first day of production, Dutton turned his back and walked away, refusing to greet them. He especially disliked Simon's presence on set, and eventually the writer decided to stay away, using as an intermediary a gentle, charming producer named Bob Colesberry, who would later prove vital to Simon's continuing TV education.

· · ·

*T*he Corner ran in six hour-long installments in April and May 2000. Critical reception was immediate and positive, with little of the backlash that HBO had feared. By any measure, it was among the most fearlessly bleak works to ever appear on TV, a film that didn't flinch from having, say, a mother ask with one breath if her son has been going to school and, with the next, whether he has any heroin she can cop. The cast is familiar, like watching an early production of *The Wire* Players: Clarke Peters, who would play Detective Lester Freamon, is Fat Curt; Lance Reddick (Lieutenant Cedric Daniels) pops up as a junkie; Delaney Williams (Jay Landsman) is a scrap metal dealer. Khandi Alexander, as Fran Boyd, gives an outrageously fierce, complicated, and devastating performance, and would later anchor Simon's *Treme*.

And yet, viewed post-*Wire*, it is obviously an apprentice effort. Before the start of episode one, Dutton delivers an earnest lecture (which he refused to allow Simon to work on) directly to camera and periodically conducts awkward "interviews" with the actors playing their characters. All feel clumsy and pedantic. More generally, *The Corner* is inhibited by the responsibilities of being a true story. It becomes the homework many viewers feared, wrongly, that *The Wire* was, without any of the mythology and invention that made *The Wire* so much more.

The Corner was a revolutionary step for both its authors and its network. But it is held to earth by mere facts. It would take the new form of the open-ended series, and the freedom of fiction, to let the truth soar.

Seven

The Magic Hubig's

D avid Simon was the master of the memo: a medium that neatly combined his two native gifts, for writing and for argument. Once the writer got a head of steam behind him, recipients of a Simon missive could find themselves alternately bullied, cajoled, flattered, talked circles around, and on the floor laughing. Very often, they also found themselves convinced. But of all his substantial oeuvre, no memos could have been more important than the ones he wrote selling *The Wire*—with the possible exception of the one he'd later write to save it.

Certainly the history of popular art features few documents as baldly, eloquently ambitious as the show "bible" that Simon submitted to HBO in September 2000. The series, he wrote, would be, just as *Hill Street Blues* had once been, a Trojan horse—nominally a police procedural set amid the devastated landscape of postindustrial, drug-afflicted inner Baltimore, but in fact something very different. *The Wire*'s audience, he predicted confidently, having been seduced by the genre, would be left with a very different reward, not "the simple gratification of hearing handcuffs click...."

The Sopranos becomes art when it stands as more than a Mob story, but as a treatise on the American family. *Oz* is at its best when it rises beyond the framework of a prison story and finds commonalities between that environment and our own, external world. So, too, should *The Wire* be judged . . . as a vehicle for making statements about the American city and even the American experiment. The grand theme here is nothing less than a national existentialism. . . .

In the few short years since Tony met his ducks, it was safe to say, TV had come a long way from pitches like "Her husband died, but he came back as her *dog*." As Simon wrote in a follow-up letter to Carolyn Strauss, explaining precisely how much the future brand of HBO depended on putting his show on the air:

> For HBO to step toe-to-toe with NBC or ABC and create a cop show that seizes the highest qualitative ground through realism, good writing, and a more honest and more brutal assessment of police, police work, and the drug culture—this may not be the beginning of the end for network dramas as industry standard, but it is certainly the end of the beginning for HBO.

Simon, never particularly diffident about his talents or ambitions, felt he was in a good position to strive so lavishly. "My attitude, and the attitude of most of the people working on that show, was, 'If this doesn't work, fuck it, we won't stay in TV. It seems like there's a window right now, but if we're wrong about that, we'll go back to books.'"

Still, that window was alluring. As much as Simon was devoted to the romance and art of journalism and, more important, to nonfiction, even he had to concede that fiction film and TV were the primary communication media of his era. "To get a best-selling novel on the *New York Times* Best Sellers list, you need to sell a hundred thousand copies. A poorly watched HBO show is going to draw three or four million a week. That's ten times as many people acquiring your narrative." And that mattered because, to Simon and his partner, Ed

Burns, *The Wire* was explicitly a piece of social activism. Among its targets, large and small, were the War on Drugs, the educational policy No Child Left Behind, and the outsize influence of money in America's political system, of statistics in its police departments, and of Pulitzer Prizes at its newspapers. The big fish, though, was nothing less than a capitalist system that Burns and Simon had begun to see as fundamentally doomed. (If Simon was a dyed-in-the-wool lefty, Burns practically qualified as Zapatista; by ex-cop standards, he might as well have been Trotsky himself.) In chronicling the modern American city, Simon said, they had one mantra, adapted from, of all sources, sports radio personality Jim Rome: "Have a fucking take. Try not to suck."

Neither Burns nor Simon would ever seem entirely comfortable acknowledging the degree that *The Wire* succeeded on another level: as beautifully constructed, suspenseful, heartfelt, resonant entertainment. They would show little to no interest in discussing such matters as character or dialogue, camera technique, plotting, the things that obsess most fiction writers and filmmakers. "It's our job to be entertaining. I understand I must make you care about my characters. That's the fundamental engine of drama," Simon said dismissively. "It's the engine. But it's not the *purpose*." Told that *The Wire* had transcended the factual bounds that, for all its good intentions, had shackled *The Corner*, he seemed to deliberately misunderstand the compliment: "I have too much regard for that which is true to ever call it journalism." The questioner, of course, had meant the opposite: that *The Wire* was too good to call *mere* journalism. As late as 2012, he would complain in a *New York Times* interview that fans were still talking about their favorite characters rather than concentrating on the show's political message.

Simon, then, was a Greek who found himself perturbed by the artistry of his own Trojan horse, annoyed that viewers were so busy marveling at its sculpted contours and realistic paint job that they barely noticed they were being attacked. Such, 99 percent of the time, are the makings of terrible drama: wooden characters, contrived plot machinations, clunky dialogue. The real miracle of *The Wire* is that, with only a few late exceptions, it overcame the proud pedantry of its creators to become one of the greatest *literary* accomplishments of the early twenty-first century.

· · ·

T he show's seventy-nine-page bible was a concession to the reality that
The Wire was not like other series—even those on HBO. Albrecht and
Strauss had not been satisfied with Simon and Burns's pilot and had asked for
two more episodes. Even then, the story had not yet introduced the eponymous wire. This was a work of art that required hours of investment just to
begin to get into, and that's no way to get an easy green light.

The spine of the story—which the bible outlined in meticulous detail—had
taken shape in Simon's Federal Hill bachelor apartment. He had recently
moved back to the city from the suburban home in Columbia, Maryland, he'd
shared with his second wife and son after starting a relationship with Laura
Lippman. In the midst of the divorce, he threw himself into writing and selling *The Wire*. "It was a really difficult time," said Joy Lusco Kecken, who
worked with Simon as an assistant during that period. "This meant a lot to
him. I think he felt he had to sink or swim with it."

The story outline hewed closely to the case that had first introduced
Simon to Burns, that of Little Melvin Williams. Little Melvin was a Baltimore
street legend, though one all but invisible to the city's white population and,
for a long time, law enforcement—a disconnect in civic realities that would
become a consistently shocking theme of *The Wire*. He had started out in
the late 1960s as a pool hustler, "playing the angles to perfection in the Avenue pool halls," as Simon wrote with hard-boiled lyricism in the first of the
five-part series that ran in the *Sun* in 1987, after Burns had finally arrested
Williams.

As Simon told it, Williams had been in the right place at the right time as
heroin flooded urban America. He spent the next two decades revolutioniz-
ing and institutionalizing its sale—through connections to organized crime in
New York above and a hierarchy of young, increasingly violent enforcers
below. He was, in position, if not in personal style, much like *The Wire*'s more
low-profile drug lord Avon Barksdale.

Williams also had a deputy, Lamont "Chin" Farmer, a ruthless manager of
the operation's young army. Farmer was an innovator in his own way, a cere-

bral drug dealer who took business classes at a local college and was once taped lecturing his older brother, another dealer, on heady points of free-market economic theory. Among the legitimate businesses from which he operated was a print shop. Here, then, was the DNA of Avon Barksdale's own, fatally flawed number two, Stringer Bell—or, as the bible had it, "Stringy."

(That these small differences in working names—McArdle for McNulty, Aaron Barksdale for Avon, Stringy for Stringer, Flubber for the ex-con who would become Cutty—are as disorienting as they are is further proof of how intimately we come to know these characters; would the phantom Tommy Soprano have possessed the same magic as Tony? The world will never know.)

The story of Williams's downfall is also familiar to *The Wire* devotees. It began with a murder: a twenty-seven-year-old graduate student found dead in her kitchen, shot through the house's back window. Burns, then a homicide detective, and a partner were assigned the case and duly investigated the crime scene—a process immortalized in a nearly five-minute scene in *The Wire* in which Bunk and McNulty use only the word *fuck*, in nearly every one of its myriad meanings, inflections, and variations. (That succinct dialogue, short on vocabulary but long on meaning, was in turn lifted from a scene in *Homicide* the book.)

The murder became a gateway for Burns to begin investigating Williams's operation. In his *Sun* series, Simon described it in terms that would not, with few exceptions, have been out of place in *The Wire*'s statement of purpose: "There were no car chases, no gunfights, no dangerous undercover assignments. The case was two years of exacting, often aggravating police work—most of it in parked cars, sipping 7-Eleven coffee, or in cluttered city offices, checking tax records or monitoring phone calls from a government desk."

The case's breakthrough was the discovery that Williams's organization exclusively used beepers to communicate. Burns got a court order to "clone" five beepers, using men stationed on top of nearby buildings to monitor when Williams's men were using their devices. The final breakthrough was cracking the simple but clever code the men were using to identify who was calling. It involved "jumping" numbers over the 5 on a standard pay phone keypad.

Almost two decades later, long after the widespread use of cell phones,

Simon worried that replicating the beeper system in *The Wire* might seem anachronistic, but Burns reassured him. "Ed hated cell phones. He carried a pager because he thought it was a discipline," Simon said. "I asked if we'd get in trouble with this old technology and he said, 'No. Anything's a discipline.'"

Soon after Marty Ward's death, Burns and his team were ordered to bring their case in. They ultimately traded a short-term gain—the arrest of Williams, Farmer, and others—for a long-term failure, the missed opportunity to delve into Williams's organization and perhaps the deeper roots of Baltimore's drug and murder trade. That would have to wait for *The Wire*.

I n his bible, Simon expended characteristically strenuous effort emphasizing "McArdle's" Celtic heritage: "the Irishman," he's introduced as. In this, his antiauthoritarianism, and his maverick role in the Barksdale case, he was clearly a version of Ed Burns, though Simon acknowledged that much of McNulty's private life—the failed marriage, the guilty absent parenting—was drawn from his own experience. Plus, "David doesn't like authority either," observed George Pelecanos, who would emerge as the most important writer of *The Wire* after its two principals.

Burns saw himself also in the wise older detective Lester Freamon, exiled to the pawnshop division for McNulty-like behavior in his youth and then resurrected for the Barksdale case. The narrative problem, he pointed out, was that McNulty's rebellious behavior often forced him to the periphery of the show's actual detective work; he spent much of *The Wire* in exile from the main action, first in the BPD's marine division and, later, coincident with the actor Dominic West demanding less screen time in season four, walking a beat.

Finding an actor to play McNulty had been a crucial element to getting the series green-lighted, and the search had not been easy. The production team first targeted a different British actor, Ray Winstone, who better matched their vision of McNulty as a man who was older and had gone further to seed. Simon, *The Corner* producer Robert Colesberry, and Clark Johnson, the onetime *Homicide* actor who was now developing a reputation as a director of pi-lots, flew to Canada to meet with Winstone at the Toronto Film Festival in September 2001. Winstone's American accent wasn't good enough to cut the role of a Baltimore cop. In the coming weeks, an astonishing range of other names was bandied around: John Hurt, Tate Donovan, Donnie Wahlberg, Guy Pearce, Josh Brolin, Tom Sizemore, Viggo Mortensen, Liev Schreiber, David Morse. In Winstone's fleshier mode, John C. Reilly was a favorite choice for a while, until word came that he was uninterested in working on a series.

Meanwhile, a tape of West reading a scene between McNulty and Bunk arrived from London. The thirty-two-year-old Yorkshire native, educated at Eton College and Trinity College, Dublin, had worked primarily on the classi-cal stage. His audition won over casting director Alexa Fogel with a McNulty-ish piece of cheek: it showed West on-screen, reading a scene between McNulty and Bunk. No matter how hard she strained, though, Fogel couldn't hear the off-screen actor reading Bunk. She fiddled with the monitor, called people in to check if she was going mad. At the end of the scenes, West turned to the camera and apologized that his reading partner had been caught in traffic. He'd been reading on his own.

He still wasn't an easy sell. Both Simon and Albrecht worried that he was too young, too pretty, and that his aristocratic accent came through his at-tempts at a Baltimore honk. Who cared? argued Clark Johnson. "I said, 'His accent sucks? Well, he came here from Dublin when he was nine and he's still got a trace of accent, so what? We'll live with it.'"

Fogel made a case for something else in West's makeup: "Chris Albrecht turned to me, because I was the one making the case for Dom. I told him that I believed he possessed an emotional damage that was the same as what David wrote. I don't know what it was, but there was serious bad business underneath the surface."

Good casting always depends on that kind of sensitivity to what's bub-bling under the surface, not just on it. On *The Wire*, that principle was ex-tended to something like an institutional ethic, a belief that almost anybody could play any part. It took viewers almost three seasons to understand why

Avon Barksdale, played by the pantherine but slight Wood Harris, had the internal stuff to rule the West Side drug game while Idris Elba's Stringer Bell, powerful, handsome, and very much Hollywood's vision of a gang lord, was fatally stuck as a number two. Likewise, Jamie Hector as Marlo Stanfield—indistinguishable physically from the gaggle of corner boys until one started getting the measure of his dead, sharklike eyes. As in life, the show seemed to say, it's dangerous to mistake looks for character.

Fogel learned her lesson about selling Brits to the powers that be: When she brought in Elba to read for Stringer, she instructed the actor to hide his natural thick Cockney accent so as not to prejudice the producers. When it came time to cast Irishman Aiden Gillen as season three's ambitious city councilman Tommy Carcetti, the notion of casting foreigners was no longer an issue. (Though that willingness would play a part in ensuring that Fogel did *not* get the job of casting director on *Mad Men* several years later. Matthew Weiner refused to cast English actors for Americans, claiming he could always tell the difference.)

In the end, what emerged was likely the largest cast of black actors ever assembled for TV. Notably, they were not all playing drug dealers or street people. *The Wire* presented a realistic world in which, without comment or fanfare, African Americans played a role in every strata of urban life—from the mayor on down. Looked at with *The Corner*, Spike Lee's pair of documentaries about Hurricane Katrina and the failure of New Orleans's levees, the movie *Life Support* starring Queen Latifah as a working-class woman with HIV, and more, it solidified HBO's unlikely role as the smartest and most sophisticated chronicler of black life in America.

As important as casting, in those early days, was the enlistment of Colesberry to reprise his role as executive producer of *The Corner*. Colesberry was a compact, quiet, patrician-looking man and the bearer of great gentle authority. An ex-army battery commander, he had studied drama at NYU and then worked primarily as a producer of features, including projects by Ang Lee, Martin Scorsese, and Alan Parker. His work on TV was as rarefied as the medium offered; in the eighties, he had produced a renowned version of *Death of a Salesman* starring Dustin Hoffman and, after *The Corner*, Billy Crystal's piece of New York Yankees mythmaking, *61**. He had an easygoing knack for diplomacy. When Charles Dutton raised objections to Simon's presence on *The Corner* set, Colesberry, who was certainly no less white, had been able to act as mediator. He was a crack logistic producer—"He'd been in the artillery," said Clark Johnson. "He did the fucking math: 'If you aim this thing over there, it's going to land within five feet of the target'"—but he was also heavily involved in creative decisions. He would sit in the writers' room, silent until he sensed that things were going off track. Often, a wince or raised eyebrow was enough for his opinion to have its desired effect.

On-screen, Colesberry became known to viewers in the small role of hapless detective Ray Cole. Most important, he was one of the men Simon trusted to both share his mission and argue forcefully, at a level approaching his high standards, when they disagreed. For all of his clarity of vision, the veteran of open newsrooms thrived on that kind of feedback. "Whether it was Bob, or Ed Burns, or David Mills, Simon always needs a bounce," said Johnson.

"One time I asked Bob something about the budget and he said, 'I don't care about money. Ask Nina,'" remembered one *Wire* director. "Nina" was Nina K. Noble, Colesberry's no-nonsense deputy, who would herself become one of Simon's most valued bounces. Like Simon, she had studied under Jim Finnerty on *Homicide*, and she became a feared enforcer of budget and time, as well as a manager of the show's outsize personalities.

Though the majority of *The Wire* would be filmed on location, Noble's first order of business was to find a place in Baltimore to build sets such as the detectives' offices and McNulty's apartment. She located an abandoned Sam's Club that fit the bill. Because the building technically required a retail tenant, moving in meant that *The Wire*, something of a Hollywood outlier in every other sense, started life as an illegal subletter. When eventually the authorities caught on, Noble briefly considered accommodating the code by opening a retail "Wire Shop" selling T-shirts and DVDs.

Baltimore had a limited prior cinematic history. There had been *Homicide* and a triptych of films by Barry Levinson, but the city's most significant and sustained exposure to film production had been through the oeuvre of another native son, John Waters. His was about as far from *The Wire*'s sensibility as it's possible to get, but the show nevertheless wound up employing veterans of Waters's experimental, over-the-top films—most notably Pat Moran, a flaming-red-haired barrel of a woman who handled casting of local extras and day players, and production designer Vince Peranio. It is the happy truth that Peranio, the man who taught America what the inside of a realistic heroin shooting gallery looked like, was the same man who taught it kitsch, in such films as *Pink Flamingos* and *Multiple Maniacs*. In the latter film, Peranio himself had appeared as a giant lobster, named Lobstora, raping a murderous sexual-freak-show operator played by Divine.

Of course, *The Wire* in its way was as much of a constructed reality as *Multiple Maniacs*. When shooting in a vacant town house or drug den, the production team would clean out piles of debris, trash, and human waste and then replace them with their own meticulously re-created versions of the same. Though the story was set largely in Ed Burns's old Western District, its exteriors were shot mostly on Baltimore's *East* Side, where, Peranio said, fewer trees and more vacant houses provided a grimmer landscape. The high-rise housing projects of the type that were the locus of Avon Barksdale's power had in fact been demolished in Baltimore several years before filming started. Scenes at "the Towers," therefore, were shot at a residence for senior citizens, with its lower floors dressed to look like projects and a green screen above, on which upper floors were digitally added in postproduction. (The residents were not overly amused by the disruption and were probably happy when *The Wire*'s reality caught up with Baltimore's and the Towers came down at the beginning of season three.)

None of this was remotely scandalous or would even have been particularly notable were it not for Simon and company's public fetish for verisimilitude. A measure of that impulse could be taken behind the scenes of Simon's next HBO project, *Treme*, which documented New Orleans in the aftermath of 2005's Hurricane Katrina. Created with Eric Overmyer, *Treme* was, if anything, even more obsessed with accuracy than *The Wire*. The walls of the show's offices were covered with photos, news stories, and dense, detailed timelines of everything that had occurred, and precisely when, in the years after the storm. Yet in a season one episode, when one of the main characters, the chef-owner of an understaffed and faltering restaurant, found herself without any dessert to serve, she reached for New Orleans's beloved local version of a Hostess Fruit Pie, a Hubig's Pie.

It was a great detail, one that conveyed deep local knowledge—not only of endemic junk foods, but of what the gesture of giving, and accepting, such a modest gift would have meant in those postdisaster days. There was only one problem: The Hubig's factory had not actually reopened until many months after the scene was supposed to take place. After much discussion, it was decided: The pie would stay. How? "Well," explained Simon, "it was a *magic* Hubig's."

That line between absolute accuracy and the demands of compelling drama remained a shifting target throughout the making of *The Wire*. Simon and Burns, the ex-journalist and the ex-cop, often alternated positions on either side of it. In matters of dealing with HBO, the logistics of filming, and other production issues, *The Wire* would always remain Simon's show. His was the autocratic final decision on all matters of substance, while Burns remained happily insulated. "I don't even really know what a producer *is*," he said, not without some pride.

In the writers' room, however, they were closer to equals. Simon's primary strengths were at once global—setting the agenda for each season—and nitty-gritty, taking the final pass on every script after the other writers had weighed in. Burns, meanwhile, emerged as a prodigious, sometimes exhausting fount of ideas, a veritable one-man plot engine. "People ask me, 'Where do you get ideas from?'" said William Zorzi, Simon's ex–*Sun* colleague who joined *The Wire* in season three. "I say, 'Ed Burns brings them in every morning. Where do you get yours?'"

"These are two guys who can finish each other's sentences," said Chris Collins, who sat in the writers' room as an assistant. "When they'd start breaking story, they'd be five steps ahead of everybody else. One would drop a name. That would remind them of something else. All of a sudden they're way out ahead."

The relationship was often contentious—uncomfortably so. "Ed was always challenging David. He'd come in with five ideas and he would fight for all of them," said Joy Lusco Kecken, a season two writer.

"I don't think there were ever names called, but things could get heated. Certainly the subtext was, 'I think you're ridiculous and that's the worst idea I've ever heard,'" said Overmyer, who also served on *The Wire* in season four. "David's pretty left-wing, but Ed, I think, is even left of him. It was like the Bolsheviks versus the Mensheviks." It would often fall to Pelecanos to suggest that perhaps it was time to move on from some point of debate. "George is a man of few words. You'd see him looking around the room while Ed and David were off debating finer points of Baltimore city politics and then say, 'Okay, so, Namond goes down to the store, that's where we were, right?'"

To Pelecanos, who commuted daily from Washington, D.C., starting in season two, it could feel frustratingly like a two-man show. "I don't even have to be here," he'd complain.

"We talked about things like changing SIM cards in a phone all year long. As soon as you thought it was over, Ed would come back from lunch and drop a whole new bunch of information. You'd be like, *'Seriously?* We're doing this *again*?'" he said.

Burns could be frustrated by the journalistic frame Simon brought to all he did. "There's a difference between fact and truth," he said. "If you stick with fact, you're fucked." At the same time, it was Burns who often raised technical objections, such as strenuously protesting a proposed shooting location for a stash because it didn't have a second exit should its inhabitants need to escape. Such details, Burns said, were like a down payment to the audience, one that earned a certain amount of suspension of disbelief later. Simon surely agreed. The two just weren't always on the same page about which details mattered and what, in fact, the truth was.

Adding to the creative tension during season two was the presence in the writers' room of the cackling Rafael Alvarez, Simon's old *Sun* colleague. Alvarez, a Baltimore native, had been brought in specifically to work on the show's dockworkers subplot. He infuriated Burns and Pelecanos with his constant snacking and habit of lying down on the floor of his office for afternoon naps.

But all of this was as Simon, the lifelong believer in the positive powers of argument, wanted it. "I never liked fighting with Ed because it was tiring and slowed the process down," he said. "But I never had a fight with him that, in the end, didn't make the show better."

And the multilayered negotiations between the demands of art and documentary truth resulted, more often than not, in the right decisions. It was absolutely correct to stick with beepers as a plot device, despite the prevalence of cell phones, just as it was correct to save the demolishment of the high-rise projects for the beginning of season three. Placed there, the Towers coming down signified the breakdown of the relative order upheld by the Barksdale regime and the subsequent rise of a new, more vicious breed of drug lord, personified by Marlo Stanfield.

Such liberties also allowed *The Wire* to invest its characters with mythical weight. Omar Little may, in his constituent parts, have been a realistic figure. As a detective, Burns had relied on tips from stickup boys, crazily brave operators who lived, albeit usually briefly, outside even the marginal rules of the drug game. And, indeed, the ranks of his informants included a soft-spoken but ferocious man named Anthony with a particular aversion to foul language. But as a fully realized character, Omar—always "Omar," not "Little"—was unmistakably something more: a larger-than-life force of nature, part Br'er Rabbit trickster, part Robin Hood outlaw hero. Likewise the meathead cop Herc, the very incarnation of the unwitting, destructive status quo. Or McNulty as hero: the One Who Sees.

Such resonance suited Simon because, when not insisting on *The Wire* as a work of politics, he found his literary comparisons centuries before most critics' preferred reference point, Dickens—centuries, even, before Shakespeare. *The Wire*, he said, was essentially a Greek tragedy.

"The ancients valued tragedy, not merely for what it told them about the world, but for what it told them about themselves," he said. "Almost the entire diaspora of American television and film manages to eschew that genuine catharsis, which is what tragedy is explicitly intended to channel. We don't tolerate tragedy. We mock it. We undervalue it. We go for the laughs, the sex, the violence. We exult the individual over his fate, time and time and time again."

In his Baltimore version of Olympus, the roles of gods were played by the unthinking forces of modern capitalism. And any mortal with the hubris to stand up for reform of any kind was, in classical style, ineluctably, implacably, pushed back down, if not violently rubbed out altogether.

"That was just us stealing from a much more ancient tradition that's been so ignored, it felt utterly fresh and utterly improbable," he said. "Nobody had encountered it as a consistent theme in American drama because it's not the kind of drama that brings the most eyeballs." It was possible in this time and place because, in the new pay cable model, eyeballs were no longer the most important thing.

Yet *The Wire* was also, inescapably, modern; its characters operated based on real, idiosyncratic psychologies, refusing to be pushed around like figures on a board. Sometimes they surprised even their creators. One passionate argument in the writers' room was about a major moment in season one's next-to-last episode, "Cleaning Up": the execution of the young drug slinger Wallace by the tougher, only slightly older thug Bodie Broadus. Just before shooting his friend, Bodie hesitates, gun shaking. Burns raised an objection: The Bodie we had seen to that point, he argued, was the very incarnation of a street monster, a young person so damaged and inured to violence by the culture of the drug game that he would never hesitate to pull the trigger, even on a friend.

"It didn't go with the character. Bodie was a borderline psychopath. I was like, 'We're leading the audience down this path, and now this guy is backing off?' That's fucked up. That's bullshit," he said, remembering his feelings on the scene.

In future seasons, though, Broadus would emerge as yet another McNulty figure: a soldier who tries to make his own way and ends up ground down by the system. His death would be unexpectedly poignant. All of that, Burns granted, was set up by his unexpected moment of humanity in season one.

"What it did was it allowed for a wonderful dynamic that went on for four seasons. It brought out a lot of comedy that psychopaths don't have," he said. "It was a learning curve for me. Originally I just didn't like it because you don't pull punches like that with the audience. Now, when I think about it, I think, 'This is cool. This is something that allowed for another dimension.' It worked. It worked fine."

I t helped that, beginning with "Cleaning Up," written by Pelecanos, a major section of voices in the writers' room belonged to novelists, for whom plot and character were almost second nature. Simon and Pelecanos had met only the previous year. Laura Lippman, a *Sun* reporter and novelist who became Simon's third wife, had suggested Simon read one of Pelecanos's crime novels, set in Washington, D.C., noting a kinship between the two writers' sensibilities. Simon later admitted it took him a long time to actually pick the book up, partly out of a native Baltimorean distrust of D.C. Soon after he finally did, the two met at the funeral of a mutual friend, and Simon asked Pelecanos for a ride from the service to the shiva call. On the way, he explained the series he had just sold to HBO—a "novel for television," he called it, with "chapters" rather than episodes. He asked if Pelecanos might like to write one of the chapters.

Simon bet, correctly, that Pelecanos's experience would be a particular asset in dealing with all the complicated narrative business that the next-to-last episode required. In future seasons, Pelecanos always wrote the script in that penultimate slot (Simon would write the first and last episode of each season), with the consequence that he became a kind of Grim Reaper, since that episode consistently boded poorly for at least one major character. Before *The Wire* came to an end, he'd be responsible for dispatching Wallace, the union leader Frank Sobotka, Stringer Bell, and the androgynous hit woman Snoop, all in climactic fashion.

Before that first script, Simon came over to Pelecanos's D.C. bungalow and the two sat on the back porch while Simon explained the process, what a beat sheet was, how each page was about a minute of screen time. Don't worry about street names or other Baltimore-centric details, he said; all that can be filled in later. That should have been the first clue that writing for TV was very different from writing novels, particularly the research-heavy type over which Pelecanos was accustomed to having absolute control. When Pelecanos received the final draft of "Cleaning Up," he called Simon.

"What the fuck? Where's all my work?" he wanted to know.

"How much of your stuff do you think survived?" Simon asked. "Thirty percent?" Pelecanos agreed. "You're doing pretty good, then," Simon told him.

Pelecanos proved a quick study in the essential lesson all TV writers must learn: that the job is to subjugate one's voice to the showrunner's and the challenge to find ways to accumulate personal creative satisfaction along the way. By the time he wrote the penultimate episode of season three, "Middle Ground," he and his boss had worked out a unique system: Instead of going back and forth with drafts, Pelecanos would tell Simon what parts of a script he was most attached to and let Simon do whatever he wanted with the rest. He estimated that as much as 90 percent of his original writing made it to screen on that episode; he called the deeply multilayered final conversation between Stringer and Avon, before each departs to betray the other, "the best thing I'll ever have my name on."

Pelecanos was only the first, and most influential, of the novelists Simon recruited to work on the show. From up and down the East Coast they came, like representatives of the crime families: Pelecanos from D.C.; Dennis Lehane from Boston; Richard Price from New York. Price's 1992 novel, *Clockers*, had anticipated *The Wire* with its tragic dual story of cops and dealers in a fictional northern New Jersey city. It also lent the show several scenes, most memorably a scene in which Herc and his partner, Carver, run into Bodie and some other corner boys at the local movie theater, all "off duty," like Sam Sheepdog and Ralph Wolf clocking out after a long day of battle in a Looney Tunes cartoon.

It was, by any measure, a heavyweight conglomeration of talent, buoyed by much mutual admiration, but not uncompetitive. "Lehane and I came up together, started writing novels at the same time. And Price was a guy we really looked up to. But, having said that, I didn't want Richard to write a better script than I could," said Pelecanos.

The men would angle to get the best scenes into their own episodes. If too much good stuff seemed to be accumulating on another guy's beat sheet, Pelecanos would grumble, "Why don't you just give him the Emmy now?" (In fact, *The Wire* would go down as the most scandalously under-awarded show of all time. It received no Emmys and only two nominations, both for writing; Pelecanos shared one of them with Simon for "Middle Ground.")

"Price was insidious, because he could take stuff that didn't look like it would be great and make it great. You'd start sweating just thinking about it. You could see his wheels turning. Like, 'This is meat. I'm gonna turn this into a whole *meal.*'"

Price, for his part, had watched the first two seasons of the show and arrived "intimidated," he told the journalist Alex Pappademas. "I put everything I *had* into *Clockers*. I didn't have some secret information in my back pocket that now was going to come out for *The Wire*."

Upon arriving in Baltimore, Pelecanos, a devoted researcher, had been pleasantly surprised by the openness of the Baltimore Police Department. "It had taken me years to get into the places I needed to go in Washington, like the homicide squad," he said. "I walked into BPD and someone tossed me a Kevlar vest: 'Come on, we're going on a drug bust.'"

Whether it was born of institutional transparency or overwhelmed disorganization, the BPD's open door policy extended to *The Wire*'s actors, many of whom were brought down for educational ride-alongs. Even for those who regarded themselves as reasonably savvy about urban realities, it was a shocking experience.

"I'd grown up in housing projects, but it wasn't blocks of boarded-up houses and naked babies in the arms of twenty-five-pound heroin addicts," Seth Gilliam said. He and Domenick Lombardozzi were assigned to a ride-along with a notoriously gung ho narcotics officer who went by the nickname Super Boy. On one ride they found themselves crouching in the backseat during a firefight. "I'm thinking, 'My head isn't covered! My head isn't covered! Am I going to feel the bullet when It hits me?'" he remembered.

Wendell Pierce, who played Bunk Moreland, and John Doman, the formidable major Bill Rawls, and West were in another group. "We went to shootings and stabbings. There was a guy with a knife still in him. Another guy who got shot and the cop was still trying to take him downtown for questioning," Doman said. "All of us were like, 'This is unbelievable.'"

Far from most of their homes and families in New York, Los Angeles, or London, the cast spent a lot of time hanging out together. At least two social groups developed. The first centered on the town house that Clarke Peters, who played Lester Freamon, had bought after season one. Peters was an erudite, fifty-year-old native New Yorker. He had left the United States as a teenager for Paris, where there were still the remnants of a great African American expat community. Within weeks of arriving, he'd met James Baldwin, Maya Angelou, and the blues pianist Memphis Slim, among others. When the musical *Hair* came to France, he worked as one of the production's costume designers and eventually joined the cast. He settled in London, acting mostly in the theater, but he had a Simonian pedigree, having played the avuncular junkie Fat Curt in *The Corner*.

In Baltimore, Peters's house became a kind of groovy bohemian salon for an older set of cast and crew members that included Doman; Jim True-Frost, who played Roland Pryzbylewski; and others. Several ended up renting rooms in the house. Peters, a strict vegetarian, would cook elaborate group meals. There was a piano and impromptu jam sessions fueled by red wine and pot smoke. For those seized by the after-hours impulse to paint, there were canvases on easels set up in the basement. Among its habitués, the house was called "the Academy."

Meanwhile, a rowdier scene existed among the younger cast members—untethered, far from home, and often in need of blowing off steam. This social group was centered on the Block, the stretch of downtown East Baltimore Street populated by a cluster of side-by-side strip clubs (and, in semipeaceful détente across the street, BPD's downtown headquarters). The cast of *The Wire* became legendary visitors to the Block, with a core group including West, Gilliam, Lombardozzi, Wendell Pierce, Andre Royo, J. D. Williams, and

Sonja Sohn—holding her own among the boys in one of many on- and off-screen parallels.

"We finished shooting at like one o'clock and, you know, normal places close at two, so we'd go down to the Block, just to feel the energy," said Royo, who played the sharp-eyed junkie, Bubbles. "The owners of the clubs would come out, the girls would come out. It was like we were heroes. The local heroes." At a cast and crew softball game, Royo hired a limousine and a team of strippers to act as cheerleaders.

West, predictably, attracted his share of female attention, professional and otherwise. "A man could live off his leftovers," Pierce would say. All were champion drinkers, and things had a way of getting out of hand. Gilliam took especially poorly to being approached while enjoying himself off duty.

"He could be an angry drunk in a minute," Royo said. "If somebody would be like, 'Oh, you those guys from *The Wire*,' Seth would be like, 'I don't know what happened to manners, but we were talking.' And these were guys who weren't used to being talked to like that. Who had already humbled themselves to come over." Yelling and pushing would often ensue, though usually not more. "Sonja would always have her eye on one of the bouncers and could give him a look. She's a sexy little chick, so they'd make sure she was comfortable."

Gilliam and Lombardozzi, the show's on-screen Bert and Ernie, shared a large apartment in Fell's Point. They hosted epic evenings of beer and video games, including Madden Football tournaments pitting "Good Guys vs. Bad Guys," cops against the drug dealers. The games would run until five or six a.m., when half the players would have to depart for an eight a.m. call. (Peters, the refined bohemian, articulated the cast's generation gap after hearing Lombardozzi brag about a particular Madden move he'd pulled off the night before: "He's going, 'Yeah, man, what you do is push x, x, y, x, y, y ...' I'm thinking, 'What the fuck? This is how they spend their free time?'")

The pent-up energy that fueled all this revelry had a darker side. For many of the actors, particularly those working long night shoots on grim streets, production was both physically and spiritually exhausting. Royo found it especially difficult to play Bubbles. As a child, with a father who owned a Harlem clothing store, he had taken special pride in his appearance, showing up for school in wing tips and double-breasted suits. He knew that the sight of him in filthy junkie gear caused his parents particular heartache—not only on sartorial grounds, but because it was the type of role African American actors were all too accustomed to finding as their only options. At his audition, in front of Simon, Johnson, and Colesberry, Royo voiced his concerns that Bubbles not be just another clichéd black junkie. "They just looked at me and were like, 'Oh, you don't know how we get down.'"

Still, Bubbles may have been more than a cliché, but it was a difficult character to play day after day. "My character's head space was not a pleasant one," Royo said. "I'd look at Idris? Nothing but bitches outside his trailer. Dom West? Nothing but bitches. Sonja? Dudes *and* bitches. Me? I'd have *junkies* out there. They fell in love with Bubbles. I'd go into my trailer and clean my shit off and come out and they'd look at me like, 'You're not one of us. Fuck you.' And then when I had the Bubbles garb back on, it'd be, 'Hey! What's up? Welcome back!' That's a head trip, man. That shit eats at you."

By the third season, he said, "I was drinking. I was depressed. I'd look at scripts like, 'What am I doing today? Getting high or pushing that fucking cart?'"

He was not alone. In the isolated hothouse of Baltimore, immersed in the world of the streets, the cast of *The Wire* showed a bizarre tendency to mirror its on-screen characters in ways that took a toll on its members' outside lives: Lance Reddick, who played the ramrod-straight lieutenant Cedric Daniels, tormented by McNulty's lack of discipline, had a similarly testy relationship with West, who would fool around and try to make Reddick crack up during his camera takes. Gilliam and Lombardozzi, much like Herc and Carver, would spend the bulk of seasons two and three exiled to the periphery of the action, stewing on stakeout in second-unit production and eventually lobbying to be released from their contracts.

Michael K. Williams, whose Omar was far and away the series' most popular figure (a *GQ* writer quipped that asking viewers their favorite character was "like asking their favorite member of Adele"), was so carried away by sudden fame that he spent nearly all his newfound money on jeans, sneakers, and partying. At the very height of his popularity, Williams found himself evicted from the Brooklyn public housing project he'd grown up in, for nonpayment. He and Royo were only two of many *Wire* veterans who said they sought help for substance abuse once the experience was over. This is not to mention those non-actor cast members brought from the real Baltimore into the fake one— among them Little Melvin Williams himself, out of prison on parole and cast as a wise, battle-scarred deacon.

As James Gandolfini could attest, the hardships of inhabiting difficult men episode after episode, season after season, were hardly limited to *The Wire*. Still, the peculiar ways in which the show affected its participants' lives seem like another facet of the intimacy and intensity with which Simon and his collaborators insisted on engaging with their story. Once rolling, it was, mostly for the better, a creative upwelling that tossed and lifted all in its wake. Henceforth, nearly all other depictions of police and city life would seem so divorced from reality that they might as well have taken place on another planet.

Eight

Being the Boss

In February 2001, New York's Museum of Modern Art screened the first two seasons of *The Sopranos* in their entirety, along with a series of films titled *Selected by David Chase*. (They included *The Public Enemy*, *Mean Streets*, and the Laurel & Hardy feature *Saps at Sea*.) It was a triumphant moment. Under the curatorial direction of Peter Bogdanovich, MoMA had played a crucial role in elevating and institutionalizing the generation of American cinema that Chase so admired. (He honored that lineage by casting Bogdanovich in a recurring role as Dr. Melfi's therapist.) To have *The Sopranos* effectively installed in that pantheon—and later added to the museum's permanent collection—was, Chase would later say, among his proudest moments connected to the series.

Other signs of highbrow acceptance abounded as the show's third season was set to begin. The *New York Times* TV critic Caryn James gushed, "As no single film or ordinary television series could, *The Sopranos* has taken on the texture of epic fiction, a contemporary equivalent of a 19th-century sequence of novels. Like Zola's Rougon-Macquart series or Balzac's 'Comédie Humaine,' *The Sopranos* defines a particular culture (suburban New Jersey at the turn of the century) by using complex individuals. So what if Tony is not a prostitute out of Balzac but a mobster out of David Chase's imagination? His outlaw status offers a way of assessing mainstream society in all its savagery and hypocrisy, even while the series creates a unique family history."

As for the other side of the coin—popular acceptance—there could be no question that *The Sopranos* had arrived at something approaching the status of a national institution. Across the country, people would celebrate the March 4 premiere with viewing parties, complete with baked ziti and costume contests for best over-the-top Jersey-wear. There had been the *MAD* magazine parody ("The Supremos"); *The Sopranos* pinball machine; a line of *The Sopranos* cigars and humidors; the official cookbook, complete with a chapter supposedly penned by Bobby Bacala titled "If I Couldn't Eat, I'd F**king Die." Shops in Little Italys everywhere were stocked with Tony-related T-shirts. When the production set up to film outside in New Jersey or New York, the location would be immediately besieged by gawkers, lending the street an almost carnival atmosphere. Vendors would materialize; businesses blared "Woke Up This Morning" from their doors. Terence Winter remembered going to a show in Atlantic City with a group of cast members, including James Gandolfini, and having the spotlight turned on their table as the whole place stood to applaud. "It felt like being with the Beatles," he said.

The cultural impact outweighed the raw numbers. That much-anticipated season premiere was watched by 11.3 million viewers, not nearly enough to crack the top twenty shows on network TV. (The reality show *Survivor: The Australian Outback* commanded an incredible 29.8 million viewers per week that season; the top-rated drama, *ER*, drew 22.4 million.) Still, *The Sopranos'* roughly 10 million viewers per week—including HBO's weekday rebroadcasts—was an astonishing number for pay cable. The newly ascendant market for DVDs, giving newcomers a chance to catch up before the premiere, only added to the eyeballs.

The show had hit the rare sweet spot of mass appeal and critical respect. It could, as the clichéd analysis had it, be enjoyed on "two different levels": for its visceral pleasures (the plot twists, the malapropisms, the blood, the sex) or for its literary ones. More accurately, it could be enjoyed in both ways *simultaneously*, the pleasure residing in the tension between reveling in the

culture and the artistry of the critique. The result was an out-and-out phenomenon.

All of this, Chase had achieved on his own terms and in the very system
that had caused him so much shame all those years. What could be more in the
rock 'n' roll, maverick spirit of what directors like Coppola and Scorsese had
done to the big Hollywood studios in the seventies? Stick it to the bastards in
their own house, right under their noses, and make them thank you for it.

More remarkable, Chase himself had become famous. In the history of
television, how many people outside the business could have identified a TV
writer by name, much less by face? Who *cared*? Yet here was Chase being
stopped for autographs on the street, the subject of adoring profiles, on the
cover of *Rolling Stone*, dead center among his cast, staring dourly at Mark Seli-
ger's lens while his feet sat buried in a metal pail filled with cement.

It was an apt image. Even in the midst of wild success, Chase was weighed
down by doubt and by dissatisfaction. He worried about those viewers he felt
just didn't get it, who tuned in each week just hoping to see "big Tony Soprano
take some guy's head and bang it against a wall like a cantaloupe." He worried
that the show's success did nothing to change the fact that he'd sold out by
being in television at all. Plot leaks, for which there was a sudden, fevered market, drove him to fits—and his employees to acrobatic precautions to avoid his
wrath. (In a *Vanity Fair* article, frequent director Tim Van Patten told Peter
Biskind, "When I'm done reading a script, I will take the first 10 pages and rip
them up into small bits, drop half into the bathroom garbage, and half into the
kitchen garbage. Then I'll take the next 10 pages and rip them into small bits,
drop half into the other bathroom garbage, and half into the incinerator in the
hallway. I've been doing that for 10 years. My fingers would be killing me by
the end of these things.") Chase worried that even HBO, for which the value of
The Sopranos had been incalculable, didn't give him enough respect; at the end
of each season, he complained, the network waited an inordinate amount of
time to commit to the next.

Joshua Brand had his former employee's number when he talked with a
Sopranos crew member sometime during season two and asked, "None of this
is making him any happier, is it?"

With great visibility had come great problems. The tabloids had feasted on James Gandolfini's marital and substance abuse problems. The actor was becoming increasingly erratic, culminating, just a few weeks before the MoMA event, in the multiday disappearance that ended at the Brooklyn nail salon. Meanwhile, activists purporting to represent the image of Italian Americans had lately been getting press by calling for a boycott of *The Sopranos*. When they briefly succeeded in barring the production from shooting in Essex County, New Jersey (causing, among other things, the relocation of the iconic "Pine Barrens" episode to Harriman State Park, just across the New York State line), Chase was apoplectic.

"How can these people cling to their victimhood so much? These mingy little barbers. Italians are very successful people. Why is it so important that they stay a beaten, oppressed, suffering minority? It makes me sick," he said several years later. "I remember thinking, 'I will shoot this show in my living room if I have to. But we'll keep on shooting it. And we'll keep portraying these people as they are, and we're not going to change one lick of hair one iota to suit anybody. I will do it in my living room for $10 an episode, but I won't stop.'" Long after the incident, he took undiminished delight in pointing out that James Treffinger, the county executive who had instituted the ban, had subsequently pleaded guilty and gone to jail on federal corruption charges.

At MoMA itself, during a Q&A with reporter Ken Auletta, an audience member had accused Chase both of sullying the image of Italian Americans and of working for the Mafia himself. That surely didn't dissuade Chase from making an announcement to the crowd that would be picked up the next day by *The New York Times* and newspapers across the country: His contract was up at the end of the next season, season four, and that's when *The Sopranos* would come to an end.

Certainly, Chase had reason to feel burned out. Since its debut, the scale and scope of *The Sopranos* had multiplied in every way—a combined result of success and narrative necessity. As Chase liked to point out, season one had been designed as a self-contained arc, one that, at the end, left no clear route forward: Tony's primary antagonists, his mother and his uncle, had suffered a stroke and had gone to jail, respectively. As often happened in the open-ended universe of an ongoing series, that necessitated introducing new characters to drive the plot: first Tony's sister, Janice—an heir to Livia Soprano's narcissistic awfulness—then her ex-boyfriend and a rival for the Mob's control, Richie Aprile, and so on. And with each new character came new sets, new groups of friends, and new story lines to explore and service in the kind of meticulous detail that made the show come to life.

The Sopranos was now a mini-empire, commanding fevered scrutiny, hundreds of people, and heady amounts of money. The number of shooting days for each script—which is the surest measure of cost—had swelled from a standard seven or eight to first ten, then twelve, then eventually as many as twenty, not counting reshoots, which could often take up several more days. The production had already traveled to Italy for one episode. No piece of music was off-limits, no matter the licensing fee. Chase had begun spending more and more of his downtime near the Atlantic coast of France, where he would eventually buy a house. He would edit from there, buying time on a satellite uplink to communicate with the rest of postproduction, nine time zones away. Cast and crew lunches often included lobster tail or prime steak. There appeared to be no checks on the size and costs of the show.

"When we got there, we were awestruck," said writer Andy Schneider, who joined in season six, with his wife, Diane Frolov. "TV was always about saving money, but HBO was paying for these lavish parties, big night shoots, things you would have censored yourself from writing before because you could never afford it. In normal television, you take out walk-ups, you take out night shoots. It takes a long time to light a street. Here you could have a quarter page saying, 'Character walks down the sidewalk and enters the house. And it's night. And it's raining.' You were free." In a world in which every shot on every page corresponds to a significant expenditure, there might be no greater indication of the power Chase had consolidated than that he occasionally shot alternate scenes—New York mobster Phil Leotardo shooting Tony at the start of season six, instead of Uncle Junior, for instance—to throw off potential plot leakers.

"No matter what we wanted, we did," said Mitch Burgess. "We wrote an episode that called for a quarry for Tony to throw Ralphie's body into, after he cuts his head off. But David couldn't find a quarry around here. So we all went to Pennsylvania, the whole company. We threw a gunnysack into a quarry, lit up like a movie. And then we went over to the Holiday Inn, went to bed, got up, and moved the whole company back."

Matthew Weiner, who joined the show for season five, said, "We were exorcising David's demons. Do you know how many decisions were based on some meeting when he was on *Northern Exposure*, or *Rockford*, or *Kolchak*, or some other show you've never heard of where he worked for three years and somebody told him 'You can't do that'?"

Chase, for instance, banned "walk and talks"—in which two characters, in the frame together, exchange information while heading toward their next destination—because it was a common network money-saving technique. "Sometimes you'd be in this amazing location and we'd say, 'Can't they just walk down the highway? You've got this strip club on one side, an abattoir over there. We can see it all!'" said Weiner. "And he'd say"—with withering sarcasm—"'Yeah. Let's lay some track and walk backwards and get out of here by four.' I just knew it was some executive at Universal that he was punching in the face, thirty years later." (Weiner never shied from expressing his gratitude and admiration for Chase, his showrunning mentor. Nevertheless, it's worth noting that another Chase pet peeve was shots that showed the backs of actors' heads. And that the first shot of *Mad Men*—indeed, its iconic logo—was the back of Don Draper's head.)

To Chase, remaining vigilant to any and all interference was vital, even in the undeniably cozy confines of HBO. "It was necessary for me to always take the point of view that I was obligated to no one and nothing. And that unless I was going to do the show I wanted, I wouldn't do it," he said. "That unless I was going to be compensated at a level I thought proper, I wouldn't do it. And that at any moment I would say, I *could* say, 'Good-bye. No more. I'm leaving. Ending, no ending. I'm out of here.' It was always important for me to maintain that position. In order to stay free."

All of this made for an exhilarating creative workplace, but it also created an atmosphere of intense pressure, most of it bearing down on Chase himself, who was overseeing not only the writing of each script, but also nearly every other creative decision of thirteen minimovies in rapid succession. "David would come in in the morning and say, about some script problem, 'I think I fixed it. I was in the shower this morning . . .' And I'd think, 'How come he's always in the shower when he thinks about this stuff?'" said Weiner. "Then I got the job and realized, 'Oh, my God, you're *always* thinking about it!'"

As Biskind observed, Chase had good reason to understand Tony Soprano's feelings upon being elevated to boss: "All due respect, you got no fucking idea what it's like to be number one. Every decision you make affects every facet of every other fucking thing. It's too much to deal with almost. And in the end you're completely alone with it all."

Or Uncle Junior's assessment: "That's what being a boss is. You steer the ship the best way you know. Sometimes it's smooth. Sometimes you hit the rocks."

The massive job was made possible at least in part by creating a world in which other people managed the rest of his life. Chase lived first in a series of apartment sublets, but once the show was a success, he moved into the penthouse of the Fitzpatrick Manhattan hotel on Lexington Avenue, with the hotel staff at his disposal. As he had in Los Angeles, he dined at the same restaurant several times a week, this time alternating periods at Daniel and Café Boulud. (The ease of getting restaurant reservations, he said later, only half joking, was one of the major reasons to keep extending *The Sopranos'* run.) At work, he withdrew behind levels of gatekeepers. Chase's assistant learned to institute a "five-minute rule" whenever bad news was delivered: the amount of time needed for the desk kicking and yelling to stop and a more rational response to commence. Not that there was a lot of bad news. "Nobody said no to David. Ever," she said. "Except Jim. And even he said no only by not showing up."

"I've met a lot of tough guys in my life," Tony Sirico, the ex-con, once told Robin Green. "But when I see David, I step back."

The bigger the show got, said Chase's assistant, the more difficult even the simplest things became. "It used to be that if David needed to get somewhere, he could take a cab or get in a shared fifteen-passenger van or fly first class on the regular airline. Then, as things got more intense, he couldn't take a cab anywhere, not even a car service. It had to be his own driver, but not in a fifteen-passenger van, in his own van. And if he couldn't have the driver he wanted . . . His needs were just greater and greater. And his ability to handle little shifts or to be told he couldn't have something was less and less." (Chase said that he was happy to take advantage of the perks that HBO offered and which, he pointed out, were not unusual for the showrunner of a successful series.)

The stress only intensified after 9/11, when Chase, the man who had been obsessed with nuclear destruction for as long as he could remember, became fearful of flying. At Silvercup, he demanded heightened security and code-activated locks to be installed on the doors to the writers' offices. The new reality of terrorist threats dovetailed with Chase's deeper worldview, said the assistant. "It's the world against him. People are horrible and they want to get him. Whatever's happening, it's an injustice against him."

To her, the trajectory seemed clear: "I remember that first year when we worked in total obscurity and how much fun we had. The more money, the more respect, the less happy everybody was. Certainly, Jim was struggling, David was struggling. The people who were getting the most fame and the most money were struggling the most," she said.

For all his other duties, the writers' room remained the most important part of Chase's work life, and it was a space ruled by his personality. As far back as *I'll Fly Away*, Henry Bromell had been surprised by the ruthlessness with which he ran his room:

"My wife and I had had a baby and she really wanted to go back to work. So I told David, 'Just so you know, I need to go home at six a few nights a week.' And he said no. He said, 'I need to know your top priority is this job, not your family. Make a choice.' And he had a cold look in his eyes. I was like, 'What, are we in the Mafia?'"

A writer in a David Chase writers' room learned to be acutely sensitive to the boss's moods—and that there was small margin for error. "David always made it clear, you know, 'I'm not running a writing school here.' Either you got it or you didn't," said Terence Winter. "People used to say, 'I don't think David likes me.' I'd say, 'You know how I know David likes you? You're still here. If he doesn't like you, you'll be the first to know. And you will be gone.'"

Chase had declined to hire back any of the writers from season one aside from Renzulli and Robin Green and Mitchell Burgess. To that number he added two more as the staff reassembled in late 1999: one was Winter, an ex-attorney from Marine Park, Brooklyn, a neighborhood much like *Sopranos* country. He had been slaving on such shows as *The New Adventures of Flipper* and *Xena: Warrior Princess*. Winter was good friends with Renzulli; both had worked for a time as New York City doormen and met on Renzulli's short-lived show *The Great Defender*. Renzulli had secretly funneled Winter *The Sopranos* scripts throughout the first season (this was long before the need for any security protocol), and Winter fell in love before he ever saw a filmed episode. Winter was working on *The PJs*, a claymation Fox series starring the voice of Eddie Murphy, while Renzulli bugged Chase to give him a chance. Chase finally offered him a tryout script ("Big Girls Don't Cry") and then a job. Unfortunately, it was for less money and a lower title than he already had. "I had to make the most horrifying phone call of my life, saying no to *The Sopranos*," he said. Luckily, Chase and HBO relented and gave him the title of co-producer.

The relationship between Renzulli and Chase had always been tense: Chase found Renzulli's incessant talking irritating and was once infuriated when he demanded a limousine for his family in New York, precisely the kind of grudge he was prone to hang on to; Renzulli was resentful of being bossed around by someone who, to his mind, didn't understand the world they were writing about as well as he did. As the writing staff's most prominent Italian American, he was especially sensitive to ethnic characterizations, almost to the degree of the protesters who had disrupted production in season two. When Todd Kessler, on Chase's instructions, included the term *guinea tee* in some screen directions, referring to a wife-beater T-shirt, Renzulli called him up. "How would you like it if I wrote 'kike glasses'?" he asked.

To Renzulli's mind, the show had broken its contract of verisimilitude as early as the second episode, when Paulie tells Christopher: "I went over [to France] for a blow job. Your mother was working the bonbon concession at the Eiffel Tower."

"I just thought, 'You can't do that. You can't.' You've just robbed Christopher of his balls and backbone and you've shown Paulie to be a no-class guy. Christopher would never forget that when he became a made guy," he said. Even worse was a season five development that he watched as a civilian viewer. To solve a thorny set of problems, Tony conspires to have a recently released mobster, Feech La Manna, played by Robert Loggia, busted for parole violation and thrown back in prison. The real-life thorny problem that the plot point addressed was the crippling difficulty Loggia was having remembering his lines. But to Renzulli's mind, that did nothing to forgive what he saw as a fatal violation of Family protocol. "The whole crew deserves to get found dead," he said.

"He's wrong," Chase said. "This is what these guys do. They send each other to jail by squealing all the time."

These would have been mere differences in opinion were it not for deeper suspicions Renzulli was beginning to have about Chase's attitude toward the characters they were creating. In the case of the Paris blow job line, for instance: "They went for the fucking line, thinking it was funny," he said. "It was clear that he found these guys amusing. And not in a good way." The characters, he came to believe, were written with more contempt than empathy: "He would run away from any of those characters he wrote. He wouldn't want to be around them for ten minutes."

To be sure, these feelings were colored by the writers' far from amicable parting. Renzulli, eager to take advantage of *The Sopranos*' success, had departed to take a development deal after season two. Before season four, he and Chase discussed his coming back to the show, but negotiations broke down over money. Renzulli insisted that he make more than what he had before leaving and, as important, more than his old protégé Winter. He was left with the feeling that Chase had gone behind his back to ensure that HBO didn't give him what he needed. "I wanted him to come back," Chase said, "When you're doing a TV series, you want all the help you can get. And he was, on balance, a help." But once Renzulli made his demand, he dropped his efforts to hire him back. "I stopped backing him," he said.

The deeper cut came when Winter and his girlfriend traveled to stay with the Chases in France. This, Renzulli felt, was an unpardonable betrayal, of the same kind he'd identified between Paulie and Christopher, Tony and Feech. The writer who may have most personally understood the codes and protocols that animated *The Sopranos'* world left, devastated and embittered that they didn't apply to the real world. The two barely spoke again.

It was not the only departure fraught with emotion. The second writer to join *The Sopranos* for its second season was twenty-six-year-old Todd Kessler, who shared an office with Winter. Kessler had grown up in Michigan and graduated from Harvard; like David Milch and Matthew Weiner, he was the son of a successful physician. In his short career, Kessler had shown a marked facility for connecting to older male mentors. As a theater and playwriting student in Cambridge, he had been taken under the wing of the playwright David Rabe. Later, Spike Lee offered him a full-time job at his production company and, when he turned that down, a chance to write a screenplay for a project Lee meant to direct. It fell through, but Kessler ended up as the youngest writer by far on the network TV show *Providence*, which debuted the same weekend as *The Sopranos*. The show featured a veterinarian character; NBC once gave him a perfectly serious note suggesting that each episode endeavor to feature a litter of puppies. When Chase offered him a chance to write an audition script, Kessler jumped.

That script—"D-Girl," revolving around Christopher's foray into screenwriting—installed Kessler as the house wunderkind. Chase flattered him, asking for advice and reassurance. "He leads with his insecurity," Kessler said. "I remember him asking, 'I don't know. Do we have a show here?' I'm twenty-six years old, giving him a pep talk. It pulled me in. Bonded me with him."

Kessler threw himself into the show, staying on unpaid at the end of the season to watch the shooting of the finale, "Funhouse," which he'd co-written. At the end of that season's shooting, he said, Chase allowed him to come to Los

Angeles to sit in on two months of editing, asking him not to mention it to the other writers. He became close with the Chase family, often going out to dinner with them. Kessler's agent, who happened to also represent Chase, told him that Chase was considering the possibility of someday handing the show off to another writer and that he, Kessler, was being groomed.

Chase dismissed that idea outright, saying he had never thought about handing the show over to anybody. In fact, he said, he had been growing increasingly unhappy with Kessler's work as the writers reconvened for season three. "He had written a really good episode, and then it seemed to me that it was declining after that," Chase said. "I don't remember a lot of this, but I imagine he was being increasingly rewritten. Some people understand this completely strange, bizarre mind-set of organized crime. Some people don't."

As Kessler remembered the sequence of events, on July 21, 2000, at about eight thirty a.m. the nominations for that year's Emmys were announced. They included one for Chase and Kessler as the writers of "Funhouse." Chase had written the first thirty pages—a long fever dream, occasioned by a bout of food poisoning and punctuated with graphic bathroom sound effects—in which Tony's subconscious reveals what he's known for a long time but refused to acknowledge: that his deputy, Big Pussy, is a rat. Kessler wrote the second half, in which Pussy paid with his life.

Kessler spent the next ten minutes fielding congratulatory phone calls. Then came one from Chase's assistant, saying that Chase wanted to see him in the office. When Kessler arrived, still buzzing from the news, Chase closed the door and sat down.

"I guess the timing isn't great," he said, "but I think I need to end this relationship."

Kessler, astonished, asked what he meant. "I think you've lost the voice of the show," Chase said.

"David, the last thing we wrote was nominated for an Emmy, less than an hour ago," Kessler said. "If you felt this way, why didn't you say something?"

Chase considered this. "I guess you're right," he said finally. "Do you want a second chance?" Kessler, more confused than ever, said yes. "Well, I need to think about it," Chase said, showing him the door.

Kessler left work and went to see his brother, Glenn, an actor and writer, at the SoHo apartment they shared. "As soon as I started to tell him what happened, I burst into tears. Like the embarrassing, childlike crying where you can't catch your breath. The show had been my entire life." As he sat on the curb, sobbing, a call came from Chase.

"He was asking my advice on writing a scene. Like, would Tony say this or something else. No mention of what had just happened," Kessler said. Two days later, Chase told him that he'd get his second chance, but that his next script had better come in "production ready," with no need of revision. Given Chase's way of working—and really any showrunner's—this was as definitive a death sentence as a fish in the mail. Sure enough, several months later— and after the two had lost the Emmy to *The West Wing*—Kessler was summoned once again to Chase's office. This time it was definitive.

"I've never seen people get fired so fast. You walk into David's office and ten seconds later the door opens and you have your shit in a box. He does not mince words," Winter said. This time, he didn't even see that much. Winter called Kessler a week later, wondering if he was sick, since he hadn't been showing up for work. Chase hadn't told anybody about the dismissal.

Chase's memory of the incident wasn't nearly as dramatic. "It's never good to be fired, maybe there's no such thing as amicable, but it didn't appear to me I was cold when I did it. Although, look at the message. It probably can't come through very nicely." About the unfortunate timing around the Emmy nomination, he said, "It's hard for me to picture getting the news the nominations came out and then telling him, 'By the way, you're fired.' I guess I'm capable of such thoughtlessness, but it's hard for me to picture." When told Kessler's version, complete with its overtones of Freud and betrayal, he said dryly, "I might have had more on my mind than he did."

A few years later, Kessler wrote the pilot for a new series of his own, to appear on FX. Rather than assume an autocratic role, he would share the duties of showrunner with his brother, Glenn, and a writer named Daniel Zelman. The series wound up running for five seasons and winning four Emmys and sixteen additional nominations; along with *Mad Men*, it was one of the first two basic cable series to be nominated as Outstanding Drama Series. The plot revolved around a terrible boss—brilliant but manipulative, vain, imperious, unpredictable—and a young, talented, but impressionable employee who finds herself seduced, repelled, and ultimately both matured and corrupted by coming into her orbit. It was, he said, based in no small part on his experiences working on *The Sopranos*. The show was called *Damages*.

C hase's announcement at the MoMA panel was only the first of several false stops for *The Sopranos*. Chase compared the show with Russia's *Mir* space station, left up in orbit long past its originally intended expiration date. At the end of each season, spent and exhausted, he considered leaving it to drift off into space. "David always said that when we have an episode about Meadow getting her driver's license, you know that we've jumped the shark," said costume designer Juliet Polcsa.

"You do all the easy ideas the first season, the first ones that come to you," Chase said. "The second season you do the next best ideas. Each time it becomes harder and harder not to repeat yourself and to come up with something fresh that feels different."

Eventually, during each hiatus, ideas would start to flow, and Chase would come back to the writers' room with a long strip of taped-together 8.5-by-10-inch pieces of paper, a miniature version of the whiteboard, on which each character's fate was plotted. Still, the process of turning that outline into episodes could be grueling.

"It became a running joke at the beginning of every year," Winter said. "We would be trying to break stories and there'd be a certain amount of despair, David going, 'Ah, it's taking so long.' I'd say, 'David, it's not taking any longer than it has any other year.'" Winter would pull out the calendar from the previous year and point out that the first outline had not been done until after another two weeks of meetings. "I'd say, 'David, we are not gonna leave this room until you're satisfied and it's great. It's okay. It will not go on the air until we think it really works.'"

The closest Chase came to actually pulling the plug was in early 2003, shortly after season four had ended. Without warning, he summoned Winter, Burgess, Green, and his wife, Denise, to his office one Sunday. HBO was asking him to commit to two more seasons. Season four had ended with the devastating episode "Whitecaps," in which Tony moves out of the Soprano house. It would go on to win Emmys for Gandolfini and Falco and Chase, Burgess, and Green. It would, Chase thought, be an honorable place to end. "He really didn't know, creatively, if he was going to be able to do it," Green said.

Winter, in particular, argued strenuously that they should go on. Eventually, Chase agreed, though he decided to take an inordinately long break. The result, over a year later, was the best of the later *Sopranos* seasons. The pattern, as the seasons had gone on, had become to sustain the plot by introducing a new adversary for Tony—first the coldly menacing Richie Aprile and then volatile, psychopathic Ralphie Cifaretto, both men who posed a physical, existential threat to our protagonist. Season five also began with the introduction of a new thorn in the Soprano side, only this time it was more complicated. Tony Blundetto (played by Steve Buscemi, who also directed several *Sopranos* episodes) was Tony Soprano's cousin, and he wreaked his havoc by messing with the Soprano gang's New York partners. This pitted Tony's loyalty and affection against his sense of business and the Mafia code—ultimately forcing him to kill Blundetto to preserve his own way of life.

I wanted out," said Robin Green of that Sunday meeting in Chase's office. "But I would never have said that. He wanted us to say yes."

By this time, the relationship between Chase and Green had long since begun to sour. The two had worked together, on and off, since *Almost Grown*. Now, with Renzulli long gone, she and Burgess were the only writers left from the original *Sopranos* staff. Long ago, she and Chase had bonded over stories about their mothers. Coming into season five, Green noticed that Chase had moved her chair around the writers' room conference table. "It was so he didn't have to look at me," she said.

As Chase told it, the problem began and ended with the pair's writing output. "From the beginning, there was something about *The Sopranos* they didn't get. They either could not, or didn't want to, understand the through-the-looking-glass quality of the wiseguy mentality. I sat there in a room while Robin argued with Terry all afternoon about whether Tony would have to kill Tony Blundetto." The result, he said, was that he ended up doing more rewriting. "And the strange thing was that, as time went on, I was having to rewrite them more. They had like a reverse learning curve."

Still, the relationship was obviously charged with long-standing emotions. "She became more and more truculent and obnoxious in the room," Chase said. "What she was good at was asking, 'Why? Why would that happen? *Why?*'"

"David's a guy who . . . you kind of hold your breath around him. There's a physical feeling of discomfort," Green said.

Things only got worse in the first half of season six, when Green and Burgess worked on a script—about Tony, convalescing from his gunshot wound, trying to relocate to a better floor of the hospital—that ended up getting killed outright, the only time that had happened. Finally, Burgess came up from covering set one day to find Green in Chase's office, getting fired. ("Nobody ever wants to fire Mitch," Green said, patting her husband's hand.)

"He had a list of infractions, some of them going back twenty years," she remembered. "He could cite the time when I drank too much at a party and interrupted a conversation he was having."

Chase agreed to give them one more chance to finish a draft of the script they were working on, but the writing was on the wall. Two weeks later, neither argued when Chase told them the arrangement was over. Burgess placed his pencil down on Chase's desk. "Well, shit, David, if you don't think the work is any good, then fuck it," he said.

The conflict didn't end there. Chase was furious when a story in the WGA's magazine, *Written By*, seemed to suggest that Burgess and Green had quit because they disapproved of the show's direction, rather than been fired—even more so when their next series, a traditional CBS cop show called *Blue Bloods*, was initially marketed as being "from the executive producers of *The Sopranos*." (The writers said that neither incident was under their control.)

For Green, the hurt feelings lingered. "I think about it all the time," she said. But not to the exclusion of remembering what it had meant to be in that particular room at that particular moment in television history.

"I have every reason to say horrible things about David," she said. "And yet, when I think back, I had more fun than I've ever had in my life writing for *The Sopranos*. What happened on that show, how it changed our lives, the excitement of it, the fun of the first season, where we didn't know it was going to happen . . . it was the most fun I've ever had in my life."

Nine

A Big Piece of Equipment

I n Chase, Ball, and Simon, the new TV revolution had found its Moses, its Mensch, and its Mencken. It remained only to find its Magus. Which is where the third David of the Third Golden Age came in.

David Milch's success—indeed, the very fact of his continued, albeit intermittent, employment—was, in some ways, the most unlikely story of the TV revolution, the extreme edge of what the moment's confluence of creative and economic forces allowed to take place.

By the time the revolution dawned, Milch had already had by far the most successful tenure in network TV of all the showrunners it would elevate. He had started his career at MTM, the modern cradle of quality television, and had been a critical figure at *Hill Street Blues*, that company's signature show. From there, he'd gone on to co-create and run *NYPD Blue*, which ran for twelve seasons and provided a crucial link to the Third Golden Age. He'd won four Emmys and been nominated for eighteen more. On paper, there was nobody better positioned to usher in, and reap the benefits of, the ascension of TV as an art form.

But on paper, the record could hardly do justice to what, with vast understatement, could be called the uniqueness of Milch's modus operandi, or to the challenges it presented. In a world that valued predictability, he was, by design and by compulsion, wildly unpredictable. In a business in which time equals money, it was one resource with which he could be amazingly profligate. The unlikely result: In a society of men loath to put value on intellectual distinction, much less give other men credit for having it, he was all but automatically referred to as a "genius."

The Milch story was no less a piece of mythology for being largely true: Born in Buffalo in March 1945, five months before David Chase, he was the son of an eminent but volatile, hard-drinking, and horseplaying surgeon. He once described himself as a "Jewish country day-school boy." In 1962, he left home for Yale and "never went back." Hailed in New Haven as a charismatic prodigy, he was taken under the wing of the critic R. W. B. Lewis and Robert Penn Warren—referred to decades later, at every possible opportunity, as "Mr. Warren." Post-graduation, Milch was tapped to assist his mentors, and Cleanth Brooks, on a landmark anthology of American literature.

He also developed several obsessive-compulsive conditions. These included addictions to alcohol and heroin, though they were not as immediately crippling to his ambitions to become a novelist as were such habits as rewriting the same thirteen pages of prose over and over again, word for word in longhand, for a year. Television proved a salvation, though not one of which the mandarins of Yale approved. Mr. Warren, Milch said, "refused to have a television set in his home, as though it was some crouching beast." Nevertheless, TV's "coercions of circumstance," as Milch called them—speed, deadlines, the constraints of genre, the necessity of collaboration—would prove to be precisely what he needed to emulate his mentor and become an author.

It was coincidence that brought him there. A Yale roommate, Jeffrey Lewis, had joined *Hill Street Blues* in its second season. Lewis introduced Milch to Steven Bochco, without mentioning any of his friend's eccentricities. "He was an English professor, and that's what walked into my office: tweed jacket, glasses, I think he was wearing a tie," Bochco said. "We started talking and he was very smart, very charming. Clearly a big piece of equipment."

Bochco assigned Milch a freelance episode centered on the rape and murder of a nun that incites a mob response in the city. The first draft was a dud. "I told him, 'David, that's not your fault, that's our fault. We didn't solve this problem in the writers' room,'" said Bochco. The two were about to break for the day when they hit on the idea of juxtaposing the nun's murder, and the police's handling of it, with that of a Latino store owner, which the department would deem all but unnecessary to solve. The story was little more than a "D" plot, a nagging, half-remembered presence at the periphery of the main action, but it underscored the rest of the proceedings and lent them a very different, more complicated tone.

"The lightbulb went off over David's head, and fifteen minutes later we had it," Bochco said.

The episode, "Trial by Fury," aired as the first of season three and won Milch his first Emmy. Bochco deemed it "maybe the best episode of Hill Street we ever did." Milch's voice is most evident in the ritual opening roll call officiated by Michael Conrad as Sergeant Esterhaus—a man whose playfully ornate language bears more than a little resemblance to that of Deadwood's Al Swearengen. At roll call, Esterhaus addresses an issue that would be of particular interest to Milch throughout his career: Police brass, the sergeant says, has demanded that Hill Street station's officers employ more linguistic discretion in their dealings with the public. On the blackboard, he has written a list of acceptable terms—"shucks," "drat," "fudge," and so on—and he offers a piece of literary advice Milch might have done well to heed himself on Deadwood: "Now [these] won't come trippingly to your tongue at first, but with time and usage, you could find them becoming second nature. Your recourse to obscenity will then be fresh and vital when you encounter those situations and individuals for whom only obscenity will suffice."

After Milch's second draft of "Trial by Fury," Bochco offered him a staff position in the Hill Street Blues writers' room. Stable employment did not exactly prove a stabilizing force. Whether he was loaded or temporarily sober, Milch's behavior became legendary. Eric Overmyer arrived at MTM for his first day as a writer on St. Elsewhere to see a man in the second-floor window peeing on the flowers below. "Oh, must be Milch," the receptionist told him.

"He had a drawer full of money and he liked to whip his dick out," said Robin Green, who worked with Milch on a post–*Hill Street* project, *Capital News*. "He's a wild man." At one point, Bochco told *The New Yorker* in a 2005 profile, he learned that his friend and employee had begun commuting from Las Vegas every morning, the better to spend long nights gambling.

None of this was enough to prevent Milch from staying employed. On the contrary: For executive-producing the last three seasons of *Hill Street Blues*, he received a $12 million contract. At least in retrospect, Bochco seemed to regard Milch's habits as the antics of a mischievous child: "He's nuts. He's just crazy. He had a recklessness about him that to this day thrills me." Still, the two could butt heads—not always a pleasant experience: "David can be very intimidating. He's almost always the smartest person in the room, and he will not hesitate to bully. He's so observant about people, he'll scope out how you're vulnerable and he can attack you."

It helped that Milch was able to remain almost demonically productive, churning out high-quality scripts at a breakneck pace. The demands of creating twenty-two episodes a season were both a creative liberation—leaving him no time to succumb to his various blocks—and, as long as he produced, a kind of insurance policy against unemployment. The train, after all, had to keep rolling. From the vantage of 2012, he said the pace of working on a hit network drama was grueling: "I've written 300 scripts in my life and I couldn't do the first 250 again," he said. "It's a younger man's game."

When *Hill Street Blues* ended its seven-season run in 1987, Milch was in a position to create his own shows. The first was an ill-fated experiment called *Beverly Hills Buntz*, in which Dennis Franz reprised a role from *Hill Street Blues*, this time in a half-hour comedy format set in Los Angeles. *Capital News* was even shorter lived. Steven Bochco had had a similar run of failures with dramas since following up *Hill Street Blues* with *LA Law* (most legendarily, the musical-drama hybrid *Cop Rock*). In 1993, the two decided to rejoin forces and created *NYPD Blue*.

The show was at least nominally based on the experiences of a tough, battle-tested New York City cop named Bill Clark, who was to Milch much the way Ed Burns was to David Simon, a kind of kindred spirit, even spiritual twin, from the other, tougher side of manhood's tracks. *NYPD Blue* announced in no uncertain terms its intention to push *Hill Street Blues*'s commitment to dramatic realism to the edge of what network TV would tolerate. Even before airing, it drew an organized protest from the conservative American Family Association, which succeeded in convincing more than fifty ABC affiliates to black out the premiere episode because of its language and partial nudity.

Part of Bochco's pitch to ABC had been the prescient notion that network TV needed to adjust its standards to compete with the coming threat of cable programming. Indeed, the series's traditionally handsome leading men—first David Caruso, who left after season one in search of success in films, and then, for five seasons, Jimmy Smits—proved hardly as important as the figure of Detective Andy Sipowicz. Played by Franz, Sipowicz—with his temper, his crankiness, his struggling back-and-forth with addiction, even his dumpy body type—heralded far more about the generation of complicated antiheroes to come than any number of bare buttocks or instances of the word *asshole*.

From the beginning, Milch fully indulged the modern showrunner's autocratic prerogative. He never convened a writers' room, instead meeting one-on-one with writers and giving vague notes for scripts that he would then almost completely rewrite. "One thing you had to come to terms with, you knew you could never get it to where he would be pleased," said David Mills, who joined *NYPD Blue* after collaborating with David Simon on their *Homicide* script. "When it came to writing on that show, that was the biggest thing to deal with. You can't outwrite him, which means that you can't even win an argument with him on a story point, so why argue?"

(In one of the great near misses of TV history, Mills arranged for Simon to write an *NYPD Blue* spec script and brought him out to Los Angeles to meet with Milch. The two got along well, and Milch offered Simon a full-time job on the show the same week that Tom Fontana did the same on *Homicide*. "It was more money, a bigger hit, but Tom said, 'Listen, I might not be able to pay you as much, but I'll teach you how to produce,'" Simon said. "I said, 'I don't want to be a producer.' He said, 'Yeah, you do. In this game, the only way you protect your writing is to produce.'" He added, "I think I would've learned to really like David Milch.")

Mills found the experience of working with such a volatile leader exhilarating. Not everybody agreed. In her book *Free Fire Zone*, playwright turned screenwriter Theresa Rebeck wrote an essay that appeared to be a thinly veiled account of her time on the *NYPD Blue* staff. She nicknamed the Milch character Caligula.

"Caligula's stories were fantastic—I mean he was a terrific storyteller—and he could really write," Rebeck wrote. "He was also, often, a terrible human being." She described bullying acts of cruelty and professional intimidation, alternating with ostentatious generosity; Milch was famous for randomly handing out hundred-dollar bills and running a weekly lottery for the entire cast and crew in which he gave away thousands of his own dollars.

"When he wasn't being a completely abusive, chaotic nightmare, Caligula was exquisitely charming. He was funny and compelling, kind, alert, and at times deeply compassionate," Rebeck wrote. "He had a prodigious hunger to believe that not only was he a good writer, he was a *great* writer, and it was pretty much understood around the building that anything he wrote, casually, on a napkin, say, was vastly more brilliant than anything the rest of the writing staff could ever hope to accomplish even with thirty years of sweat and hard work." (Rebeck also charged that "Caligula" once hired a prostitute to service himself and his friends and then attempted to expense her fee as show payroll.)

However you cared to analyze Milch's behavior, *NYPD Blue* quickly became a very strange place to work. At some point, Milch stopped committing scripts to paper at all, preferring to come to set and extemporaneously dictate lines to the actors. "There was usually a draft he was working from, but those drafts bore no resemblance to what we ended up doing," said Mark Tinker, one of Grant Tinker's sons, who was an executive producer on the show. "You never knew what you were going to shoot the next day or where it fit. A lot of times the murderer would change in the course of his rewrite."

This often forced the entire production to wait around without any idea of what to do. "We'd say, 'Okay, David, we're going to be done in an hour.' He'd come down and act out a scene. Everybody would stand around and watch. He'd go up to get it transcribed while we guessed at what the staging would be, because the actors didn't have any lines to go on yet. It was crazy," said Tinker.

If there was a method to this madness, it seemed to be that of a fireman setting blazes only he is capable of putting out, thus ensuring his own heroic indispensability and heroism. "It was narcissistically brilliant, in that it essentially disempowered everybody else. Because nobody could do their job," said Bochco. "Everybody became completely dependent on David showing up, David being so brilliant on his feet, he could make up a scene. And so he became the absolute center of a completely dysfunctional universe."

Milch himself saw it in a slightly different light. "The entire television construct is organized around fear. Everyone feels expendable, so they try to make themselves necessary. And the reason they insist on punctuality is that they don't know what the fuck *works*, so at least they're not going to be vulnerable by being tardy," he said. "In a way, that's a liberation for people who are fear based, because they can say, 'What are we going to do?' I believe that deep down people who are governed by fear want to be governed by faith."

Put more simply: "What I am demonstrating is that if it fails, it's going to be *my* fault. And so that's a guarantee of future employment for the people whose fault it isn't."

Whatever the underlying motive, there was a general feeling that the chaos could not be stopped, that to force Milch into more traditional, accountable ways of working would be to squash his creativity—and, not incidentally, the success of a highly rated show. "We were all his enablers. Enabling his bad behavior so we could get the show done," Tinker said. "Mostly we didn't know he was using again, we just thought he was crazy. But we would put up with his crazy behavior when we shouldn't have, in order to keep the train moving down the tracks."

Inevitably the process began to take its toll, first on Milch's health—he suffered a series of serious heart complications requiring time off from the set—and eventually on his relationship with Bochco. As the show became a bigger and bigger success, Milch began to demand more and more money.

"It was a constant," Bochco said. "Finally he came in one day and said, 'I need more money,' and I lost my temper. I said, 'You're already the highest-paid writer-producer in television. You're making more in fees on this show than I am!' And he went off on me and I went off on him and we were nose to nose, shrieking."

That night, Bochco said, he was too upset by the fight to sleep. The next day, he called Milch into his office and said he couldn't stand fighting with a friend and creative partner and had a solution: "I said, 'Go back to your office, talk to your agent, and tell me everything you want. And I'll give it to you. Whatever it is. So, think about it because you're not going to hear the word *no* from me.'"

Milch left and, ten minutes later, was back. "I know what I want," he said. Bochco readied a pen and paper to take down his demands. "He said, 'Promise me that you'll have lunch with me once a week.' I said okay and he turned around and walked out. We never had another conversation about money ever again."

Ultimately, though, Milch's behavior began costing in the metrics that really mattered. "We went from half a million underbudget to a million and a half over," said Tinker. Jimmy Smits, fed up with the strain of trying to prepare without a script, left the show. And the plots, inevitably, grew more and more incoherent. After the seventh season, Milch left the series. By that time, anyway, network TV had all but given up reserving a time slot for risky, prestigious adult fare, the equivalent of a movie studio's Oscar-baiting Christmas releases. A few years later, that niche would have migrated to HBO. And so, naturally, had Milch.

Carolyn Strauss claimed to have never heard the stories about David Milch when she and Chris Albrecht met him for lunch in early 2002. HBO was riding about as high as it ever would then, with *The Sopranos* having concluded its third season, *Six Feet Under* about to start its second, *The Wire* set to debut, and, with the exception of rumblings on a revived basic cable station called FX, little challenge anywhere on the dial.

For all his craziness, Milch had always played relatively well with suits.

He could take notes, at least when he thought they made the work better. And he had been remarkably successful at pitching. While he was trying to make it as a literary writer, he said, editors had begun to sniff him out immediately. "I had such an immature relationship to that world, I'd just be out to steal the money. I didn't like the people, I didn't like any of that, so I enjoyed fucking them up a little bit. But by this time, I wanted to tell stories and they could sense that." Besides, he said, he had a track record; we might not know what the hell he's talking about, he imagined executives thinking, but "you throw a piece of meat in a room and after a period of time he comes out with a script."

Even for those, such as Strauss and Albrecht, who had already weathered a David Simon statement of purpose, Milch's pitch must have been a heady experience. The story was about Roman centurions, city cops, in the time of the apostle Paul, just after Christ's death. That only began to suggest the underlying themes as Milch saw them.

As he later described it, he began with reference to the Christian existentialist theologian Paul Tillich, who said (in Milch's paraphrase) that "an effective symbol partakes of the reality it represents."

> I was interested in the way that Christianity, which was origi-
> nally based on the lived experience of Christ, came to be accepted
> more universally and how the symbol of the cross became the orga-
> nizing principle, detached from the suffering body of Christ. And
> how that allowed a much more complicated and extensive social
> organization.

From there, he diverged into a piece of abstrusely metaphorical social biology:

> I used the example of baboons: Baboons can only move in groups of
> forty-four because they have to be able to see the leader. If they can't
> see the leader, it's like the current has been turned off. The leader is
> in the center.

And then a profane retelling of Bible lore:

> Paul, who was the first guy the city cops in Rome arrested, for prose-
> lytizing, had an epileptic seizure and a vision. Paul had murdered
> the first of the apostles, St. Stephen, because he said if Christ is truly
> the Messiah, then this is the end of days. If this ain't the end of days,
> he's not the Messiah and these people are apostates. So he went out
> and organized the stoning of St. Stephen. The Pharisees said, "This
> guy is a little fucking crazy. You should go to Damascus. You'll
> be strong in Damascus." And on the way to Damascus he had a sei-
> zure, experienced Christ. What he then began to say was, 'You don't
> have to be a Jew. You do not have to be circumcised. All you have to do
> is confess Christ crucified and believe in his symbol.' And so the sepa-
> ration of the symbol from the lived experience, now Christianity
> spread everywhere.

It was, in other words, a classic Milchian rap: funny, lyrical, part lecture, part
hustle; designed to both flatter and intimidate the listener; so packed with
ideas that it veered toward incoherent; but also, if one could grope his or her
way through the allusions, the discursions, and the puffery, containing much
deep and fascinating thought. This was Milch's all but constant mode, often
verging on self-parody. Talking with him, you could find yourself playing a
kind of game in which you asked the simplest possible question—one calling
for a yes or a no or some fundamental declaration of fact—to see if he would
still find the answer by launching into a discussion of the Tao or Kierkegaard
or St. Paul. Most often, he did.

The rap, one suspected, was equally that of a former wunderkind—one
who at age sixty would, within ten minutes of meeting, still show visitors
the elaborate acknowledgment to himself in R. W. B. Lewis's 1991 biography of
the James family—and of a genuinely unique and fertile mind. It also had a
practical function. Who, in the face of such erudite and celestial musings,
would be vulgar enough to press the point on crass, earthbound matters like,

say, budgets or deadlines—or, for that matter, what was actually going to *happen* in a proposed show?

In any event, it is both a credit to Strauss and Albrecht and an indication of the strangeness of the moment in TV history that their response to Milch's Roman centurions was, "That's the best pitch we've ever heard. Unfortunately, we already have a show set in Rome in development. Have you ever thought about doing a western?" And it's a credit to Milch's supple, idea-based sense of narrative that he was able to say, "No problem." If the Roman show was to be about civilization organizing around a common symbol—the cross—then why not substitute an equally potent "agreed-upon lie": gold. Thus, *Deadwood* was born.

I t was no surprise that HBO's next act should be the western. After all, just as the auteur films of the sixties and seventies had done, the TV revolution began by inverting classic American narratives—the outlaw saga, the family drama, the cop show, and so on. In its violent, muddy revision of the ur-American myth of the frontier, *Deadwood* followed squarely in the tradition of Sam Peckinpah's *The Wild Bunch*, Robert Altman's *McCabe & Mrs. Miller*, and others.

As if to underline the point, filming took place at the Melody Ranch Motion Picture Studio, an ersatz pioneer town in the Santa Clarita Valley, once owned by Gene Autry, where such figures as Roy Rogers, Tom Mix, Gary Cooper, and the cast of *Gunsmoke* had applied themselves toward inventing the myth of the American West. The set would be soaked down every day before shooting, to create the appropriately primordial slurry of mud, blood, and manure from which *Deadwood* imagined civilization lurching spasmodically to life. The pilot was directed by the great western director Walter Hill.

One of Milch's great themes was the loss of religious ritual as the central organizing principle of the modern world—and what flows into that vacuum to replace it. Without the Church in any of its myriad manifestations, he seemed to feel, we are so many children in the wilderness, oyster spat drifting in search of something to attach to. This both was the subject of *Deadwood*—as

the muddy community groped fitfully toward some kind of organization—
and, to his mind, what explained the moment in history that allowed the show
to exist, at the expense of what had once been the dominant mode of popular
entertainment: film.

"The whole idea of going out to a movie was really a secularized version of
going to church. And there was a certain expectation you brought to the movies which has taken all this time to be demystified," he said. (Or perhaps still
hadn't been: David Chase still liked to invoke the idea of the movie theater
as "cathedral," long after multiplexes had become more like parking garages,
at best.)

In Deadwood, South Dakota, outside the "churches" of the law and country, in Indian territory, the most potent religious symbol in 1876 was yellow
and glittery and found in surrounding streams. "The agreement to believe in
a common symbol of value," as Milch put it, "is really a society trying to find a
way to organize itself in some way other than, say, hunting or killing."

The man who understood that fact most of all, the man at *Deadwood*'s
center, was the most "anti" of all HBO's antiheroes—Al Swearengen, the
greedy, profane, grasping, murderous, all but prehistoric proprietor of the
Gem saloon and whorehouse.

"While I agree with you that gold is worth $20 an ounce, my gift is not for
prospecting, because I don't like water freezing my nuts," Swearengen said in
the vulgarized, bordering-on-Elizabethan voice that closely mimicked his
creator's. "But I will bring you women, and to the extent that we agree on the
value of the gold, then a woman sucking your cock or doing one or another
thing is worth gold in the amount of X, Y, or Z."

Milch added, "And that's how the town of Deadwood"—and, by extension,
society—"is born."

Swearengen was played by Ian McShane with a ferocity that must have
shocked an older generation of British viewers who knew the actor as a
kindly, crime-solving country antiques dealer on the long-running series
Lovejoy. (Equal cognitive dissonance would have greeted Americans had the
role gone to Milch's reported first choice, Ed O'Neill, best known as Al Bundy
on *Married . . . with Children*.)

Pitted against Swearengen—and those elements of Swearengen in himself—was Timothy Olyphant's Seth Bullock, a former Montana marshal pulled reluctantly into the same role in *Deadwood*. Bullock was precisely the kind of character—the taciturn, duty-bound, unflinching lawman—who would have automatically been the hero of the films or TV shows previously made at Melody Ranch. Yet in keeping with the rules of the new TV, it was almost possible to forget he existed.

Swearengen and Bullock, like many of *Deadwood*'s characters, were historical figures into which Milch breathed his particular brand of life. So was Wild Bill Hickok, who arrived in Deadwood in the show's pilot, the very picture of ruined, worn-out American celebrity. Even those familiar with the historical record—and, by now, the tendencies of HBO series—were shocked to see him gunned down at a poker table in the fourth episode, the death as sudden, brutish, and inglorious as Omar Little's would be in *The Wire* a few years later.

Around the central characters was arrayed a panoply of grotesque and damaged souls: the East Coast girl, cosseted in privilege and a morphine habit, until perversely blossoming in Deadwood's primordial soup; the epileptic preacher; the shattered doctor, clinging to his sense of duty; the whores sold as little girls and now doing the same to others, an entire citizenry of lost, orphaned, and brutalized children—including Swearengen himself. All, despite the lofty rhetoric about Gold, God, and other capitalized Big Ideas, were caught up in the same affairs that consumed the characters in *The Sopranos*, or *Six Feet Under*, or *Rescue Me*: death and love, parenthood and power, loss and longing, and, above all, the search—usually frustrated—for some form of human connection, down in the muck.

With the reduced pace of twelve episodes instead of twenty-two, the limits of shooting on the ranch, and a sober Milch (he claimed to have been fully clean since 1999), the *Deadwood* set wasn't as frantic and insane as *NYPD Blue*'s had been. But the process was no less bizarre. Once again, cast and crew would gather, many days, with little sense of what they would be shooting. The director Ed Bianchi showed up for his first assignment on *Deadwood* and found himself wandering the sets for two days. On the third, he had lunch with Milch, who asked how things were going. "I said, "To tell you the truth, I'm a little anxious. I've been here for two days now and I haven't seen a script.' He said, 'Oh, I can't help you with that.' That was his little joke." Nevertheless, Bianchi—who also directed multiple episodes of *The Wire*— agreed to sign on as a producer for season two. "He does write scripts late, but what makes it okay is that he'll sit down with you and tell you what the story you're going to do is. Then he writes that same story. He knows what he's going to do, he just hasn't put it on paper yet. He's totally functional."

Nor was Milch insensitive to the demands of production. If, for instance, certain actors were on call for a particular week, or certain sets were out of commission, he would write to fit his producers' needs. "We'd say, 'It would be good if we could shoot in the Gem all day.' So he would write scenes for the Gem. And a lot of times one of those scenes might be a three-quarter-page monologue that Ian would have to deliver and that he'd get the night before. He'd come in knowing it fucking cold. It's an English acting thing," Bianchi said.

In guiding actors, Milch was more likely to deliver historical context— say, on nineteenth-century views of medicine—than concrete notes. The actor Garret Dillahunt, who first played Wild Bill's killer and then the character Francis Wolcott, was given and asked to study 190 pages of biographical material about a sixteenth-century heretic named Paracelsus. "None of it ever appeared," he said. At the same time, Milch could seem genuinely open to—even dependent on—what his actors brought to the table. Often, character details were drawn from the real-life production—as though the band of actors, writers, and crew people out in Santa Clarita were itself a microcosmic gold rush town. Once, he observed the actor Dayton Callie self-consciously showing off a new coat to crew members. Transposed onto Callie's character, Charlie Utter, the new coat became a metaphor for Utter's changing role in the community.

"I didn't know Charlie Utter until I knew Dayton Callie playing Charlie Utter," he once wrote.

How you experienced working with Milch depended much on your own personality, said Mark Tinker, who followed him from *NYPD Blue* to *Deadwood*. "If you're an actor who can't go with the flow, you're fucked. If you're a producer who must have everything in order, you're fucked. But if you can relate to the creative process and you get enthralled with David's brain and his approach to work and the heart that he exhibits, then you're going to be fine." He paused. "For a while."

Tinker himself reached the outer limit of his ability to work with Milch during the filming of *John from Cincinnati,* the inscrutable and brief follow-up to *Deadwood.*

"I'd had enough. So, we went for a little walk around the *Deadwood* lot, which was where we were also shooting *John.* I said, 'David, I gotta go eat McDonald's for a while.' His work was just too rich a meal for me to comprehend and digest. No day was ever the same. You never knew what was going to set him off, what was going to please him. . . . I needed something where I knew what it was going to taste like every day," he said.

At the time of this retelling, Tinker was executive producer of *Private Practice*, an hour-long spin-off of *Grey's Anatomy*, about oversexed doctors in Los Angeles. So, how did McDonald's taste?

"Be careful what you wish for," he said.

If all showrunner-writer relationships, fraught as they are with approval and rejection, discipline and reward, take on a distinctly Freudian tinge, it's no surprise that Milch's were especially susceptible. He explicitly fostered a mentor-mentee, if not outright paternal, dynamic with chosen writers, telling Mills, for instance, that he would teach him everything he knew, until the younger man had had enough and was forced to leave. His professional relationships were particularly intense with the female writers who came into his orbit. Theresa Rebeck, after detailing the many crimes of "Caligula," turned more self-reflective: "I both loved and hated this guy. I was desperate for him to think highly of my writing. . . . I needed to pretend that anything he wrote on a napkin was vastly more brilliant than anything I might write, ever, because it was simply true," she wrote. "For months [after leaving the job] I wallowed in the confusion of wondering whether I was any good as a writer and why I couldn't get Caligula to see that I really did have the talent and ability to be a great writer of his show. Why couldn't I get Caligula to value me and treat me with just a shred more respect so that I could have stayed and let him destroy me more?"

Others had a very different, though equally loaded, experience. Regina Corrado was another New York playwright lured to Los Angeles to write for TV. At the recommendation of a friend, she wound up in the *Deadwood* writers' room. From the beginning, she felt immense, loving support from Milch. "I can't say enough wonderful things about him. He just so effortlessly changed my life," she said. She was aware enough to note the personal significance of starting to work on the show the same year she lost her father, who happened to also be a charming, highly educated drinker. ("You've been training for this job your whole life," one of her sisters said.)

And she could see Milch's potential to be more brutal—particularly with male writers. She and fellow writer Liz Sarnoff would watch writers walk away from meetings with the showrunner, shoulders slumped, and half joke to each other, "Another spirit broken."

"He was more liberal with his abuse of men, in a way," she said, invoking a *Deadwood* scene in which Swearengen slaps another man across the face and tells him, "See that? It didn't kill ya!" "He was saying, 'You take your beatings like a man and give some back. It doesn't have to be that your ego gets crushed every time.'"

But none of this diminished her sense of genuine connection, whether it was sitting in Milch's office, watching him work—"I remember once, he wrote this line for Calamity Jane, 'Every day takes figuring out how to live again,' and he turned around to me with tears in his eyes"—or accompanying him to the track and picking up his winnings, in one case $90,000 in a paper sack.

The angriest Milch ever got with her, Corrado said, was when she tried to get out of moving up to become an on-set producer. "Get the fuck out of my office!" he told her, furious that she would turn down the opportunity for which he had groomed her. After working on *John from Cincinnati*, Corrado left to work on another, more traditionally run show, but she thought often of her days with Milch.

"I miss it. It was always so filled with excitement," she said. "But Liz told me, 'Once you leave David, you can't go back.' You can't be in that world if you're not in that world. You can go back and visit, but it's never the same.' He used to say it was the killing off of the father. You have to kill him off."

M ilch's feelings about working with others were as complicated as everything else about him. This was a battle every modern showrunner faced in one way or the other: the push and pull of auteurship and collaboration. Few scenes could embody it more vividly and literally than Milch's method of composition. It was practically a piece of performance art on the theme. He had begun developing the process as far back as *Hill Street Blues* and had fully refined it by *Deadwood*. And he was well aware of what it looked like to an outsider.

"This will be easy to dismiss if you think it's just an ego trip," he warned a visitor about to observe the same process on the HBO series *Luck*, which premiered in 2012. "But it's not. It's something else."

A group of *Luck*'s writers, interns, and various others, predominantly young and female, were waiting for Milch outside a darkened room in his Santa Monica offices. They resembled vestal virgins. Milch entered, arranged some cushions, and lowered himself to the floor. He assumed a position to accommodate his bad back: head propped up on one arm, one leg bent awkwardly at the knee so that the foot faced upward. It was not unlike an especially awkward male pinup pose.

In front of Milch, at eye level, was a computer screen. At a desk to his right sat a typist/transcriber and the assigned writer of that episode's script, taking notes. The vestal virgins filed in and silently occupied the couch and chairs behind Milch. He called for the writer's first draft of a scene to be put up on the screen and began to dictate.

"Is it better 'This is how church is lately now, too'?" he said. "I like that better."

"Yeah," said the writer.

"'This is how church is lately now, too.' Go forward. Stop. Go forward." The cursor dutifully followed his directions, and the gallery followed along.

Milch described this process as "problems of spirit turned into problems of technique." Laying hands on the keyboard himself, he explained, would be too powerful a trigger for his obsessive-compulsive tendencies. The audience, in addition to witnessing his brilliance, was a kind of disciplinary force, pushing him forward.

Eventually, he came to a section of scene description, interspersed with a few lines of dialogue, in which several characters—including a trainer named Turo Escalante and a couple of wiseguys, Bernstein and Demitriou—watch a horse, Mon Gateau, deliver a mighty performance on the track. The resulting monologue could have been a lost Samuel Beckett prose poem, in which the disembodied authorial voice labors to get his story just right:

Lose the rest. Stop, please. *Descending toward the* . . . Starting *toward the winner circle* . . . *Starting his* descent *to the winner's circle.* Double dash. Comma. *Perfunctorily acknowledging a patron.* Double dash. Now the patron's gonna speak. *"Candy* comma *huh, Turo?" Perfunctorily acknowledging a patron's congratulations. Starting his descent to the winner's circle. Descending to the winner's circle.* Stop. *Close on Escalante, descending to the winner's circle, perfunctorily acknowledging.* . . . *"Candy, huh, Escalante?" Escalante: "He run good, yeah."* Period. *"He run good, yeah." Close on Escalante making his way to the winners' circle.* . . . Lose the "s" in congratulations. *"He run good, yeah."* . . . *Bernstein and Demitriou. On their feet, watching Mon Gateau gallop out. Far in front of the remainder of the field* . . . *Of the* rest *of the field. Far in front of the rest of the field.* Double dash. *On their feet,* comma. Go forward. Lose *the rest* there. Lose *among the horses.* Lose *and.* Lose the last two lines starting with the assistant. Go forward. Stop.

Milch was not wrong that the process would appear to an outside observer as a piece of astonishing, self-aggrandizing theater, a kind of religious rite in and of itself, with Milch acting as shaman. The content, though, was remarkably quotidian, consisting largely of the kind of fitful process—adding emphasis here, cutting a word there, then replacing it, then cutting again—that most writers suffer alone and in silence. Likewise, he had a need to express out loud, and record, the larger, underlying thinking—about themes, subtext, resonance, and so forth—that for other writers would remain intuitive, hidden, and unarticulated.

Just as Milch's rap eventually began to seem oddly guileless—it was, you came to believe, the only way he knew how to speak—so too did this séance style of writing come to seem like something more than just absurd showmanship: an actual attempt, perhaps informed by the rigors of rehab, to achieve communion with other creative souls—what he referred to as a "going out in spirit." Corrado once wondered aloud whether she, or any of the other writers, had any effect on the work they were supposedly involved with. Milch stopped and looked her in the eye. "The essence of this work is the essence of you," he told her.

When asked if he would prefer, given the luxury of time, to write every episode of a series himself, he admitted that it was a tempting idea.

"The '(b)' answer is, I'd write it all myself," he said. "Which is to say that in my vanity and egoism, I would think that that would be the way to proceed. But I know deep down that the better answer is: Even having all the time in the world, it's better to collaborate with your brothers and sisters. It's ultimately the richest experience. It's a much more eventful journey."

In this struggle, Milch himself was not unlike the citizens of his Deadwood or, for that matter, any of the difficult men who populated TV's Third Golden Age, from Tony Soprano on. All of them strove, awkwardly at times, for connection, occasionally finding it in glimpses and fragments, but as often getting blocked by their own vanities, their fears, and their accumulated past crimes.

"We're in a stream or river or something," Milch said. "We are being carried along on something, in which technology has taken over from religiosity. And the story which is being told is the story of the individual trying to learn how to fucking swim."

Ten

Have a Take. Try Not to Suck

In December 2003, five white men in various stages of middle age gathered at a hotel in Tarrytown, New York. By day, they played competitive racquetball games. Somebody with a little foresight, and a concern for productivity, had chosen a hotel that didn't have a functioning bar. Instead, at night they shot pool for money until an employee kicked them out of the rec room for gambling. In between, meeting in the living area of a hotel suite, they decided to elect a white mayor in an overwhelmingly black city, reform a major police department, and, just as a policy experiment, legalize drugs.

The Wire was on hiatus between its second and third seasons, and the men in Tarrytown were the show's brain trust: David Simon, Ed Burns, Bob Colesberry, and George Pelecanos. Also there was William Zorzi, one of Simon's old colleagues from the *Sun*. Zorzi was working on a book project that he and Simon hoped to get off the ground in nearby Yonkers, so Simon invited him to sit in on what Colesberry had arranged as a kind of brainstorming retreat for season three. Simon had an ulterior motive, too: Zorzi had been a political reporter, and despite the pronounced grumbling of his main collaborators, Simon planned to use season three to take on City Hall.

Viewers of *The Wire*, what relatively few there were at that point, had already learned that they might be expected to follow the show in unexpected directions. Season one had been a beautifully self-contained tragic drama. Like season one of *The Sopranos*, it had also ended in something of a narrative dead end. The eponymous wire was dead; the investigative detail had been broken up, with McNulty banished to the marine division; Avon Barksdale had reclaimed his hold on the Western District's drug trade; and, generally, the powers that be on both sides had groaned, possibly swayed a bit, but then settled back into place, as implacable and unyielding as ever.

Even given that narrative challenge, though, season two came as a shock, relocating a major part of the action to Baltimore's dying waterfront and introducing an entirely new cast of characters. Cynics suggested that the shift to a subplot that included mostly white characters was a pandering response to the show's poor ratings. Nothing about Simon's personality made that seem likely, though. And if the goal was giving HBO's viewership faces to which it could relate, a roster of roughneck stevedores, truck drivers, and union leaders would have to be seen as a questionable strategy, at best.

In fact, Simon's fallback plan, if *The Wire* didn't get off the ground, had always been to continue the series of year-in-the-life, nonfiction books he'd begun with *Homicide* and *The Corner*. He had even discussed the next installment with his editor, John Sterling, who envisioned the series in the grandest terms. Simon, he said, was turning Baltimore into his own version of William Faulkner's Yoknapatawpha County. The proposed third book would follow four longshoremen as they dealt with an industry that was disappearing, if not already vanished, in cities up and down the eastern seaboard. As Simon put it, about season two, the story was about "the death of work."

Not everybody was happy about *The Wire* shifting to tackle that topic. "It just didn't feel like *The Wire*," said Burns. But Simon was vehement: by turning their attention to a different sphere early, he argued, they would be claiming the prerogative to do anything they wanted later. "We claimed the whole city," he said. "If the show survived, we could go anywhere. And if it didn't survive, if it was only going to survive as a cops vs. gangsters thing, then fuck it, I didn't want to do it. There wasn't enough there to waste five years of my life on. It had to grow. So, let's take our shot now." The result would be like a brass rubbing, each season uncovering a new section of the landscape, until by the end, an entire panoramic metropolis was revealed.

If, in light of that goal, the title *The Wire* seemed oddly literal and unambitious, Simon disagreed. "In my mind it was never just about the wiretap. It was about the delicate high-wire act, about the connections between people. It worked on that level. We're all connected in some way."

Some critics regarded season two of *The Wire* as the weakest of the first four seasons, the one in which romanticism most clouded Simon's usually clear-eyed judgment. Certainly it was a premonition of the far more serious problems to come in season five. But it was also the season that revealed, thrillingly, the scope of what *The Wire* project would be.

At the end of the season, *The Wire* won its one relatively easy renewal from HBO. Simon even began thinking of a spin-off focused on politics and tentatively titled *The Hall*. When that failed to get off the ground, he decided that *The Wire* could accommodate an area of the brass rubbing even farther afield from its original focus. The story he brought to the table was based closely on the career of Martin O'Malley, the young white Baltimore city councilor who improbably split the black vote in 1999 to be elected mayor and later became governor of Maryland. "The journey of the serious journalist is 'Why?'" he explained. "Who, what, when, where, how—a fourteen-year-old with a phone and a formula can write those stories. *Why* did something happen is epic. So if we're trying to explain why the American empire is in decline, why we can no longer solve our problems, or even address them, then we *have* to introduce the political realm. And so what if it was an editorial?"

Once again, he faced resistance from his fellow writers. All of them.

"I thought it would be boring. We're barely holding on by a thread [ratingswise] anyway. Let's not do something where the audience is going to take a piss break every time the mayor shows up," said Pelecanos. "The discussion went on all season. I'd argue against those scenes, and David would say, 'You just don't want to write them.' Yeah, because they're fucking *boring,* David. Give me a scene with Bunk and McNulty in a bar talking about their dicks. That's what I want to write."

The battle was a matter not just of taste, but of real, quantifiable space. Even given the expansive scope of serialized TV, screen time is a zero-sum game and every minute given to a new character or plot arc means one fewer for everything else. Viewers of a show deep into a long run often look back on early seasons with something like the nostalgia of a firstborn child: "Remember when it was just us?"

"If you look at season one or two of *The Wire*, you'll find an A story line, and a B story line, with maybe a small C. All of a sudden, we started having A-line, A-line, A-line, B-line, B-line, C-line, C-line . . . and it's like, 'What the fuck are we doing here?'" said Burns.

This was the flip side of Simon's determination to expand *The Wire* each season. You can see it in Pelecanos's story notes and beat sheets, handwritten on legal pads, which begin season three in neat, amply spaced penmanship and grow increasingly more cramped and chaotic—filled with arrows, crossouts, reorderings, and parentheticals—as the episodes progress. The notes are also tantalizing glimpses into phantom story lines left on the cutting room floor: at various points, the plot included Omar kidnapping Poot, the hapless Everyman corner boy, and, as disturbing, Herc wooing Beadie Russell.

The squeeze wasn't felt just by writers. A character with less screen time can't complain, but that character's corresponding actor may need some significant ego massaging. In season two, Seth Gilliam and Domenick Lombardozzi found themselves in a position almost precisely parallel to that of their characters, Carver and Herc: relegated to the sidelines of the action—which meant shooting mostly second unit with Bob Colesberry—and increasingly frustrated. "We would bitch and moan and complain. It got to the point where we were calling our agents, 'Get us off this fucking show,'" Gilliam said. "I told Dom, 'I feel like George Steinbrenner signed me because I used to be a guy who beat the Yankees. And now I'm sitting on his bench just so I don't beat them.'"

Eventually, a meeting was set up with Simon. "We told him, 'We're very frustrated.' He's like, 'That's great. Frustration is good.' We say, 'Yeah, but we're *really* frustrated.' He's like, 'Your characters are frustrated. You have to use that. But trust me, in season three you guys are gonna have a lot more to do. Season three is gonna be great. I'm still developing it, but all I know is Herc and Carver are gonna have a lot more stuff to do. And for right now, frustration is good.'"

Burns was never entirely convinced that the real estate spent on the political story line was worth it. "You could have played it a lot of ways without going all the way up to the mayor. It takes up an awful lot of room. And we'd tend to get stuck on whether O'Malley did something or not."

Pelecanos, though, was a convert. "The kicker was, once I saw what we did, the political thread kind of made the show whole, took it to another level," he said. "Up until that point, you didn't understand how things connected, why there was a breakdown in the system. To me, that's what made it. David was right all along."

There were two other major arcs to be plotted out that season. Years before, while doing their reporting for *The Corner*, Burns and Simon had found themselves one evening on West Baltimore's Vine Street. "The sun was coming down, there was this redness in the sky. And somebody must have had some good shit out there because everybody on the street was fucked up except David and me," Burns remembered. "And David says, 'You know, if we could put 'em all here, it'd be great. This is what they ought to do. Put them all in one place, so the cops can do their job and the neighborhood can breathe freer.'"

The result was a fascinating, if credulity-stretching, thought experiment: What would happen if drugs were legal? This plot, too, required the introduction of a new character: veteran police captain Bunny Colvin, who had made a brief appearance in season two. Fed up with the endless cycle of petty drug violence in his district, Colvin decides single-handedly to establish a free-trade zone—"Hamsterdam"—in which dealers may operate with impunity as long as they don't impose on the rest of the neighborhood.

"'We're all good liberals here,' we thought. 'Let's put our money where our mouths are. Really see what would happen,'" said Pelecanos. "We didn't want to push an agenda that said this was going to solve all the city's problems." Far from it, in fact. In constructing Hamsterdam, the writers followed the experiment to its logical, and apocalyptic, conclusion. By the end of the season, Bubbles wanders through a free zone that has turned into a Hieronymus Bosch painting: fires burning, bodies in doorways, women being raped, children running in unsupervised packs. To get the scene right, said Pelecanos, "we shot for two days straight, just to make sure everybody looked really fucking tired."

Said Burns, upon seeing the final scene, "All we did, basically, was take the walls off the houses in Baltimore. That's the shit going on inside."

Finally, season three would both refocus on the Barksdale regime and chronicle its ultimate downfall, accompanied by the rise of the "New Avon," as Pelecanos's notes from Tarrytown had it. (Later, he added the name of the "New Avon": Marlo.) And, as important: "Stringer Bell—Killed by Omar or B. Mouzone."

To be an actor on a TV show during the Third Golden Age was to live in a permanent state of anxiety, one's mortality (and unemployment) forever lurking around the next plot twist. For some, death was just the beginning of a long, fruitful run of ghost and dream sequences. Most, though, understood that one of the period's signature tropes—that, as in life, anybody could check out at any time—had significant implications for their job security. Even James Gandolfini admitted that he didn't sleep entirely easily knowing that Tony's fate lay in David Chase's hands.

The situation turned actors into forensic Kremlinologists, deep-reading every set of new pages for the slightest hint of impending doom. "Every time you read the script, you're looking for a hint: if too much of your story is being told, 'Oh shit, they're building it up. I'm gonna go,'" said Andre Royo. He and Michael K. Williams decided between themselves that one of their two characters, either Omar or Bubbles, was bound to buy it before the series ended. (Williams won that Pyrric victory.) After a few seasons, Royo even developed a kind of Stockholm syndrome. He went to Simon and asked whether keeping

Bubbles alive wasn't a disservice to the story's realism, given the usual life span of a junkie snitch.

"David looked at me and was like, 'Shut the fuck up,'" he said. "'I don't know what's going to happen, but I do know there has to be some hope or people aren't going to get out of bed in the morning.'"

The Wire actors' anxieties may have been compounded by the fact that communication with actors wasn't foremost among Simon's showrunning skills. "David had a problem about telling people how they were gonna die. He'd never just say, 'Look, you're gonna die.' There was always this weird energy," said Royo. Larry Gilliard Jr., who played D'Angelo Barksdale, had been infuriated by how he learned about his early departure in season two: Simon had run into him on set and said, "You're going to love the stuff I wrote for you this episode." "Great!" said Gilliard. "I mean, it's probably your *last* episode . . . ," said Simon.

The lesson went apparently unlearned by the end of season three. By all accounts, the producers honestly meant to sit down and talk with Idris Elba about the timing and manner of Stringer Bell's death. Instead, that meeting never happened, and he learned about it by reading the script—and subsequently hit the roof. Making things worse was the script direction that had Omar standing over Bell's body and urinating on it, apparently a real Baltimore gang tradition. Elba headed to the set and started telling fellow actors he wouldn't shoot the scene, enlisting some in his cause.

"He was pissed, man. And I got it, because, in effect, we were firing him," said Pelecanos, who wrote the episode. "David and I went to his trailer and tried to talk him down. We said, 'This is the end of the character. We can't keep his story going, it's not logical. And this is exactly the way he would probably go out.'" Elba fixated on the pee. Omar wouldn't be peeing on him, Simon and Pelecanos said; he'd be peeing on a fictional character. "Not on *my* character," Elba told them.

Simon and Pelecanos could have invoked a favorite David Chase line when faced with similar protests: "Whoever said it was *your* character?" Instead, they cajoled and apologized until Elba relented. The death scene was shot at an empty Baltimore warehouse and wrapped at four a.m. On his way down a dark street to his car, Pelecanos heard pounding footsteps behind him and turned, cringing. It was Elba. "I just want to shake your hand," he told the writer. "It's just business."

T he Stringer Bell controversy was an instance that would have benefited greatly from the equanimous presence of Robert Colesberry, but he was no longer there to provide a diplomatic, even keel. In January 2004, just before filming on season three was about to start, Colesberry had gone to the doctor to see about a procedure for a chronic throat issue; he had problems swallowing and would occasionally choke on food. While there, tests revealed severe arterial blockage and an emergency double bypass was ordered.

Before going in for the six-hour operation, he talked about *The Wire* with his wife, Karen Thorson, who supervised the making of each season's main title sequence. Colesberry spoke excitedly about using the Blind Boys of Alabama to record season three's version of the Tom Waits song "Way Down in the Hole." The last thing he said to Thorson was that they needed next to turn their attention to a sound track for *The Wire*, collecting all the music the show had employed over the years. (Like *The Sopranos*, the show didn't use a score.) Then he went off for the routine surgery.

The surgeon, Thorson remembered, emerged from the procedure confident that all had gone well. Then, at one a.m., she received a call. "They said, 'We want to do an MRI, because he's unresponsive.' They said it like they were delivering a newspaper: 'Robert's unresponsive,'" she said. Colesberry, it turned out, had suffered a stroke. Over the course of the next four days, he swam in and out of consciousness. Simon, Nina Noble, editor Thom Zimny, and members of the family gathered in the hospital room. Simon brought in a boom box and played fifties R&B and music from the show. On February 9, with the whole group gathered around his bed, Colesberry died. He was fifty-seven.

There were several official memorial services for Colesberry, the last of which was held in Baltimore just before shooting began. Simon addressed cast and crew, assuring them that the production would soldier on. Many said it was a crucial moment for Simon, the point at which he ceased to be a journalist working in TV, or even just a TV writer, and became a full-fledged producer in the best sense of the word. There were implications for other members of the team, too. Pelecanos and Burns were given more responsibility, with Burns assuming the title of executive producer. Nina Noble, whom Colesberry had mentored for many years, stepped into his shoes and would be a crucial partner for Simon for the rest of *The Wire*'s run and beyond.

There was one more memorial to come. In the third episode of season three, a wake was held, in accordance with Baltimore police custom, at venerable Kavanaugh's Bar. Ray Cole, the character Colesberry had played, was laid out on the pool table. It was Dennis Lehane's episode, but Simon wrote the tribute delivered by the character Jay Landsman. In it, Landsman praises the work Cole did "on that arson down in Mississippi" and "that thing on Fayette," references to *Mississippi Burning*, which Colesberry produced, and *The Corner*. Finally, he concluded, "Ray Cole stood with us. All of us. In Baltimore. Working. Sharing a dark corner of the American Experiment. He was called. He served. He is counted."

Before filming started, Thorson and Simon had taken Colesberry's ashes in a piece of Tupperware and, with a plastic spoon, spread them around the sets of *The Wire*.

With the third season completed, HBO certainly had every reason to feel it had done right by *The Wire*: it had allowed the show to run for thirty-seven episodes, despite small ratings and few awards. Now the story that had started it all, the effort to bring down Avon Barksdale and Stringer Bell, had played itself out. From a business standpoint, it was hard to argue that it was owed any more time or space.

But then, of course, hard arguments were David Simon's chosen art form. He and Burns had already sat down and discussed ideas for two more seasons. Burns was intent on visiting the public school system, to explore the world he had experienced as a teacher. Simon, in turn, had always believed that the only proper ending for the series would be to turn *The Wire*'s roving gaze on the world *he* knew best: the press.

"The last critique we wanted to make was of ourselves, our media culture," he said. "It was a critique of newspapers, but it was also a critique of the audience, of how stupefied and simplified the audience has become. So that Americans can no longer recognize their own problems, much less begin to solve them."

Later, rumors surfaced that a sixth season, focusing on Hispanic immigration, had been scrapped, but Simon dismissed them. A season on that theme had been proposed by David Mills, he said, but it would have needed to be inserted before the events of the fourth season, which led to the series finale, were put in motion. It would also have required everything to stop so that the writers could do the research necessary to maintain the show's level of verisimilitude. And time was one thing Simon did not have, as he tried to save his show before it was scattered to the wind. Already, in the long hiatus, uneasy actors were investigating other jobs; Andre Royo went deep into the audition process to play "Crab Man" in the NBC sitcom *My Name Is Earl*.

Simon and Burns sat down and worked out a story that focused on four elementary-school age boys losing their innocence in various heartbreaking ways as the season progressed. We would be introduced to them by the ex-cop Roland Pryzbylewski, who, like Burns, had left the force in order to join the public schools. (There had been a time, during the brainstorming for season three, when the character of Carver had been the one the writers pointed toward becoming a teacher.)

Then Simon marshaled all his powers of persuasion: the tantalizing storytelling, the moral dudgeon. And the begging. "I don't mind kissing ass when the ass then moves and does what it's supposed to do," he said. "Give me that familiar HBO ass and I'll pucker right up."

Every time *The Wire* had come up for renewal, Chris Albrecht remembered, the HBO fax machine would leap to life. "David would send these letters—intense, single-spaced, pages long—explaining why picking up this show was something we absolutely had to do. You would get to the third page and be so exhausted you'd say, 'Just tell him to come in.'"

Carolyn Strauss had always considered *The Wire* a favorite child—or at least the one most in need of protection. "I suppose it was because *The Sopranos* got all the attention," she said. "And my little baby did not." Still, she knew that more seasons would be a tough sell and which way the wind was blowing. "I understood the business pressures that Chris was under. And I knew it would be a painful decision."

Said Albrecht, "We had taken the show to three seasons. Season three had ended in a great place. Arguably, the story was complete. So, let's declare victory for a show that nobody was watching—and not a lot of people were writing about, either—and move on." On the other hand, he was willing to hear Simon out. "We didn't shut the fax machine down. We didn't refuse him entrance to the building."

Instead, Simon was summoned to give the pitch of his life. Characteristically, its theme was less about the specifics of the proposed season four story than about a singular artistic appeal: he wasn't done, he had more to say. When Simon left, Albrecht turned to Strauss. "He was like, 'We've got to do this,'" she said. "And I was like, '*Duh.*'"

"It was one of those meetings that played out as you would've hoped," said Michael Lombardo, then the executive vice president of business affairs, production, and programming operations, who was in the room. "A passionate, smart writer gave a beautiful explanation of what he was wanting to do, and the network responded appropriately. Chris listened, understood, and responded. I was very proud of him. It was a good day to be at HBO."

"Honestly," said Albrecht, "I think it was easier to do the fourth season than to have to call up David and have another meeting."

Production on season four was, Nina Noble said, the high point of the near decade of *The Wire,* despite being a flagrant violation of the old show business imprecation against working with children or animals. "Just personally, for David and me, we had spent the third season still trying to deal with Bob's death and figuring everything out. The fourth season was really when we felt like we were standing on our own again."

The kids were not the only thing different about season four. Dominic West had been growing increasingly restless. With a new baby back in London, he was putting his wilder days behind him, and it was hard to be an ocean away, occupying the same head space as the hard-drinking, skirt-chasing McNulty for yet another season. There were also the temptations of bigger stages. Almost alone among *The Wire* actors, West had become moderately famous thanks to the show. There were murmurs about his becoming the next James Bond.

For all these reasons, West had asked to be put on the back burner for season four. The previous season had ended with McNulty busted down to beat cop and happy about it. That's where he remained for most of season four, seemingly done banging his head against the police department's walls and shacked up in domestic bliss with the harbor policewoman Beadie Russell.

Still, West was needed for at least brief scenes in every episode, and the production often tied itself into knots attempting to accommodate his schedule—often cramming scenes from several different episodes into his visits to Baltimore, about a week per month, so he could hurry back to London. This was already causing some stress among what was usually a strikingly peaceful ensemble. When West began showing up unprepared and grumbling, his fellow actors felt it was time for some self-policing. A group of them—Sohn, Royo, and Gilliam, and others—rented a hotel room and staged a gentle but pointed intervention.

"They wanted to tell him, 'Look, get with it. When you're here, you've got to be here,'" said Noble, who didn't hear about the meeting until after it was over. "It's the kind of thing that I would have had to do eventually, but they just took care of it." West, she said, shaped up quickly.

Unlike other seasons, this time the production had the luxury of shooting all twelve episodes before any began airing, which made things at least marginally less stressful. (Simon's production company, went a quip popular with nearly everybody who knew him, was called "Blown Deadline" for a reason.)

The schedule was helpful in another, vital way. By now, the revolution in viewing options was well under way. In 2001, HBO had launched its on-demand service. The next year, DVD sales eclipsed VHS for the first time; an industry report cited the release of entire seasons of *The Sopranos* and other TV shows as one of the driving factors in the technology's growth. Meanwhile, TiVo and other digital video recorders had made their debut, further detaching any given program from any particular night.

The network now brought some of those changes to bear on its last-ditch attempt to build *The Wire*'s audience. The three previous seasons were released in DVD sets. Meanwhile, critics received all thirteen episodes of the new season and were asked to watch it in its entirety before it even began to air. This was a tacit admission that one of the strengths of the new TV—the ability to draw out stories as if in a novel—could also be a weakness: it could take three or four or five hours of viewing before the show became addictive, just as you might need to read one hundred pages of a novel before getting hooked. This had been a particular problem for *The Wire*, which with its complicated jargon and byzantine plotlines gave even less quarter than most when it came to easing a viewer in. The biggest obstacle lovers of the show faced when trying to recommend it to friends was dislodging the suspicion that it was homework, TV that was good *for you* but not at all a good time.

Critics had always been kind to *The Wire*, if not overtly messianic (this was before the era of twenty-four-hour tweeting and recapping). After watching season four, they began beating the drum in earnest. "This season of *The Wire* will knock the breath out of you," wrote the *The New York Times*. "This is TV as great modern literature, a shattering and heartbreaking urban epic," said *TV Guide*. James Poniewozik, in *Time* magazine, wrote, "They have done what many well-intentioned socially minded writers have tried and failed at: written a story that is about social systems, in all their complexity, yet made it human, funny and most important of all, rivetingly entertaining."

To further entice people to watch, HBO confusingly began to offer future episodes for on-demand viewing, almost immediately after a previous episode had aired. This may have felt somewhat desperate, and it undercut some of the sense of occasion that longtime fans felt as Sunday night approached, but it did allow more viewers the chance to find their way to the show. Certainly, something worked in its favor: the average weekly rating for season four was, depending on whose numbers you trusted, somewhere between 4.4 and 5.5 million viewers, up dramatically from 3.9 million during season three. That was still a shockingly small number by the standards of mass media. But a better measure was the degree to which *The Wire* suddenly penetrated nearly every conversation among a certain class of educated, liberal, city-dwelling HBO viewers. Legions of these now scurried back to watch the first three seasons while taking in the fourth in real time, making the series perhaps a unique instance of a narrative experienced out of order by a majority of its viewers. In some circles, to not have seen *The Wire* had become a shocking breach of social protocol.

F or these, among other reasons, perhaps the deck was stacked against *The Wire* as it moved into season five. For many involved, there was a palpable sense of having peaked.

"I thought that no matter what we did after the kids' story was going to suffer. Emotionally, you weren't going to top that," said George Pelecanos.

HBO, too, seemed to think that the best was over and it was time for a denouement. The network had committed to doing one more season, but it was adamant that it be shorter than the previous three. Simon pitched hard for the usual twelve or thirteen episodes, but HBO stood firm at ten.

Under any circumstances, this would have been disruptive. Twelve or thirteen one-hour episodes had proven over the past half decade to be organically, almost magically, well suited for the telling of certain kinds of stories. By some accounts, the number thirteen was merely a fortuitous holdover from the days of twenty-two-episode seasons, when networks would order that many episodes to start and then another nine on the "back-end," if all went well. David Milch had a more numerological explanation for the use of twelve, which became the alternate standard for HBO shows after *The Sopranos*:

"To the extent that the corollary theme is what we learn or fail to learn over the course of time, then form and content inform each other. So twelve,

which is formally just an attribute of the calendar, becomes a thematic principle," he said, also noting that days consist of two twelve-hour halves.

Whatever the underlying reason, the new genre of drama seemed invariably to lose its way when its usual rhythm was disrupted—either by a shortened season or lengthened double episodes. The pacing would seem off, the
storytelling judgment flawed. Since even in a full-length season *The Wire*
would have more story than the allotted time would allow, being limited to ten
episodes was bound to be an issue.

And Simon had plenty to say—a decade's worth of fuming passion about
where his beloved *Baltimore Sun* had gone wrong. In particular, he took aim at
two star editors, John Carroll and Bill Marimow, who had taken over the *Sun*
in the early nineties. The outsiders, to Simon's mind, had instituted a corrupt
and cheapened culture more concerned with winning Pulitzers than serving
the community—or, for that matter, getting things right. In 2000, Simon had
denounced a *Sun* reporter, Jim Haner, in the magazine *Brill's Content*. Haner, a
prize-winning star at the paper, Simon charged, repeatedly embellished and
perhaps fabricated stories, while Marimow and Carroll looked the other
way. For his trouble, Simon was painted as an angry, vindictive ex-employee.
Now, with more visibility at his command, he revisited the same turf, creating
a fictional *Baltimore Sun* led by imperious, detached editors and harboring a
serial fabulist.

Underpinning the story, beyond whatever grudges were being worked out,
was a serious point about how the media is fatally detached from the reality it
purports to cover. This, to Simon's mind, was the final piece in the big "Why"
of *The Wire*. It was summed up in one scene, perhaps the best of the season,
when Omar, who had loomed so large throughout the previous fifty-seven
hours of the show, a walking myth whose name literally rang out as he walked
down neighborhood streets, failed to merit even a mention in the city's paper
of record when gunned down. Even to the reporter and editor whom Simon
clearly admires, he's just another "thirty-four-year-old black male, shot dead
in a West Baltimore grocery."

It was an elegant, devastating scene, one that said everything about the
two radically different worlds inhabited by the show's rich and poor, black and

white, powerful and disenfranchised characters, and about the futility of ever
bridging the divide between them. Unfortunately, there was much more newsroom plot. The simple truth was that in several important ways, season five
was a failure, dramatically. All of the concerns Simon's fellow writers had in
previous seasons about new characters and story lines crowding out old ones
came true: Pelecanos's ex-con Cutty was all but gone. Pryzbylewski, gone.
Two of the four kids from season four, gone. And so on. Only this time the
losses came without the compensatory pleasure of rich, three-dimensional
replacements. Simon's newsroom felt schematic, its villains too obviously evil,
its heroes too ruggedly saintlike. (Even the name of the fabricator, Scott Tem-
pleton, was a ham-handed reference to the rat from *Charlotte's Web*.) Many
devotees, watching the shortened clock run out on this universe they had
come to love, couldn't help resenting every minute spent in the company of
these interlopers. And the characters' woodenness planted a seed of doubt in
those for whom the newsroom was the most familiar of *The Wire*'s worlds. If
he's this wrong about these guys, the thinking inevitably went, maybe he was
wrong about all those *other* guys, too.

In the writers' room, oddly, there was more dissent about a different story
line: one in which McNulty (reactivated for this final season), in a final, desperate effort to direct the department's energy toward the drug infrastruc-
ture, invents a false serial killer. Simon had been toying with the story for
many years; it had started as part of an aborted novel he had begun to write as
far back as 1996 and of which he had completed one hundred pages. The plot
would not seem to be any more of a radical departure from reality than Hamsterdam had been, but it was the cause of much conversation both in the writers' room and among viewers who felt it finally exhausted their suspension of
disbelief.

All of this led to something unique in the history of *The Wire*: a chorus of
bad reviews. "What Happened to Our Show?" pleaded the title of a representative essay in the *Washington City Paper*. "Simon may yet right the ship," the
article read, but *The Wire* was "thudding to a close, stuck in a stereotypically
TV-like world it's heroically avoided until now."

Simon did not respond to the criticism with grace and stoicism. In fact, he created an angry and airtight syllogism: If the media had a problem with season five, he said, it was because they felt threatened by its critique of the media. It was, necessarily, a matter of thin skin. (Never mind that the degree of association between modern TV critics and traditional hard-news journalists of the type he was portraying was slight, at best.) His lengthy lectures on the subject to anybody who raised an objection were successful in drowning out more substantive criticism of the season's artistry, but it was hard not to feel that the argument would not have passed muster at the Simon family dinner table in Silver Spring.

How did it happen? How did such an acute and assured show lose its way in its waning moments? One popular answer was that Simon was too close to the material, that his judgment was impaired by the strength of his lingering resentments. But Simon himself seemed to nail a more subtle diagnosis. He was talking about the role he had played in season four, when Burns was intent on critiquing the school system: "Everybody, if they're trying to say something, if they have a point to make, they can be a little dangerous if they're left alone," he said. "Somebody has to be standing behind them saying, dramatically, 'Can we do it this way?' When the guy is making the argument about what he's trying to say, you need somebody else saying, 'Yeah, but . . .'"

In season five, there may have been nobody in *The Wire* writers' room with enough power to say "Yeah, but" to Simon. He had lost his all-important "bounce." Pelecanos openly admitted that he himself had at least partially checked out: "I'm pretty sure we all felt we had no dog in that fight," he said of the newsroom story lines. "There was no passion there for us." More important, Burns was largely missing. Early on, he had been dividing his energies between the show and the miniseries *Generation Kill*. Several episodes into *The Wire*'s season, he left to begin prepping for the miniseries' shoot in South Africa, Namibia, and Mozambique. Throughout the triumphant fourth season, Simon had been there to assist Burns's vision and rein in his ever-expansive impulses. When it came time for season five, though, Burns wasn't there to return the favor with his gift for ingenious plotting and deft characterization. Indeed, he said he had never watched season five in its entirety.

Similar problems would nag at *Treme* Simon's next, Burns-less, HBO

series about post–Hurricane Katrina New Orleans, which was long on atmosphere, politics, and passion, short on compelling plot and nuanced character.
Meanwhile, despite a head bursting with projects, Burns produced nothing
publicly for at least a half decade following *The Wire* and *Generation Kill*. The
truth—no graver than the difference between Wings and the Beatles—may be
that the two men, auteur's egos and all, simply needed each other to do their
best work.

Y ou've got to write for yourself, yourself and the other writers. That's it,"
Simon said, looking back and employing a favorite analogy. "If you go
with the audience, they'll always ask for ice cream. 'You gotta eat vegetables,'
you say. 'No, I want ice cream. Give me more ice cream. The last time you gave
me ice cream and I liked it.' The audience is a child."

At the end of sixty hours of television, season five included, Simon could
rest easy that he had served up something unique to, and yet also uniquely *of,*
television: a work of literature with the nutrition of broccoli and the flavor of
ice cream and the show—five years after leaving the air—most commonly referred to as "the best show ever on television." It may also have been the last
time HBO could unequivocally claim that title.

PART III

The Inheritors

2001 | 2002 | 2003 | 2004 | 2005 | 2006 | 2007 | 2008 | 2009

SHO

Weeds
1 · · · 2 · · · 3 · · · 4 · · · 5

Dexter
1 · · · 2 · · · 3 · · · 4

The Sopranos
3 · · · 4 · · · 5 · · · 6 · · · 6b

Six Feet Under
1 · · · 2 · · · 3 · · · 4 · · · 5

True Blood
1 · · · 2

Oz
5 · · · 6

John from Cincinnati
1

Deadwood
1 · · · 2 · · · 3

The Wire
1 · · · 2 · · · 3 · · · 5

Rome
4 · · · 5 · · · 6 · · · 2

Big Love
1 · · · 2 · · · 3

Generation Kill

Carnivàle
1 · · · 2

The Shield
1 · · · 2 · · · 3 · · · 4 · · · 5 · · · 6 · · · 7

Damages
1 · · · 2

FX

Nip/Tuck
1 · · · 2 · · · 3 · · · 4 · · · 5 · · · 6

Sons of Anarchy
1 · · · 2

Rescue Me
1 · · · 2 · · · 3 · · · 4 · · · 5

Mad Men
1 · · · 2 · · · 3

AMC

Broken Trail

Breaking Bad
1 · · · 2

2001–2009

Eleven

Shooting the Dog

I n the spring of 2012, HBO debuted *Girls*, a half-hour series about four women in their early twenties navigating life in post–*Sex and the City* New York. For about three weeks, the show was all that anybody talked, tweeted, blogged, or otherwise electronically bloviated about—at least in the world in which any new HBO show was discussed with talmudic intensity. *Girls* became a vessel for all that attention because (a) it was good—though perhaps not hefty enough to support the weight of all the Rorschach-like baggage commentators brought to it; (b) it was created and run by a woman, still an unfortunate rarity more than a decade into an otherwise deeply fruitful artistic revolution; and (c) the woman in question, Lena Dunham, was only twenty-six years old.

To Dunham, then, thirteen years old when *The Sopranos* debuted, the notion that TV was a wasteland must have seemed like a rumor from another universe, in the same category as the fact that phones once came with cords. In this, she was just the most dramatic example of the group of showrunners and TV visionaries who inherited and solidified the Third Golden Age. Though only a decade or two younger than the men who pioneered the transformation of TV, they came from a very different place. They were not aspiring filmmakers, or journalists, or novelists who had lost their way. They were television people through and through—unburdened by any of David Chase's chest-beating grief about the direction of their careers. If they'd spent time toiling in the old network trenches, it had been just long enough to instill in them a taste of the hunger for something bigger and more fulfilling, something that then came to them, almost as their due. But though it was HBO that opened the door, it was not the home to this generation's best work. That would happen instead on basic cable, broken up, just like the bad old days, by commercials.

T here was nothing secret about the HBO formula," Chris Albrecht would later say. "It was a good formula: You don't have to do twenty-two episodes. You don't try to program ten new shows in one month. You don't try to figure out what the audience is going to watch. You try not to interfere in the creative process too much. And you put a little money against it. After a while, we proved that you could have both creative opportunity and big success, i.e., *money*. And once you have those things, there's going to be a lot more people looking to be in the game."

Back when the Fox broadcast network was ascendant, it had made a fateful bargain: If cable operators wanted the right to carry it—which is to say NFL football, *The Simpsons*, and other highly desirable properties—the operators would have pay not only in cash, but in bandwidth. Fox, in other words, wanted channels—which is how it ended up with a curious appendage called FX that it had no idea what to do with.

Original programming had actually been one of the calling cards for FX (or, as it styled itself then, fX) upon launching in 1994: "TV Made Fresh Daily," as the motto had it. Emanating from "the Apartment," a 6,500-square-foot space in Manhattan's Flatiron District, the offerings included slapdash shows on such topics as pets and antiques and were anchored by a strenuously wacky morning show called *Breakfast Time*, co-hosted by Laurie Hibberd, Tom Bergeron, and a puppet of undefined species named Bob. (Bergeron would go on to host *America's Funniest Home Videos* and *Dancing with the Stars*. In fact, fX's most lasting contribution to the future of television might have been the employment of eventual reality TV hosts; it also featured Jeff Probst of *Survivor* and Phil Keoghan of *The Amazing Race.*) The rest of the network's schedule was packed with reruns.

By 1997, only the reruns remained. The now uppercase FX did little more than show properties of its parent company, particularly those geared toward men in their late teens to late thirties. The network reached barely thirty million homes; it was not available in New York City. In terms of ratings and public profile, it may as well have not existed at all.

Then, in 1998, Peter Chernin, the president and COO of News Corp., tapped a tall, affable Bronx native and vice president of marketing named Peter Liguori to run the network. As Liguori remembered it, Chernin delivered the news this way: "I have good news and bad news. The good news is, I'm giving you a network to run. The bad news is, it's FX, it's total garbage, you're probably going to fail, and I'm going to have to fire you."

"The subtext was, 'This can't get any worse, so go for it,'" Liguori said.

Liguori had a pedigree when it came to networks seeking to define themselves. He had been vice president of consumer marketing at HBO under Michael Fuchs and had been present as the network began setting its sights on original programming. He had even played some role in the birth of the line "It's Not TV. It's HBO" (the authorship was also claimed by the advertising agency BBDO), though he just as happily took credit for what he called "the worst line in the history of HBO": "Something Special's On."

Now, to help him reconceive FX, he recruited another executive close to the roots of the TV revolution. Kevin Reilly had helped midwife *The Sopranos* at Brillstein-Grey but was looking for new opportunities. Having started his career at NBC, he did not relish a return to a broadcast network. And he had begun to see the opportunities in a changing cable universe.

Still, he was skeptical when he agreed to a lunch with Liguori. The men discussed looking to the Lifetime network, at that point the most successfully branded cable station, with its cheesy but instantly recognizable original movies for women. Liguori imagined doing something similar for young men, a station modeled on *Maxim,* the crude British-based lad magazine that dominated American newsstands in the late 1990s. The new regime had opened with shows like *Son of the Beach*, a parody of *Baywatch* executive-produced by Howard Stern, and a raunchy variety hour called *The X Show*.

"I thought the strategy was terrible," Reilly said.

As lunch progressed, though, Reilly began to change his mind. Liguori was talking less about any particular kind of programming than he was about giving FX a recognizable identity, one informed by HBO, where *The Sopranos* and *Six Feet Under* were suddenly making waves. "He was smartly saying, 'It's a general entertainment network, but it can be branded through *tone*,'" Reilly said. "And the more he talked, the more he started to sound like what he really aspired to do was HBO. I thought, like, 'Well, I can do *that*.'"

That became the men's shared buzz phrase: "Free HBO."

"I just looked at the landscape and thought, 'Here's HBO, that gets accolades for authentic programming, that doesn't shrink from presenting adult themes and adult issues in an unvarnished fashion. And here's the general interest networks: TNT, TBS, USA.' And there's nothing in the middle," Liguori said. "My hunch was there was an underserved audience of people who weren't in the pay category. I laid that out for Chernin and Murdoch: 'There is no reason why those guys have a monopoly on authenticity.'"

The Fox brass agreed but left little doubt that FX remained an ugly stepchild. The network's offices were located on downscale Sepulveda Boulevard, far from the luxurious Fox lot in Century City. Reilly, who had taken an enormous pay cut—half what he was making at Brillstein-Grey, he said—remembered being shocked.

"I had come from a place where they literally had museum-quality art on the walls. If you wanted a new coaster, there was a house designer who would have to come in and approve your $500 coaster. I walked into the FX offices and there was a huge stain in the center of the carpet. There was a hole in the wall, half-covered by a picture. I asked the office manager, 'Do you think I can get two chairs that match?' She said, 'I'm sorry, we can't do that.' I remember my assistant, who came with me, looking white as a ghost, like, 'Why did I follow you here?'" Casting was done in a conference room wallpapered in what

Liguori remembered as some form of green velvet. "You kept looking around for the avocado refrigerator in the room," he said.

Nor was that the most significant shock for Reilly. "I looked at the ratings and, you know, I'd never seen the decimal point on the left side of the number before. I'd seen a 7 rating, but I'd never seen a .7 rating," he said. "I asked, 'What's success? What does Lifetime do?' They were doing a 1.5. But the word was, 'Oh, we'll never get there. If we can do a 1, we'll be thrilled.'"

For Liguori, though, low expectations were part of the promise of the nascent network, the thing that would allow them to be creative. "That was the thing: we didn't have to hit it out of the park in terms of ratings," he said.

Reilly began calling in writers and showrunners to pitch material for the new network—so many that a shocked security guard at the Sepulveda building, unaccustomed to signing so many people in and out, vocally complained. Reilly and his boss were clear about what they were seeking.

"I don't think they've cornered the market on antiheroes at HBO. They're on in twenty-three million homes; we're going to be in seventy-five million. So how about we snuggle in as close as we can? We're not bound by the FCC either. Let's just do something that's going to blow them back on their heels."

O f all the strange inlets in the flow of TV history where talent has pooled for a time, none—not even *The White Shadow*—was as unlikely as *Nash Bridges*. The show, which ran from 1996 through 2001 on CBS, was an entirely conventional hour-long drama starring Don Johnson and Cheech Marin as irreverent detectives solving crimes while cruising around San Francisco in a big yellow convertible. If the show had its sights set anywhere, it was backward on a previous generation of Stephen J. Cannell productions that mixed comedy with formulaic cases of the week. "It really should have been in the eighties," said Shawn Ryan, who secured the show's place in history as an unlikely incubator of a basic cable revolution.

Ryan was a large-framed, balding guy with the air of a former jock gone slightly to seed. He subscribed to the David Simon school of showrunner antifashion, favoring high-top sneakers and T-shirts. It was easy to imagine him playing beer pong or slumped on a couch, holding a video game controller.

Raised in Rockford, Illinois, Ryan had studied playwriting at Middlebury College in Vermont, then made his way to Los Angeles. For three years, he learned his craft at *Nash Bridges* and then spent a year writing for *Angel,* Joss Whedon's spin-off of *Buffy the Vampire Slayer.* He also wrote two pilots with decidedly ungroundbreaking premises: one about a former wild girl returning to her hometown after her father died, to keep the family business going, and one a workplace comedy set in a veterinarian's office. Neither went anywhere, but they were enough to land Ryan a modest development deal at Fox Television Studios. He spent his first nine months unable to come up with any mutually agreeable comedy ideas. In semi-desperation, Ryan offered to try his hand at drama instead and began sketching out the beginnings of a police series.

"At its heart it was, 'What's a cop show I'd want to watch?'" he said. "I felt a lot of things on TV—even that I'd worked on—were bullshit. In my head, I saw something very different from what I had ever seen. But it's hard to pitch 'different,' so I just started writing the first five or six pages of the script."

A handful of characters quickly took shape around a police station in a crime-plagued East Los Angeles neighborhood: an older African American detective with a younger, ambitiously brainy partner; a Hispanic captain with political aspirations; a rookie cop hiding his homosexuality. Notably absent was anything resembling the rough-and-tumble, morally compromised antigang team that eventually defined what would become *The Shield.* The team entered the picture only after Ryan had gotten a tentative go-ahead to finish a pilot script.

At that time, Los Angeles was still reeling from the fallout of the Rampart scandal, which had revealed astonishing levels of corruption in the LAPD's antigang "CRASH" unit. Delving into the scandal, Ryan shifted the pilot's focus to what he redubbed the "Strike Team" and its intense, charismatic leader, Vic Mackey. He began to get excited by the possibilities.

"I was jazzed. Coming off of three years of *Nash Bridges*, where the guys were real heroes and never made mistakes and always did the right thing, I wanted to write something where people could be assholes," he said.

The pilot for the show, then titled *Rampart*, dropped viewers in medias res at the Barn, a converted church being used as a police station in the Farmington District, or "the Farm." All is not nearly well. Mackey's team, a squad of testosterone-fueled, hyperaggressive dudes, has clearly been operating rogue for some time, sticking their hands into the pockets of the gangs and drug dealers they'd been given carte blanche to control. Mackey finds an instant adversary in the new captain, David Aceveda, who insinuates his own man, a spy, into the Strike Team. In the episode's final moments, Mackey, who has engineered a chaotic drug raid for the purpose, shoots the interloper point-blank in the face. Meet your new hero.

Ryan had certainly succeeded in banishing any ghosts of *Nash Bridges*. He had also, he assumed, written his way out of any possibility of having his pilot produced. *Rampart* had been a fun exercise, but he was resigned to it ending up a writing sample, nothing more.

Indeed, that's how it ended up on Kevin Reilly's desk, in a stack of spec scripts he'd called in to find new writers. He and Liguori were still casting around for what the shape of their new "free HBO" would look like. One thing they were not interested in was a cop show; *everybody* did cop shows. But when Reilly read Ryan's script, he thought, 'Holy shit. I don't know if people are going to love this or hate it, but it's definitely not going to go quietly.'"

He called Ryan and said, "We're going to make it."

"What do you mean?" Ryan said.

"We'll make it."

Ryan began to form the opinion that a friend was playing a prank on him. "Who is this?" he asked. And then: "*That* script?"

"We're going to make *your* script."

Reilly did worry whether the pilot's ending was a step too far. *The Sopranos* "College" episode may have aired two years earlier, but this was asking the audience to accept something of a different magnitude: a protagonist murdering a fellow police officer in cold blood. More important, it was asking advertisers to place their products next to the protagonist doing so.

"You've got to realize, this is what we're going forward with, *forever*," a worried Reilly told Liguori. "This is a guy who killed his partner. This is going to live forever."

Liguori played the Bronx card. He pointed out that, as in "College," the victim was a snitch. "I said, 'Kevin, you're from Port Washington'"—on Long Island's affluent north shore—"'I'm from the Bronx. In the Bronx, rats lose. And I think there are more people out there with the mind-set of the Bronx than of Port Washington.'"

The pilot was shot fast and cheap, under the supervision of Scott Brazil, whom Reilly had brought in to assist and mentor the novice Ryan. Brazil was a veteran of network fare good and bad, going all the way back to *Hill Street Blues*. Clark Johnson was hired to direct and instituted a spontaneous run-and-gun style, shooting in Super 16 mm and relying heavily on handheld camera work and Steadicam. Spotting a pack of stray dogs near the location of one scene, he grabbed a piece of salami off the craft services table and tossed it into the frame. "Shoot the dog! Shoot the fucking dog!" he yelled as the strays came running. "Shoot the dog" became on-set shorthand for a style that came to define the show for the length of its run. In the third season, writer Charles "Chic" Eglee was shocked to show up on set and see its Emmy-nominated star, Michael Chiklis, shooting a scene in which he plunged into real-life East L.A. traffic, a Steadicam operator in dogged pursuit.

"It was very much a 'knock the bullshit off of it' attitude that we had to shooting. There was a sheen to a lot of shows that we didn't want," said Ryan. "I would always talk to the directors about that: 'Go for the most truthful moment.' There are lots of shows where if you don't get certain shots of coverage, they'll fire you. One of the first things I'd say is, 'I'm not going to get upset if there's some piece of coverage we don't have, as long as the moment feels real.'"

Chiklis had hardly been the obvious choice to play Mackey. He was well-known to TV audiences as the genial dad/cop of *The Commish*, a network show that went a long way toward making *Nash Bridges* look edgy. Nevertheless, he and his wife were friendly with Ryan and his wife, and he had read the pilot. "If this gets made," he told Ryan, "I want to play that role."

Ryan was dubious, as was Liguori. "All Kevin and I were thinking was, 'The fat guy from *The Commish* is *not* this guy," Liguori said. "But he kept calling. I said, 'Michael, you're a star. I'm not going to insult you by asking you to come in and audition.' Meaning, I guess, 'I don't want to have to tell you no.'" Chiklis's own agents were in agreement, for different reasons. "The agencies were not being supportive at all," said Ryan. "They certainly didn't view it as an opportunity. We had tons of actors who either wouldn't consider it for a moment or took the position, 'If you want to offer me the role, maybe I'll think about it.'"

Chiklis, though, could not be dissuaded. An audition was finally arranged in FX's green-wallpapered conference room. On his way in, Liguori passed a bald, buff guy in a skintight black T-shirt. "Where's Chiklis?" he asked the room. "You just passed him," was the answer. The actor came in, gnawing on a mouthful of Nicorette, and proceeded to blow the room away.

"He scared the crap out of all of us," was how Liguori remembered it. "He leaves and there's no oxygen left in the room. No one's saying anything. Finally, I break the ice and I go, 'I don't think he just won the role, I think he *is* the role.' The only question left was whether we were going to have the balls to put the future of this show in the hands of a guy known for comedy."

The rest of the cast came together in almost as guerrilla a style as the shooting. Johnson had worked with the actress CCH Pounder on his first movie and pushed for the black detective, Charles, to become "Claudette" instead. For her partner, Ryan tapped one of his best friends, Jay Karnes, whom he had met at a college playwriting retreat. With the main characters cast, there was almost no money left to secure actors long-term, in case the show actually went to series. So Ryan dipped even deeper into his personal Rolodex. He persuaded another friend, Dave Rees Snell, to work for extra's wages, $85 per day, with the promise that he'd get more lines in later episodes. Snell's character, Ronnie Gardocki, went on to be an enigmatic central figure for seasons to come. For Mackey's wife, meanwhile, Ryan turned to his own wife, Cathy. "I know I can get *you* back," he told her.

The most spectacular casting story, however, involved a forgettable role and an actor who didn't win it. The part was for a young dealer who taunts Mackey that he's too late to catch him with drugs. Mackey chases him, knocks him down, pulls down his pants to reveal a bag taped to his crotch, and delivers the line: "Too late, huh?" Clark Johnson described the audition tape:

> The kid comes in, stands at the mark. The casting associate says, 'Okay. State your name. Are you ready to go? Whenever you're ready.' And all of a sudden the kid takes off running! You can hear his footsteps receding down the hall. She's in there by herself, going, 'What the fuck?' She starts to go toward the door and you hear the kid run back in. The kid runs back to his mark. He punches himself in the stomach. He pulls his *own* pants down, and he's got no underwear. There's his dick hanging there. He yanks the drugs from his crotch. And then he says Chiklis's line: 'Too late, huh?'"

Johnson paused, grinning, for the kicker.

> "And then he stands there, smiling, and goes, 'Scene.'"

Once the pilot was shot, a screening for Chernin was arranged. For Reilly, it was a flashback to showing *The Sopranos* to Chris Albrecht. "The reaction was just silence. You thought, 'Okay. . . .'" After some consideration, Chernin gave the go-ahead. "I don't think it's going to work," he said. "But go for it."

The troops inside FX's offices were more fired up. Only weeks before, twenty-four-year-old Jeremy Elice had taken a temp job in the public relations department, thinking he'd work for a brief spell and then return to New York, where he was interviewing for a position in features producer Scott Rudin's office. One night, the head of the department, John Solberg, sent him home with a VHS copy of the pilot. "I just thought, 'They can't do this.' I didn't know much about the place, but one thing I did know was that they had advertisers," he said.

"Hell, yeah, we're putting this on fucking TV!" cackled Solberg, a large, excitable Texan, when Elice approached him the next day. "We're gonna shove it up HBO's ass!" But where was the good guy? Elice wanted to know. "He *is* the good guy!" Solberg hooted.

Elice called Rudin's office and withdrew his name from the job search. ("Can you spell that?" the features people asked when he told them where he was going. "F," Elice explained patiently, "X.") A few years later, he would be a key part of bringing *Breaking Bad* to the air.

It remained, crucially, for Reilly and Liguori to get advertisers on board. The men flew to New York to host a screening. Before it started, Liguori tried to prepare the audience. "I want to show you a show that I think is going to represent where FX is going, and I want to talk to you about it," he said. "But while you're watching this, think of one thing. If you could put an ad in *The Sopranos*, would you do it?"

"The room was stone silent when the lights came up," said Reilly. "People's faces were like peeled back. A couple of guys slinked out the back door, looking at their shoes."

"How many of you liked the show?" Liguori asked those who remained. Most hands went up. Liguori nodded and asked the more important question. How many would buy advertising for their clients during the program? Every hand went down.

"I said, 'Guys, I could bring you this kind of programming,'" Liguori recalled. "'You think it's good. I think it's great. But I can't put this on unless I have you. I would expect 95 percent of your clients would never come within a hundred miles of this, but there's 5 percent that will. Think about that 5 percent. Video game companies. Beer companies. Fashion companies. Guy-type things. Just please support the show.' And that's what they did."

One more major hurdle remained. *The Shield* was officially green-lighted on August 30, 2001. Had the powers that be waited another twelve days, it's likely the show would never have gone forward. Even then, in the aftermath of September 11, there was enormous doubt about whether they could proceed. All the conviction that the network had about people's willingness to accept the show was thrown into question anew. This was a time, the common wisdom went, when the public would be craving hero-heroes, not antiheroes—and certainly not a *cop* antihero.

What became clear, once *The Shield* debuted exactly six months and a day after the terrorist attacks, was that it now resonated in ways that its creators could never have anticipated. The moral heart of the show was the question of to what degree Mackey's behavior was justified by the results he got. The Farm, his character would argue, was in a state of war, demanding extraordinary measures. As Claudette put it in the pilot, after the captain has compared Mackey to Al Capone:

> Al Capone made money by giving people what they wanted. What people want these days is to make it to their cars without getting mugged. Come home from work and see their stereo is still there. Hear about some murder in the barrio, find out the next day the police caught the guy. If having all those things means some cop roughed up some nigger or some spic in the ghetto . . . well, as far as most people are concerned, it's don't ask, don't tell.

In Ryan's original conception, the question of exactly what behavior one might be willing to tolerate in the name of security was focused on Aceveda, whom he envisioned struggling with how much he should or should not lean on Mackey to get what he wanted. Making Mackey himself the main character posed a more direct and discomfiting challenge to an audience that would soon be grappling with myriad real-life versions of the same quandary, from Guantánamo Bay to Abu Ghraib to domestic surveillance.

Still, as the debut approached, Liguori had little idea what to expect of the show on which he may well have bet his network presidency. The night before, he called a company-wide meeting and spoke passionately about how proud they should be about the risky work they had done together, regardless of what the ratings turned out to be. Privately, he was praying to at least double the network's baseline prime-time rating of .8. A 1, he figured, would represent a raging success.

"The ratings come in at four forty-five a.m. on the West Coast. My home phone was ringing. At that point I still had a pager and it was going off. My cell phone was ringing. I knew it was the rating, one way or the other, but I didn't want to give the impression that it was all about the rating for me. I needed to walk the walk," he said. Finally, he arrived at the office, deliberately late. Every person at the network was waiting. He checked the number: it was 4.1, the highest-rated basic cable debut of all time.

"Soon people started writing, 'This is HBO, but free,' and we were like, 'Holy shit. They're putting it in the reviews now!'" said Reilly.

That fall, *The Shield* was nominated for three Emmys—Chiklis for Outstanding Lead Actor in a Drama Series and Ryan and Johnson for writing and directing the pilot. Liguori and Reilly were so convinced that there was no chance of winning that they didn't buy tickets for the traditional postceremony Governor's Ball. "They were like $2,000 apiece," said Reilly. "We went to the show, but, fuck it, we'll go out after and get drunk. We're not paying $4,000 to eat bad breadsticks at the Governor's Ball."

When Chiklis unexpectedly won—beating out the two leads of *Six Feet Under*, Martin Sheen of *The West Wing*, and Kiefer Sutherland as another compromised, post-9/11 cop in *24*—the FX team was stuck on the outside, trying to crash. "It was me and Chiklis, trying to scam our way in," Reilly said. "He got busted. They stopped him at the door. He's just too guilty looking."

The Shield debuted three months before *The Wire*. (This was also the era of *The Job*, *The Unit*, *The District*, *The Practice*, and others; "People love articles," Liguori said.) The proximity, name similarity, and broad overlap of subject matter guaranteed a certain amount of comparison between the two shows, at least among a passionate fan base with a new medium—the Internet—on which to express their loyalties. "It was the same old argument: 'I love the Beatles, so the Rolling Stones have to suck,'" Ryan said. Fans of *The Shield* complained about how boring and slow-moving HBO's show was, while *The Wire* partisans attacked *The Shield* for being unrealistic.

Both assessments suited each show's creators just fine. Ed Burns was sent

a screener of *The Shield* pilot: "In the first half hour, the guy yelled at his supe-
rior officer in the squad room, which you never do. Even *I* wouldn't do that.
Then he has this hooker who's an informant and he gives her dope and then
money so she can buy something for her baby. And then he killed a cop. So I
said, 'We don't have to worry. This show is going nowhere.'"

As for the other side: "My issue with *The Wire* as a viewer was that it took
too long," said Ryan. "They could afford that, being on HBO. But I didn't believe in having an episode that set up something cool three episodes later. I
wanted *that* episode to be cool. I felt an obligation for every single episode to
have one or two 'Holy shit' moments in it."

He had a similar assessment of *The Sopranos*. "They were always promising a different show than they delivered. Their promos were always action-
packed: Somebody's betraying somebody else. Somebody's going to get
whacked. And then the next week it would be a very well-produced, well-
written family drama."

Ryan believed in a brand of proud TV populism that would have had David
Chase choking on his braciola. "Our show was a show that was trying to
sell Budweiser and detergent," he said flatly. Even more scandalous, he was a
defender of that supposed scourge of nonpay TV television, the very thing
that supposedly would prevent basic cable from ever approaching the rarefied quality of HBO: commercial breaks or, more precisely, the "act-out" preceding them.

"I believe in act-outs. I *like* them," he said. "They give a little jolt to your
heart, if done properly. They give you three or four minutes to think about
what you've seen and what you think is going to happen next." In the editing
room, he would obsess over those moments: five of them, in an episode that
had a pre-credits teaser and four acts. Because he was prone to moving scenes
around in postproduction, directors were instructed to treat every scene as
though it could be the end of an act: he was looking for what he called "buttons." "It could be a look, a line delivered strongly, a reveal—anything, but it
has to be a point of view: 'This is something. It's important. *Bam*. You're out.'"

Complaining about the necessities of the form, he said, was an old-
fashioned brand of snobbery. "There are people who don't want to believe

they're making television. It's easier for them to believe they're film auteurs than to embrace that this is a different genre and that there're ways to take advantage of that genre," he said. "I wasn't going to Scorsese film festivals in Greenwich Village as a kid. I was watching *Brady Bunch* repeats. I didn't walk into this business with an attitude toward television."

Indeed, *The Shield* was giddy with TV love in the same way Quentin Tarantino movies are geeked on films. Its realism was the heightened realism of boys acting out a cop show in the backyard: sneaking up, crouched, on a suspect and gesturing a partner on with a drawn gun; getting shot and dying in elaborate slo mo; dramatically taking sunglasses on and off to make a point.

The show's testosterone-fueled spirit was reflected in a rambunctious writers' room. "We had a bunch of writers who had very little experience and who were just trying to one-up each other by getting crazier and crazier and further out there," said Glen Mazzara, a writer Ryan brought over from his days at *Nash Bridges*. "It was like, 'Let's put on a show.'"

The staff included a few veterans—among them, James Manos from *The Sopranos'* "College"—but was dominated by younger talent. Two of the more influential writers—and future showrunners—had never written for TV before: Kurt Sutter and Scott Rosenbaum. Story-breaking sessions often ran deep into the night; writers would sleep in their offices, then begin again the next morning.

It was a fun room but often the scene of vicious battles over the show's direction. "The writers were all brutally honest people. All very talented, but hard hitting. Nobody could pitch an idea unless they were ready to have it completely eviscerated and ripped to shreds—so much so that people were emotionally destroyed by some of the criticism," Mazzara said.

Sutter, a long-haired, tattooed ex-actor and former addict, was the source of frequent battles with fellow writers. Several believed his more gonzo impulses held too much sway with Ryan, who presided over the battles as the final arbiter. "Anything that seemed rash, grim, grueling, over the top, like a guy getting his head pushed down on a skillet—that would be Kurt," one writer said. It was emblematic that one of his biggest battles with Mazzara was over whether a character should wield a gun or a hand grenade in a crucial scene. As it would be several years later on his own, aggressively violent FX show, *Sons of Anarchy*, several years later, Sutter's philosophy could be summed up as never using a mere gun when an awesome grenade could do.

For all its cartoonish aspects, there was no mistaking *The Shield* for *The A-Team*. From the beginning, the show plumbed the same modern obsessions that occupied HBO's more refined shows: power and violence, work and family, addiction and sexuality. Mackey was given unexpected depth by his attachment to his wife and autistic son, even as he inexorably drove them away.

But Mackey also remained a vivid expression of a man struggling with his inner beast—and, for the audience, of the beast himself, simultaneously seductive and repellent. It could be a dangerous game. Even the character's creators found themselves underestimating the boundaries of fans' love for their monster.

"If I said to you: I'm going to have a story about a corrupt cop who murdered another cop and stole a bunch of money. And that there's a pretty virtuous Internal Affairs detective who starts digging into the case and becomes hell-bent on bringing this man to justice. Who would be the hero of that piece?" Ryan said, referring to the character played by Forest Whitaker who enters in season five and sets the final downfall of Mackey in motion.

"But our audience viewed Vic as the hero. They wanted Vic to get away with it. They found every negative thing to say about Whitaker's character they could think of. When we wrote it, I was convinced: 'Boy, we're really going to make it tough for the audience. They're not going to be sure who to root for.' I was an idiot. They knew who to root for."

H aving inadvertently gained extra resonance after 9/11, *The Shield* continued to reflect current events—and never more so than in its fourth season. In that, the show's most self-contained and best season, the Barn receives an imperious new captain, Monica Rawling, who is intent on occupying the Farm and crushing the local drug regime regardless of the morally charged costs and, in some ways, oblivious to the reality on the ground. "We were very aware that we were writing about Bush's invasion of Iraq," Mazzara said.

Season four was notable in another way that would affect the course of FX's fortunes and the cable revolution. In looking for someone to play Rawling, the show needed "an actor that could match up to Mackey, not as a physical force, but as a force of nature," said John Landgraf, who took over as president and general manager in 2005. Throwing out dream names in the writers' room—Annette Bening was one of them—Ryan and his team hit upon Glenn Close. TV had made a few gigantic stars, but it was still all but unheard of for a major film actor to become a series regular. Ryan, Landgraf, and Liguori flew to New York to pitch Close at her apartment. They left with a promise that she would at least watch some of the previous three seasons on DVD. Excited by the depth of the character, and coming from a movie world in which opportunities for great female characters were ever harder to come by, Close dived in.

There was some discussion about continuing the Rawling character for another season, but Close insisted on returning to New York, where her daughter was still in high school. The experience had apparently been fulfilling enough, however, that Close agreed to take on an even bigger television role, as Patty Hewes in *Damages*, the series created by *Sopranos* alum Todd Kessler. In her hands, Hewes became the one central female character of the Third Golden Age to match her male counterparts in complexity, power, and capacity for monstrous behavior.

As for movie actors being willing to work in television, Close proved to be at the vanguard of a nearly complete reversal. Actors it would have once been unthinkable to see on the small screen were, soon enough, clamoring for the kinds of multifaceted, complicated roles TV offered. For actresses in particular, the relative bounty of roles for women over the age of thirty was a powerful allure compared with the limited options of film.

*D*amages capped off a golden initial run for FX that was comparable, at least in defining the network's identity, to HBO's first flurry of original shows. *The Shield* had been followed by *Nip/Tuck*, Ryan Murphy's salacious, darkly comic series about plastic surgeons. Then came *Rescue Me*, a collaboration of Denis Leary and Peter Tolan, a veteran of *The Larry Sanders Show*. The two had first worked together on a half-hour ABC series called *The Job*, featuring Leary as a New York police detective. Despite being what Leary called "quite possibly the darkest situation comedy ever seen on network television," the show won critical acclaim and renewal for a second season but was put on an extended hiatus after September 11, on the assumption that American audiences would not tolerate anything that even mildly sullied the reputation of police officers. It was revived the following January, only to be summarily canceled, and Leary and Tolan resolved that they were done with the conventional networks.

"There are people who panic and run and hide and cry in response to almost any crisis," Leary wrote. "Ninety-five percent of them work in network television."

Still, *The Job*'s demise turned out to be a blessing in disguise. *Rescue Me*— inspired in part by the death of Leary's cousin, a Worcester, Massachusetts, firefighter, in a devastating warehouse fire—took the base materials of the truncated sitcom and alchemized them into something deeper, more resonant, and, not coincidentally, funnier. It grafted a workplace comedy onto the family saga of an alcoholic fireman living, literally, with the ghosts of September 11. It was the first show to deal head-on with the terrorist attacks and the closest thing FX ever did to HBO's best work.

A ll of these shows, and the wave of original programming that soon followed across basic cable, had *The Shield* to thank for the opportunity. On a content level, it had further institutionalized—to something approaching the point of cliché—the Troubled Man as the Third Golden Age's primary character. In order to pitch FX, hopeful TV writers reported being flat-out instructed that their shows had better revolve around flawed but ultimately sympathetic men. Inexorably, the network would find itself going from edgy to something like Edgy™.

But what FX had amply shown was that the signatures of HBO shows— shorter seasons, higher production values, better writing, more complicated storytelling—weren't virtues found only in a subscriber-based TV model. In that, the value of *The Shield* would be incalculable.

"I wish I *could* calculate it," Ryan said with a wry smile.

He was not the only one. That question—exactly what quality was *worth*, especially outside of HBO's rarefied atmosphere—would persist and fuel TV's biggest negotiations over the next few years. Meanwhile, HBO would never again be alone at—or even necessarily at the top of—the quality heap.

The threats to that reign did not all come from barbarians storming the gates. HBO faced equal problems on the inside. On the one hand, they were the kinds of growing pains that were inevitable in any organization that had undergone a major transition in stature, visibility, and productivity in less than half a decade. On the other, they were deeply human, involving vanity, fear, competitiveness, the existential perils of getting what you want, and the twin remoras that attach themselves to any success: arrogance at how you got there and fear that it will all go away. The stuff, in other words, of a fine series on HBO.

In 2002, Jeff Bewkes had moved up to become the chairman of Time Warner's entertainment and networks group. Chris Albrecht became HBO's CEO while also maintaining control over programming. He had reason to feel confident: his two dramatic series *The Sopranos* and *Six Feet Under* were riding high, *The Wire* had just debuted, and *Deadwood* was in the early stages of development. Other divisions were doing just as well, with *Sex and the City* and *Curb Your Enthusiasm* doing an equal job of defining the network's comedy side, and high-prestige miniseries like *Band of Brothers* and *Angels in America*, starring Al Pacino and Meryl Streep, foreshadowing the future migration of movie talent to TV.

In 2003, *Variety* named Albrecht "Showman of the Year." An accompanying article stressed HBO's climate of hospitality to artists. "We are the network and we don't always agree with the final product of the things that we put on the air," he told the magazine, an astonishing assertion. "But everybody can walk away feeling a little bit better because we haven't screwed up somebody's good idea." In a *New York Times* profile, he compared the network to the Medicis, Renaissance Florence's patrons of the arts. It was a high-minded allusion, to be sure, but also, in its way, a call back to the philosophy of MTM's Grant Tinker, who had taken pains to insist he was no artist himself, just a facilitator.

That same year, though, marked HBO's first significant failure with a one-hour drama since *The Sopranos* had debuted. *Carnivàle* was a visually sumptuous, magical-realist drama set in the Depression-era Dust Bowl. Its creator, Daniel Knauf, who had only two episodes of a network show and a 1994 HBO movie under his belt as a credited writer, supposedly had a six-season plan, but those around the show worried that it had no discernible direction or leadership, and viewers felt the same.

"We fell in love with the genre more than what the writer had to say, which is a more cynical way of programming," said Michael Lombardo. "You're guessing what people are going to respond to, when what people respond to, for us, is great writing executed really well. If we think we can guess the genre, we're in the same game as the networks."

There were other duds to come: *Lucky Louie*, which debuted several years later, was a half-hour comedy from Louis C.K. The comedian's sensibility would later prove to be the perfect foundation for a boundary-pushing, if overly self-satisfied, show, *Louie*, on FX, but in this first go-round, the point seemed to be less his take on domestic life than the form of the show itself: an old-fashioned multicamera sitcom filmed mostly on an ostentatiously fake, one-room set in front of a studio audience. In theory, perhaps, this was the perfect counterintuitive move for the network that had shot *The Larry Sanders Show* with a single camera, back when that was almost unheard of for a half-hour sitcom. In practice, though, it felt cheap and odd and—crucially, for a business built on brand—simply wrong. Some internally urged Albrecht to run the show late at night, framed as an experimental piece rather than announcing it with the usual HBO fanfare, but he refused. He was heard to say that with *Lucky Louie* he was creating his own *The Honeymooners*, about as sacred a reference as it's possible to make in the world of TV, especially by a onetime comedy agent.

Yet another series, *Tell Me You Love Me*, about three couples with various intimacy issues, defied even the prurient interest spurred by (false) rumors that its sex scenes involved actual sex to debut to a dismal 910,000 viewers in September 2007.

Of course, not every series that HBO aired could be a hit. Albrecht believed that the backlash was inevitable after such a string of successes. "The story that HBO was brilliant and the best thing that ever happened, that story had gotten old. So at some point the story has to become, 'Well, what's wrong with these guys?' I mean, with *Lucky Louie*, I still think it was ahead of its time. But you would have thought we had done something sacrilegious. We were taking a chance that nobody would have paid attention to before, and now they were reacting like you insulted their mother!"

Nevertheless, there was a sense inside and outside the company that with success, the powers that be had begun to fatally change their approach.

"Something changed," said Henry Bromell, who briefly executive-produced *Carnivàle*. "It was like they convinced themselves that 'it wasn't David Chase, it was us! It wasn't Darren Star who did *Sex and the City*, it was us!'"

"We were lucky: we had these zeitgeist shows that just walked in the door," said Richard Plepler, then the executive vice president of communications. "The truth has always been that we are only as good as the people we work with."

The bigger problem for HBO may not have been what was in development, but what was not. The network's signature hits had been the product of what Albrecht liked to call "the HBO shrug"—that devil-may-care attitude that comes with low stakes and lower expectations.

"I think that, from a creative standpoint, to have hit a home run so quickly with *The Sopranos* became a little bit of a creative albatross," said Lombardo. "Our ethos had always been to be fearless, take risks, but once you had an enormous success, it became almost impossible for people not to on some level start gauging everything against it. We had evolved into a culture of saying the smart 'no,' which is a lot easier and less ass exposing than 'yes.'"

To some who had reason to expect they'd be welcomed warmly into the

HBO family, the "no" was surprising. Terence Winter and Tim Van Patten, both high-ranking members of the *Sopranos* family, each had a development deal at the network. One day, on set, they got to talking about outlaw motorcycle gangs. "Hey, this is a TV series!" Winter said. When he called Strauss, however, he was shocked by the executive's lack of encouragement. "We're getting paid whether we work or don't work," he said. "To me, the only logical answer is, 'Great! Why don't you go write a script and bring it back to us.' It doesn't cost them a dime and, God willing, we have a show." Instead, the idea died on the vine. (Kurt Sutter apparently had the same experience pitching *his* outlaw biker show, *Sons of Anarchy*. "Yes, we left your pitch meeting scratching our heads, wondering if the executive who was yawning, staring at her watch, putting her feet up on the table, and sighing exasperatedly was somehow testing our resolve," he wrote in an open letter to HBO on his blog. *Sons* would find a successful home at FX; Winter and Van Patten would go on to executive-produce HBO's *Boardwalk Empire*; and HBO would finally try its own biker show—a failed pilot from screenwriter Michael Tolkin, titled *1%*.)

At the precise time that there were more and more varied options for TV writers with serious visions, the impression began to spread around Hollywood that HBO's door was closed more than it was open—and then only to well-established writers.

"David Chase, remember, had worked on all network shows," said Lombardo. "We had gotten to the point where we might not have taken a pitch from him. He might not have been on our level."

N one of this would have been apparent to the viewing public. The cancellation of *Deadwood* in May 2006 certainly was. As Albrecht told it, that surprising turn of events started as a normal internal discussion about renewal that quickly snowballed out of control.

"By the third season of *Deadwood,* the show had found its core audience," he said. "It was a show that had accomplished what we felt it could accomplish. It wasn't growing as a franchise. And David had talked to us about some other ideas that we were excited to move on to. It was about, 'How do we maximize our David Milch relationship.'"

It could not have hurt that several very real business considerations were working against *Deadwood*. Like any period piece, the show was expensive to produce. The situation was compounded by the fact that, unlike most of its shows, HBO did not own the series outright; Paramount, with whom Milch had an overall deal, owned the foreign rights, thus cutting off a future revenue stream. In that light, the same problems that plagued a show like *The Wire*—a passionate but small, and declining, audience, critical acclaim, but little Emmy consideration—loomed far more seriously.

In the New York offices on a Friday, Albrecht called Milch in Los Angeles and told him that he wanted the showrunner to begin thinking about wrapping up the show in one more season. Might he be able to do so in six or eight episodes, instead of the usual twelve? Albrecht said he got the distinct impression that Milch was unenthusiastic about continuing at all, or at least in a shortened season, but that the conversation was the first of what he imagined would be many more.

Upon hanging up, however, Milch felt duty-bound to call Timothy Olyphant, who was in the process of buying a house, to let him know that the show might be coming to an end. Olyphant, in turn, called his agent. "The next thing we know, it's Saturday and we're getting calls from all the trades, saying, 'We hear you canceled *Deadwood*,'" Albrecht said. "By Monday, it was a story. We couldn't get David on the phone. And it just went from the air going slowly out of the balloon to the balloon totally collapsing." There was a flurry of talks, reviving the idea of a shorter season, but Milch demurred. "I didn't want to limp home," he told a reporter. "My old man used to say, 'Never go anyplace where you're only tolerated.'"

Looking back, Milch (who had left *NYPD Blue* before its conclusion and would later have *John from Cincinnati* and *Luck* end prematurely) was philosophical:

"You try to live your creative life as you would live your actual life, which is, if it turned out to be your last day, you wouldn't be ashamed of the way you finished up," he said. "I think that, in some sense, the idea of an 'ending' is constantly redefining itself. Something is ending in one sense, but it's the beginning of something further. So it's not a question that I allow myself to linger over." With a wry smile he added, "There are some series that end halfway through and just don't know it."

As he told another interviewer, "It's a child who believes that such things go on forever. It's a child also who believes you can't start over. But you can, and you have to."

Inside HBO, though, the decision reverberated as a serious blow to morale, if not an out-and-out identity crisis. Being "Not TV" had become a point of pride in the offices on both coasts—was it still true? Several executives feared privately that to kill *Deadwood* was to irreparably damage HBO's brand.

As important was a different bond of trust, one between the network and its audience. This, as much as technologies like DVDs and DVRs, had made the resurgence of serialized television possible, the tacit agreement that if we, the viewers, invested time and emotion in a show, they, the makers, would compensate us with the confidence that we were *in good hands*: not that we would necessarily be happy with the way things turned out—the average series death toll was evidence enough that *that* wasn't going to happen—but that there was a plan in place, attention would be rewarded, perhaps above all that the show would not simply disappear before fulfilling its creative arc, like some normal network TV show. Whatever one might have thought of *Deadwood*, its cancellation helped break the spell HBO had held over its audience. The network would never again be seen as something utterly different from those springing up in competition.

By this time, Albrecht's portfolio was growing larger. He moved back and forth between Los Angeles and New York; some said he was stretching himself thin. Albrecht pointed out, correctly, that the network's development and production pipeline was in full swing in early 2007, as *The Sopranos* finale approached: *The Pacific*, *John Adams*, and *Generation Kill*, all miniseries, were in various stages of development; the fifth season of *The Wire* was about to begin broadcasting, along with a new season of *Big Love*. On the comedy side, *Entourage* was a hit, with its brand of insider, name-dropping consumption porn, while the experimental five-night-a-week, half-hour drama *In Treatment* was in production. Most important for the future of the network, three series on which it would bank for years to come—*True Blood*, *Boardwalk Empire*, and *Game of Thrones*—were all in development, though only *True Blood* was in active production.

For all that, when it came to hour-long dramatic series, the programming most likely to benefit from the boost of following the *Sopranos* finale—easily the biggest cultural event in HBO's history—there were strikingly few options. Which is the best and most plausible explanation for how *John from Cincinnati* came to be broadcast on an American television network.

The series was one that Milch had pitched verbally to Strauss and Albrecht while *Deadwood* was still on the air. In terms of coherence and narrative niceties, it made his earlier show look like *Murder, She Wrote*. It took place in a gritty San Diego surf community, into which a mysterious supernatural visitor makes a disruptive appearance. Even those working on it seemed to know little more than that. "We would sit, the producers, and joke among ourselves: 'What is this about? Nobody had a clue,'" said Mark Tinker, who was an executive producer and directed two episodes.

The most generous assessment was that in *John from Cincinnati*, Milch was groping toward a kind of new narrative language. "My understanding of the way the mechanism of storytelling works is [that] any story is constantly appending specific values to the meanings of words, and of the actions of characters. And the fact that story uses as its building blocks words or characters that the audience believes it has some prior recognition or understanding of, is really simply the beginning of the story, but not its end," he told one blogger. The least generous assessment was it was an inchoate mess.

I will go to my grave saying the first four episodes of that show were as interesting and valid as any show I've worked on," Albrecht said, blaming at least some of the harsh criticism on residual anger over *Deadwood*. In any event, by the time *John* aired, Albrecht was no longer at HBO. A month before, early on the morning of May 6, he had been arrested outside the MGM Grand casino in Las Vegas, where Floyd Mayweather had just defeated Oscar De La Hoya in a light middleweight fight broadcast by HBO pay-per-view. Police reports described him dragging his then girlfriend, Karla Jensen, toward the hotel with both hands around her neck. He slurred his speech and smelled of alcohol. After being pulled off Jensen, who was left with red marks around her throat, Albrecht was booked for suspicion of domestic assault and spent that night in the Clark County Detention Center. He would eventually plead no contest to misdemeanor battery, pay a $1,000 fine, and attend domestic-violence counseling.

The career ramifications far outweighed the legal ones. Time Warner Chairman and CEO Richard Parsons immediately announced that Albrecht would take a leave of absence. Albrecht released a statement saying he had lapsed in his treatment for alcohol abuse and would return to Alcoholics Anonymous. Several years later, in an interview with *GQ* that portrayed him drinking while on a business trip in Dublin, he would disown that statement, saying instead that the story about his alcoholism had been cooked up by HBO's PR team and that he had reluctantly gone along with it in an effort to save his career. "After years of reflection and working with specialists, I have recognized that alcohol is not an issue in my life," he told reporter Amy Wallace. "What I really needed to get at the heart of was my complicated and often very difficult love relationships with women."

Whatever the truth, Albrecht's story and HBO's damage control strategy lasted only a few days. On May 9, the *Los Angeles Times* ran a story revealing that in 1991, HBO had paid a settlement of at least $400,000 to a network executive with whom Albrecht had been having an acknowledged affair and who had accused him of physical abuse. (Albrecht denied any such abuse.) Blogger Nikki Finke followed with suggestions of a history of hidden, contentious relationships with female co-workers and subordinates. On May 10, Parsons announced that Albrecht, who at fifty-four had spent nearly his entire life working for HBO, would no longer be employed by the company.

It may have been a measure of both the power Albrecht had consolidated successfully and the conviction that, after all, it had been too much for one man to handle that Bewkes created a whole new power structure for HBO. Chief Operating Officer Bill Nelson took over as CEO, while creative leadership was divided between Plepler in New York and Lombardo in Los Angeles. If it seemed ominous to some that neither man had come up through the ranks as a programmer or developer, it was also seen as reaffirmation of the principle that executives were there to facilitate creativity, not indulge dreams of creating themselves.

Carolyn Strauss, meanwhile, remained as president of entertainment, but it was a short tenure. She and Albrecht had been well suited as partners, in part because Albrecht was more than happy to handle the charismatic, schmoozing duties to which Strauss was almost pathologically averse. Over the course of twenty years, those roles had grown more calcified and extreme.

"Over time, she leaned into what she was, which was the really smart but not very sociable executive. And he became a little bit too much of the gladhander who said he'd read the script but hadn't really," said a former colleague at the network. "So when he was not there anymore, the balance fell apart. It was one thing when Chris was there, because Chris gave a great meeting. He made talent feel comfortable and welcome and smart, never left anybody feeling like they had wasted his time. And he hadn't trained or encouraged Carolyn to do those things because it had worked. That duality worked." Once Albrecht was gone, though, the colleague went on, "All an insecure writer could see was that she's texting while he's trying to pitch."

A writer who pitched Strauss during that period confirmed that impression: "She wouldn't look you in the eye, couldn't give you a fucking coherent response. She was just weird. You didn't walk out saying, 'Boy, I want to work with this person.' Not at all."

"She really is incredibly shy," said Sue Naegle, who was both a friend of Strauss's and her replacement when Strauss was forced out in 2008. "She doesn't go out to lunch with everybody. She was incredibly uncomfortable in those situations." After some time on the job, Naegle had reason to be sympathetic. "You're going to say no to 99.9 percent of the people who knock on your door, and that's it," she said. "That's the job. So she'd been here a long time, saying no a long time. And people were so tired of sitting through the Emmys watching HBO win everything, so tired of hearing how great *The Sopranos* and *The Wire* were. When they had a chance to watch the prom queen lose her crown, they couldn't wait."

The fact remained that, whatever the reason, the perception that HBO had become a hostile place to bring new material was real—and it had very real consequences.

"The word had gone out: 'These guys are a fucking pain in the ass,'" said an industry executive close to HBO programming. "And the greatest case study for all this arrogance was *Mad Men*."

Twelve

See You at the Emmys

Matthew Weiner would not have disagreed with that executive's diagnosis, nor would he have missed an opportunity to remind anybody who happened to be listening. Even before *Mad Men* had
reached the critical mass that made it the biggest quality-television phenomenon since *The Sopranos*, Weiner would happily relate the story of how HBO
blew off the pilot script he'd sent them—the one that he'd nursed for seven
years, that had landed him a writing gig on *The Sopranos*. The network, he
said, had never even bothered to call him with a no.

Weiner, like David Simon, was born in Baltimore, the second-youngest
child of a high-achieving, argumentative, left-wing Jewish family. His
father, Leslie Weiner, was one of the most eminent neurologists in the country, responsible for breakthroughs in the treatment of multiple sclerosis and
Ronald Reagan's personal neurologist. Weiner's mother had given up a career
in law to raise her family. When Matt was nine, the family relocated to a gaudy
manse in Hancock Park in Los Angeles, so that Les could join the Department
of Neurology at the University of Southern California. He would eventually

become chairman of the department. Theirs was an intensely close but intensely competitive family, with enormous pressure put on the children to achieve. Both parents could be demanding and severe. Television was mostly off-limits; homework was taken as seriously as an army drill. Later, Weiner's blend of supreme confidence and blatant insecurity would reflect the mixed messages of such an upbringing: You're better than everybody else, and you're never good enough.

"If everything David Chase ever did was about his mother," said one person who had worked closely with both men, "everything Matt's ever done is about his father." By other accounts, not least a barbed *New York Times* piece on holiday giving penned by Weiner himself, he harbored as many complicated feelings about his mother as Chase ever had. In any event, the Weiner family dynamic remained both close and fraught enough that, as late as 2009, at age forty-four, Weiner asked a reporter not to mention his having a cigarette before their interview, because his parents didn't know that he smoked.

Weiner's siblings more or less fell in line with their parents' expectations. The oldest and youngest became doctors and Matt's nearest sister a lawyer, though she would eventually end up in entertainment journalism. Matt was less clearly directed. He was the salutatorian of the tony Harvard School for Boys but then decamped for Wesleyan University to study liberal arts. He aspired to be an actor, but, cognizant that acting would not be an acceptable academic major in the Weiner family, he chose a multidisciplinary humanities program, which gave evaluations instead of grades. ("I can read," said Les upon seeing one of these. "And I can see you got a C.") When college friends decided to experiment with mushrooms, he was pointedly uninvited, perhaps having been deemed the person most likely to set off a bad trip. As for the family business, Weiner did take a class called "The Human Brain." He failed. At times he must have felt like the *Mad Men* character nicknamed HoHo, the son of a shipping magnate, determined to turn jai alai into the next sports sensation to both tweak and impress his father.

Weiner said he gave up acting when it became clear he wouldn't be a leading man. "I didn't realize there was anything else to be," he said. Upon his return to Los Angeles, he resolved to go to film school at USC. The primary achievement of his two years there was a well-received twenty-minute documentary about paparazzi. It was also the era, he later noted, during which the school added the word *television* to its name.

After graduate school, Weiner married Linda Brettler, an architect. The connection between her profession and his, he later suggested, is hardly as tenuous as it might at first seem. Both are rooted in a fine, "pure" art—drawing, writing—but then move out into the real, physical world, drawing dozens, if not hundreds, into their construction. If that means compromise with the realities of the outside world, it also offers a different level of satisfaction. As Weiner would say, once his work started to be produced, "We're drawing plans, we're doing the plan check, we're going through the city, we're finding materials—and then they *build the building.* I walk on set and I see the person that I've cast, the costumes I went to the meeting for, somebody's done something amazing with the set, all these people's creative input comes into it. It's ridiculous." (The veteran Hollywood producer Mitch Glazer, who created and ran the series *Magic City* for Starz, had a slightly different spin: "It's like being an architect, except if Frank Lloyd Wright went to the bank to get money for Fallingwater and they said, 'Sure. Does it have to be over a waterfall?'")

Weiner and Brettler began a family that would eventually grow to four sons. Professionally, though, he spent several long years in the wilderness, without work or prospects, supported by his wife. Eventually, he self-produced a metafeature, *What Do You Do All Day?*, in which he played an aimless aspiring filmmaker and compulsive gambler, being supported by an architect wife, played by Brettler in her one film role. The movie went all but unnoticed, save for a blistering review from the critic Emanuel Levy. But Weiner saw within it the first intimation that he could take control of his own career, the faint stirring of a future auteur.

First, though, work had finally begun to come. Through a friend, he landed a job writing jokes on a show called *Party Girl*, then moved to *The Naked Truth* and, finally, *Becker*, starring Ted Danson as a doctor cranky enough to be the palest premonition of future antiheroes to come. (The third act of Danson's career—on *Damages* and then HBO's *Bored to Death*—would be one of the nicest side effects of the Third Golden Age.)

Becker was a plum job, but Weiner was unsatisfied. (His feelings about the show were perhaps best expressed in an episode of *The Sopranos* several years later, when he placed *Becker* creator Dave Hackel's name on a gravestone about to be desecrated by teenage goths.) At night, Weiner began working on another kind of story. He had always been taken with the decades of his parents', and his grandparents', youth—those years' shiny, attractive surfaces and the darker realities beneath. (In high school, asked to dress as any historical figure, he had chosen Joseph McCarthy, donning one of his grandfather's suits.) In another act of self-confidence, a bet on himself, he hired an assistant, Robin Veith, to take dictation as he began to tell the story of a slick, mysterious, but troubled traveler through the upheavals of the 1960s.

There was more to the idea than mere nostalgia. As he told Terry Gross on National Public Radio's *Fresh Air*, he remembered the thought that led him to first hearing Don Draper's voice: "I was 35 years old; I had a job on a network sitcom; it was rated number nine . . . there's 300 people in the country that have this job, and I was one. I had three children, and . . . this incredible life— you know, I was like, 'What is wrong with me? Why am I unhappy? Why is there so much going on in my head that I can't express to other people because it's all awful? And what is enough? And I'm going to die one day.' And I'm looking at it and saying, 'This is it?'"

As it happened, a show about exactly those feelings was about to transform television. Weiner watched the first four seasons of *The Sopranos* as a rapt fan. He was thrilled by the new, sophisticated rules that David Chase had imposed on TV. "*The Sopranos* was saying, 'Guess what? You don't know who the show's going to be about this week. You don't know who's going to die or disappear, even if you love them. We're not giving you a formula.'"

By this time, he had been carrying his script for the pilot of *Mad Men* around with him—literally; it never left his briefcase—for four long years. Though not yet forty, he categorized himself as a hopelessly late bloomer. David Chase's story of a long struggle in the trenches was an inspiration. (It was telling, if puzzling, that he often invoked the Beatles, who were world-famous before age twenty and finished before thirty, as kin in this late success.)

Weiner lobbied his agents to send his script to Chase, who was staffing up for the beginning of season five of *The Sopranos*. Since Todd Kessler's dismissal, the show had made do for a season and a half with the tiny staff of Terence Winter, Robin Green, and Mitchell Burgess and the contributions of freelancers. The agents were reluctant but finally agreed. Within seventy-two hours, Chase was on the phone with Winter: "I'm sending you this thing called *Mad Men* to read," he said. "I'm flying this guy out and, if he's not a complete asshole, I'm hiring him."

Chase did hire Weiner, though whether that was a definitive verdict on the "complete asshole" question was open to interpretation. As a sitcom writer, Weiner had demonstrated a certain difficulty playing well with others, an ability to rub people the wrong way. He would later recount the story of one actor getting so angry with him that the actor literally kicked him in the ass and challenged him to a fight. (The Web site Splitsider.com hypothesized that the actor was Mark Roberts, who himself went on to become showrunner of the sitcom *Mike & Molly*.)

Upon arriving at *The Sopranos*, by then a well-oiled juggernaut, Weiner made immediate waves. He could be funny and charming, colleagues said, but also childishly underhanded. At times he seemed a classic bully: obsequious toward those above him, condescending and harsh toward those he perceived as having less power to help or harm him. After one confrontation, costume designer Juliet Polcsa began carrying a minicassette recorder to tape her interactions with Weiner. In a more serious incident, Weiner was on a location scout with co–executive producer Henry Bronchtein, himself a combustive personality with whom Weiner had a contentious relationship. Upon wrapping up somewhere in New Jersey, Weiner, by then an executive producer, had not made it back to the van when Bronchtein ordered it to depart, leaving Weiner stranded and furious. The incident caused a several-day internal

dustup, with Weiner demanding that Bronchtein be fired, though Chase ultimately kept him. And although it had clearly been a breach of protocol on
Bronchtein's part, it was also an indication of the kind of dynamic that Weiner
brought to the workplace. It was rumored, though Carolyn Strauss flatly denied it, that her eventual rejection of *Mad Men* sprang from a personal desire
to never work with Weiner again.

All of this was balanced, of course, by the fact that he was undeniably
good at his job—brilliant, even. The writers' room, with its competitive atmosphere and opportunities to shine, had always suited Weiner to a T. Here, if
nowhere else, he had a thick skin. "I think that part of my success climbing the
hierarchy of the writers' room was that I knew that when the boss came in, no
matter what mood they were in, I was not going to take it personally," he said.
"I'd be like, 'You don't like that? Okay. Well, I've got something else. No? I've
got something else. Did you actually say "Fuck you" to me? Okay. Well, you
don't mean it.'"

How had he developed that skill?

"That's the way my family is. You can't take it personally," he said.

Inevitably, such a strong voice affected the dynamic of the room. Even
Winter, a friend, admitted, "There were some days where it'd be nice if he
stopped talking. But he was always interesting and funny and smart. He never
talked just to hear himself talk. He always had a point . . . just *a lot* of it."

His presence also dialed up the already high level of tension between
Chase and Robin Green. "Matt was a comedy writer, so he was always vibing
the room," Green said. "He had his head so far up David's ass. . . . I would be
trapped in the room with the two of them. They would just smack their lips
over all these French foreign films. It became increasingly intolerable." Chase
said that Weiner's growing prominence made Green jealous.

If Weiner had none of the New York street cred of Winter or Frank Renzulli (he would later joke, perhaps to Green's further consternation, that he
was the "first female writer on *The Sopranos*"), he connected with Chase and
the show in other ways that were clearly a perfect fit.

"Matt went to film school, David went to film school. They'd both watched
all these movies I'd never heard of," said Winter. "I used to sit there thinking,

'God, between the two of you guys, you've read every fucking book ever writ-ten. I feel like an idiot.'" Weiner also brought a sense of nuance and a view of human interaction—how people rarely say what they really mean—that Chase immediately recognized as suiting the show perfectly. In "The Test Dream," credited to both men, Tony, overwhelmed by complications involving Tony Blundetto, retreats to the Plaza Hotel. There, he falls into an extended dream sequence that was equal parts Freud, Fellini, and the Three Stooges, a fantasy of alternating power and performance anxiety that culminated in Tony's high school coach taunting him for being "unprepared." The twin codas seemed to sum up the range of both Chase's and Weiner's worldviews: at dawn, Tony calls a sleepy Carmela and tells her he's had one of his "Coach Molinaro dreams," perhaps the most tender moment the couple share in the entire se-ries. Also, Tony decides he's going to have to kill his own cousin.

Weiner clearly treated his time on the show as a master class—not only in the art of television storytelling, but in how to be a showrunner. He left seem-ingly determined to emulate Chase, his mentor, for better and for worse.

Five years before, if HBO doesn't call Matt Weiner back, *Mad Men* never sees the light of day. Period," said one TV executive. Ironically, it was a company owned by Charles Dolan, the man who dreamed up HBO, that saved the universe of the Sterling Cooper ad agency from that fate. AMC had been, for most of its twenty-two-year existence, a commercial-free network show-ing older, cheaper-to-acquire movies. "It was like 'the not-good Turner Classic Movies.' We had black-and-white movies, but not the great ones," said Rob Sorcher, the executive who would oversee the network's transformation. Even more than FX, AMC was in a position to take a risk, to create an identity—Don Draper–like—out of almost nothing.

"It started with Josh Sapan"—the chairman of what was then called Rain-bow Networks—"coming into my office and saying, 'Look, we need *The Sopra-nos*,'" Sorcher remembered. Sorcher had taken the job of senior vice president of programming, packaging, and production in the spring of 2002, just as AMC was undergoing its transformation from a commercial-free network to one that accepted advertising. He was an intense, mile-a-minute-talking vet-eran of the advertising business who had spent several years at the Cartoon Network, Fox Family, and USA. Since arriving at AMC, he had concentrated on programming that played directly off—and could be surrounded by—the network's sole strength: a large library of movies. "We did documentaries about Hollywood, reality shows about making movies, some very interesting stuff, but that stuff didn't pop, because nobody really cares," he said.

Now his boss was demanding that, starting from scratch, he produce an original, scripted series to rival the most important TV show in a generation. Sapan had good reason for the strategy: Cablevision, which owned AMC, was not a company on the scale of Viacom or Time Warner, which could use the le-verage of many channels to force cable carriers to keep them on the air. "He was afraid that, in the digital age, a world of consolidation, the network was just going to drop into oblivion," Sorcher said. "He wanted something of distinction. A signature show that viewers would care about, the press would care about, and that would give us some leverage going into talks with cable operators."

And Sapan also said the magic words: "He told me, 'I don't care about ratings.'"

Nevertheless, Sorcher remained cautious, unsure of whether the com-pany had the mettle and wherewithal to do what it said it wanted to do. He was reluctant even to hire a full-time staff member for what would be the net-work's development department, reasoning that he didn't want to lure some-body out of an existing job for one that might go nowhere. Instead, he made the unorthodox choice of hiring Christina Wayne as a "consultant." Wayne had spent the past decade working as a screenwriter in New York and Los Angeles, writing and directing one independent feature, *Tart*, in 2001, and working as a writer-for-hire on many others. She had no TV or development experience and had barely heard of AMC. Still, in January 2005 she agreed to meet with Sorcher.

"I spent the first fifty percent of the meeting just sitting there, pretending I knew what the hell he was talking about," she remembered. "But then he got to the part about having $70 million to launch a scripted division and needing someone to go out there and find great projects. I thought, 'Oh! That could be fun.'"

Wayne set about doing just that. Sorcher's strategy was to start with a miniseries, something contained—in both cost and commitment—that would serve to get the network's feet wet. One of AMC's perennial strengths had been westerns, so Wayne found a script for a two-hour movie called *Daughters of Joy* to which Robert Duvall and Walter Hill were attached. Stretched to a four-hour, two-part miniseries and renamed *Broken Trail*, it went into production. The process was rough. Hill and Duvall were at each other's throats throughout. In postproduction, Duvall broke into the editing bay, took the raw footage, and made a cut of his own. But *Broken Trail* burst out as the highest-rated basic cable miniseries of the year. It was nominated for sixteen Emmys and won four.

Cablevision, which had its corporate headquarters on Long Island and network offices across from Madison Square Garden, was hardly a glamorous Hollywood studio. The original-programming department—Sorcher, Wayne, Vlad Wolynetz, who would become head of production, and Jeremy Elice, brought in to open a West Coast office—were like peacocks in a chicken coop.

"It looked like the office in *The Office*," Wayne said. "Vlad used to say it was where mediocrity came to die." Elice remembered the first time he and Wayne were to make a presentation to a meeting of the other Rainbow networks. Wayne met him backstage with a ten-gallon hat.

"What is this?" he said.

"This is our part," said Wayne. "We're playing prospectors for AMC: 'We're out there developin'!'"

"It's fair to say," Sorcher summed up dryly, "that it was very unlikely that interesting programming would come from that environment."

With the success of *Broken Trail* under their belt, Sorcher and Wayne now went looking for a series. "I came up with this spiel. It was really just a wish list of what I wanted to watch on TV: 'We want to do high-end, one-hour dramas. We want them to feel more cinematic and told the way a novel is told—slow-paced, slow burning, character driven." The team had a rule, almost a mantra: "No doctors, no cops, no lawyers." But looking at the shows that had done well for the network, they made a determination: a period piece would be okay.

Ira Liss, a talent manager at Industry Entertainment, handed Wayne *Mad Men*. Despite David Chase's recommendation, and to his puzzlement— "Here's the guy who you've declared a 'genius'"—himself—"telling you that a show is really good and you don't even answer?"—HBO had ignored the script.

"This has been passed on by everybody for eight years," Liss told Wayne. "But I think you'll like it."

Wayne, who had once tried to option the rights to Richard Yates's *Revolutionary Road*, did. And Sorcher, who had started in advertising, did, too. Certainly the obstacles were clear: "Everyone smokes. They're unlikable. It's about *advertising*—there's no international value in that. It's slow. It's period. It's the worst idea ever," Sorcher summed up. But in the particular economics of the moment, a big strikeout was better than a weak half swing. "I thought, if we put on these shows, and they're low to middle quality, they'll come and go and nobody's going to care. But if I choose quality, some crazy insane thing, and I know that ratings don't matter, at least I've taken the shot. In a way, it's a safer course than getting stuck in the middle," he said. The goal was clear and defined. No basic cable show had ever won the Emmy for Outstanding Drama Series. "One hundred percent, this is the show that is going to win," Sorcher told his staff. "It was built to win that award. That's what it was designed for. If it doesn't bring us that award, the system doesn't work."

If the *Sopranos* myth was of two notes (on the title and on "College") and *Six Feet Under*'s was of one note ("Make it more fucked up"), then Weiner characteristically upped the ante by later claiming that he had received *no* notes on the *Mad Men* pilot. Still, as taken as she was with the script, Wayne did have a worry: "How do you get people to come back week after week to watch a show about advertising? That's not going to be enough. There has to be what we called a 'water cooler moment,' where you go, 'Oh, my fucking God. I have to watch next week!'"

Weiner, then still working full-time in the *Sopranos* writers' room, took two months to come back. When he did, it was with an entire twelve-episode arc, plotted out in breathtaking detail. At its heart was the backstory of Don Draper, prince of Madison Avenue but, like Jay Gatsby, a remarkable act of self-invention. He was, Weiner explained, born Dick Whitman, the illegitimate son of a prostitute, and had stolen a dead man's identity in the Korean War. It was a story he'd been thinking about for years but never grafted onto the pilot. Still, he was willing to make only the smallest concessions to the script as written: one shot of a Purple Heart, hidden in Don's desk, and the subtle sound of distant bombs when he stared into a light fixture. No extended flashbacks. No dramatic reveals.

Apparently, it was enough. The AMC team went looking for a studio to partner with in making the pilot. For all the same reasons that had kept *Mad Men* unbought for eight years, nobody wanted any part of it. Finally, Sorcher decided to take a leap of faith; AMC would foot the $2 million bill for the pilot itself and hope to partner with a permanent studio later.

O f course, it was crucial to find the right actor to play Draper—that charming, enigmatic vault of secrets and shifting identities. "What I needed was an actor who could have one thing on the outside and something else on the inside," Weiner said.

The process followed a by now familiar trajectory. Jon Hamm, like Weiner, had been struggling in Hollywood long past his ingenue phase. A St. Louis native, he had watched ex-roommates like Paul Rudd get famous while he drew only the occasional guest role on cop shows. He was thirty-six, ridiculously good-looking, but well past the age of the kind of man-children then the vogue in Hollywood star making. It was, Hamm said, from the vantage of his later success, a blessing in disguise. He had seen the toll early stardom could take.

"I see actors in this town who make it big young. They don't understand the word *no*," he said. "'What do you mean I can't kill this elephant, drop it on a car, set it on fire, and then snort it?' Well, you just *can't*."

And, it happened, Weiner was looking for something precisely like what Hamm offered: an unknown face, as James Gandolfini's had been, and a full-grown adult—the kind that had once been common on TV and in the movies.

"He reminded me of an old-fashioned leading man," he said. "James Garner, Gregory Peck, William Holden. They're handsome. They're a little bit funny. They've got this wiseass-ness." Not coincidentally, they were also precisely the kind of leading men who, in 1960, when *Mad Men* began, would soon be eclipsed by a new breed of counterculture heroes more on the order of Elliott Gould. How Don, his family, the ad firm of Sterling Cooper, and various other characters would survive the onrushing ruptures of the sixties was one of *Mad Men*'s most suspenseful ongoing mysteries.

Matinee idol looks alone, though, wouldn't have been enough for Hamm. As it turned out, his own history carried some emotional echoes of Don Draper's world. He had grown up in St. Louis. His mother, Deborah, had moved there from a small town in Kansas at eighteen years old to find work as a secretary. She met and married an older widower, Dan Hamm, whose fortunes were going the way of his family's business, hauling freight from the Mississippi to points around the country. Dan—nicknamed "the Whale" for his six-foot-three, three-hundred-pound frame and outsize personality—sold his business and looked for work in the New Economy. He peddled cars for a while. He dabbled in advertising.

Hamm's parents divorced when he was two, and he lived mostly with his mother. When he was ten, though, the two were on a trip to the St. Louis Art Museum and Deborah disappeared into the bathroom and didn't come out for a long time. Hamm had to ask a stranger to go in and check on his mother, who had fallen ill. Not long afterward, he came home from school to find his father waiting with the news that she was in the hospital. Doctors had removed her cancer-stricken colon along with two feet of intestine, but it was obvious the malignancy had spread much further. "From then on," he said, "it was just pain management and deathwatch."

Hamm wound up living with his father and grandmother in a musty old house filled with stultifying sorrow. He spent most of his time at friends' houses, cared for by a loose confederation of women he called "the Three Moms." Then, when he was in high school, Dan too became ill, at one point losing 120 pounds from advanced diabetes. During Jon's second semester at the University of Texas, Dan died and Jon dropped out. (He would eventually finish college at the University of Missouri.) Not much later, he lit out for Los Angeles.

All of which is to say that Hamm, more than most good-looking, out-of-work actors biking to auditions down Santa Monica Boulevard, was in a position to know well the lessons of Don Draper: how quickly one's world can be upended and how costly is the freedom to reinvent yourself and follow the American dream.

By the time he was cast, Hamm said, he had read practically every scene in the pilot for auditions, beginning with one in which Don dresses down the oily, entitled salesman Pete Campbell, telling him that he'll "die in that corner office."

"You could get a chimp to come in and read that scene and you will cast him," Weiner said with characteristic modesty. "But the 'It's Toasted' thing?"— a scene in which Draper comes up with the famous motto of Lucky Strike, while putting the audience in the strange position of rooting for a cigarette ad campaign—"Not everybody can do that."

More important, when Hamm left the room, Weiner turned to the casting director beside him. "That's the guy," he said. And: "That man was not raised by his parents."

Predictably, AMC raised a concern. "They thought he wasn't sexy and he had a shitty résumé and, in the end, they were getting cold feet about hiring an unknown," Weiner said. Using frequent flier miles, Weiner flew Hamm to New York to meet with the network's executives. The night before the audition, he met Hamm and some of the actor's friends at a bar. "I told him: 'You need to go in there with the confidence that I've told them I won't do the show if you're not in it,'" he remembered.

It wasn't strictly a bluff. Ten years into the Third Golden Age, the autocratic showrunner in chief was an institutionalized position. And as his model Weiner had Chase, who had given him instructions he would later use in two contentious contract negotiations: "You have to be prepared to walk away, and you gotta mean it. If you're bluffing, if you're not really there, don't say it."

If now, before the pilot had even shot, Weiner had hardly achieved the stature or success that allowed Chase that attitude, he was committed to proceeding as though AMC needed him more than he needed them. "There was some talk about the network needing to oversee how Hamm was directed. I said, 'No. You're VIPs on set and I value your opinion, but I know what this thing is and that's why I came here,'" he said. He told Chase about the conversation.

"Well," said Chase, "it better be good."

With the cast in place, the pilot shot at Silvercup Studios over ten days while *The Sopranos* was on hiatus, borrowing heavily from that show's crew and creative staff—including director of photography Phil Abraham and production designer Bob Shaw. With the final product in hand, Wayne and Sorcher once again toured the studios. This time, Lionsgate bit. Immediately after wrapping production on his final *Sopranos* episode—the next to last of the series, in which Bobby Bacala is killed and Silvio ends up in a coma—Weiner headed to L.A. to start writing.

W hen the *Mad Men* writers' room convened, eight years of thwarted ambition was unleashed. Among those in the room were the husband-and-wife writing team of Andre and Maria Jacquemetton, whom Weiner had known since film school; an old colleague from *The Naked Truth*, Tom Palmer; a longtime sitcom veteran named Lisa Albert; and two young writers with little experience, Chris Provenzano and Bridget Bedard.

For the first week, Weiner spoke almost nonstop. He had spent years imagining plotlines, reading reference materials, even collecting music that he wanted to use on the show. Now he downloaded reams of information while his writers scribbled furiously. At one point, he had written about 80 percent of a screenplay about Don Draper's backstory, which he recounted in intricate detail. "He knew every side character, what towns they'd lived in, everything," Bedard said.

Every writer was tasked with bringing in a handful of random plot ideas— "An Episode About Brassieres," "Pete Gets a Haircut"—which were written down on three-by-five index cards and pinned to a bulletin board, to be used in a pinch.

Weiner paced nonstop, speaking in the voices of his characters, in particular the imperious office manager Joan Holloway. "It would just overcome him, as if he were in a trance," said Provenzano. "Of course Joan is the bitchiest character. And Matt is a quintessential Queen Bitch. He could write that character for days and days."

He also held forth on details of the period, wheeling in a television for group screenings of *Sweet Smell of Success* and *Bachelor Party*. He assigned reading lists—*Sex and the Single Girl* and *The Feminine Mystique,* John Cheever and David Halberstam, David Ogilvy's *Confessions of an Advertising Man*. On either end of the room were huge calendars crammed with month-by-month details from 1960.

"He had fully internalized the movies, the literature, the topical news, the restaurants, the *New Yorker* articles. It was a world inside his head he knew inside and out, like uncorking a vintage wine that had been sitting on the shelf, waiting," Provenzano said. When the writer began working on his first assigned episode, the WGA-nominated "Hobo Code," Weiner plied him ceaselessly with notes, once even forcing Provenzano to pull over his car to get them all down. He was especially concerned with the "Sketches of Spain" scene, in which Don gets high with his mistress and other beatniks, while listening to that seminal Miles Davis album. "He'd say, 'This scene is about America and corporations and Norman Mailer and "The White Negro."' I'm thinking, 'There's no way I can cram all these ideas into a single scene. This guy wants *The Great Gatsby* distilled into three and a half minutes.'"

Early on, the writers' room had been collegial. The staff, Weiner included, often decamped from Los Angeles Center Studios in downtown L.A. to cocktail bars in the rapidly gentrifying neighborhood nearby. (If there's any justice in the world, they were heavily comped for the boost they were about to give the vintage cocktail revolution.) It was only when the first new episode—the second of the series—was submitted to AMC and Lionsgate that the tension began to rise. In it, Pete Campbell, a major figure in the pilot, was totally absent, off on his honeymoon. Conversely, the episode lingered primarily in Ossining, with Betty Draper, a character who had barely appeared in episode one. In came the notes from Lionsgate: Where were the cigarettes? The old-fashioneds? The sexy single broads? Had they been baited and switched?

Sorcher, too, remembered having to swallow hard. "I think it was the first time the enormity of what we were getting into hit home," he said. "'We're really going to do this? And this slowly?' We were in, but at the same time we wanted something to happen, instead of *nothing* to happen."

Staffers could hear Weiner's heated arguments with the network through the walls of his office. Meanwhile, the next episode, "Marriage of Figaro," was *Mad Men*'s "College." In it, Don, clearly chafing in his domestic life, gets drunk while building a playhouse for his daughter's birthday and ends up missing the party altogether by never returning from a trip to get the cake. When he does return, long after the guests have departed, it's with a new dog, to smooth things over. In a show that would go on to be filled with bad mothers and fathers, this was the first example of flagrantly awful parenting, on the part of a character we were growing to like. "They're never going to let me do this to this character," Weiner predicted, girding for battle.

HBO may have shunned Weiner, but he seemed intent on pretending his show was on the network. He could recite by rote exactly the quota of curse words he was allowed per episode. As for act breaks, he ignored them altogether, refusing to hit any of the "buttons" that Shawn Ryan so celebrated. Instead, commercials appeared haphazardly, almost always awkwardly, as though being punished for their presence. "Let the network figure that out," Weiner said.

And if any question was left about how he would view network interference, Sorcher and Elice were equally shocked and amused to show up at the first table read at Los Angeles Center Studios only to be handed nondisclosure contracts to sign. "It was a very strange thing for a writer to be handing his executives," Elice said. "Why would we leak something about our own show?"

Once production began, tension in the writers' room ramped up dramatically. Weiner tended to respond to work that fell short of his expectations with withering disappointment, as though it were a personal affront. "He would get so annoyed, like, 'Why would she say that?' 'Why would she do that?'" said Bedard. "He took it really personally. And then it would all get worked out and he'd be thrilled beyond belief. He's elated when things are what he wants." It became routine for writers, leaving note meetings on their scripts, to hit the bathroom in order to let the tears subside.

Equal pressure was placed on writers covering set, who would find themselves in a state of terror over missing something important that Weiner wanted, or didn't want, in a scene. Infractions could be as tiny as a gesture: Hamm repeatedly brushing ashes from his suit sleeve once drove Weiner to castigate the writer on duty for not catching and stopping it.

"It was like a parent. Like you had taken a shit on the rug and he was like, 'What did you do? Bad! Bad!'" Provenzano said.

Weiner demanded a strict protocol in the room. "There is deference based on age and experience, and it better be there," he said. Frank Pierson, the legendary screenwriter of *Cool Hand Luke, Cat Ballou,* and *Dog Day Afternoon,* as well as TV going back to *Have Gun—Will Travel* and *Naked City,* started making weekly appearances in the room during the show's later seasons. One day, he was telling a story about his dog, and a young writer made the error of interrupting with a story of his own pet.

"This was somebody who was very low on the totem pole," Weiner said. "I literally pulled them aside afterward and said, 'No one gives a *shit* about your dog.'" When Pierson was talking, he said, "only *I* interrupt him."

For all that, Weiner insisted that the room was vital to his process—as a source of stories and bits of dialogue and as an audience, a kind of creative conductive jelly in which to immerse himself, not dissimilar to David Milch's hushed vestal virgins. Michael Patrick King, the longtime showrunner of *Sex and the City*, had given him a piece of advice on building a writers' room: "Find people that make you sparkle."

"And it's true," he said. "You want people who haven't heard your story, and who make you behave better, or think better, that you want to try and impress on some level. And then it becomes what Pierson once said to me. He said, 'I honestly feel like there's a kind of psychoanalysis that goes on in that room, and that everybody on some level is helping you discover what the story is.'"

A MC, deciding to build on its identity as a classic movie network, made an early decision regarding how it would promote *Mad Men*. The PR campaign, the network's PR team decided, would focus not on Hamm or any of the beautiful women in the cast, but on Weiner himself. In effect, AMC was claiming auteurship as its brand. "Honestly, it was all we had," said one person instrumental in building the strategy. "Our tagline was 'Created by the Executive Producer of *The Sopranos*.'"

It was a measure of just how far television had come from the days of the anonymous, presumably replaceable, showrunner. And Weiner was the perfect person for the job. He could be a dazzling speaker—eloquent, confident, persuasive, a natural storyteller with a world of anecdotes and references at his fingertips. At an early press event—the presentation of clips to specially selected "tastemakers" at Michael's restaurant in midtown Manhattan—he wowed the room, outshining such other speakers as Arianna Huffington and Jerry Della Femina.

Though he treated upcoming plot developments with the overwrought secrecy of nuclear codes, once they had aired, Weiner was willing to expound at astonishing length upon themes, references, callbacks to previous episodes, inside jokes, important costume decisions, and other aspects of his grand design. "Wasn't that amazing?" he would say. Or, "That was hilarious." And it would take an interviewer—used to the usual rules of human discourse—a moment to remember that Weiner was speaking unabashedly about his own work.

Indeed, for somebody who had not grown up, say, in the wilds of Africa, Weiner could be shockingly oblivious or indifferent to how the things he said and did appeared to others. Either that or he genuinely could not control his most self-aggrandizing and competitive impulses. In one characteristic, oft-repeated piece of industry gossip, he was introduced to the showrunner of a hugely successful and popular network hit. On the way out, Weiner stopped to say, "See you at the Emmys." "Actually, we're not nominated," the man said. "That's right," Weiner said, turning on his heel. "You're *not*."

At the same time, he could inspire fierce loyalty among colleagues. The negative stories, Christina Wayne insisted, were the product of jealousy and grudge holding. "I'm sorry, people got fired from that writers' room"—Weiner seemed determined to eclipse even Chase in writer turnover—"because they weren't any good," she said. "Him being 'difficult' . . . I think of it as his passion, and I respect it. I've been on the other side, when people took my work and tried to change it. So, whenever Matt got upset, or pissed off, or screamed, I felt like, 'Yeah, you're right. Protect your work.' That's your *goal*, to work with somebody like that. When I work with somebody who doesn't care, or phones it in, that's what pisses me off. That's when I feel like, 'You're a fucking douche bag.' I'd work with somebody like Matt, who gives it all up, hands down any day."

Weiner, of course, had been raised to not shy away from accomplishment. His biggest fear, at *The Sopranos,* had been that nobody would ever know how much he had written. (A first-time visitor to the set once made the mistake of chatting with the director about the episode being filmed; Weiner, who had written it, pulled him aside. "In TV," he said after introducing himself, "the director means *nothing*.")

Having his own show was vindication. Because of the writers' strike that stretched between 2007 and 2008, neither cast nor crew could attend that season's Golden Globe Awards, gathering instead on the top floor of the Chateau Marmont to watch on TV. When the show won for Best Television Series, the party erupted. Weiner climbed up on a chair to make a speech. "This is what you wait for," he said in this, his moment of triumph, "so you can tell all those people who ever said anything bad to you to *go fuck themselves!*"

And he had zero qualms about making sure that the world knew exactly how much of the show belonged to him. A writer's draft, he maintained, was almost always just a shadow of a blueprint for the eventual episode, the frame of a house with barely any walls, let alone wallpaper. "The problem for many writers," he said, "is that once they've executed the outline, they feel like it's finished. And you know that it's nowhere near finished. And you know that that's a stab at it. Actually, I don't think they could even work if they knew how unfinished you know it is."

Rewriting, even drastic rewriting, had always been part of the showrunner portfolio. According to custom, except in extreme cases, the first-draft's writer's name would remain alone atop a script, no matter how much work the showrunner had done. His or her involvement, it was understood, was implied by the job title. Chase, as time had gone by, had grown increasingly frustrated by the fact that this often meant his work was going unrecognized. As *The Sopranos* proceeded, he had added his name to the authorship of scripts with growing frequency. Weiner, though, brought the practice to an entirely new level. He adopted a rule that if more than 20 percent of a writer's script remained, he or she would retain sole credit. If not, Weiner added his name. A measure of how difficult that benchmark was to reach: Of sixty-five episodes through season five, fifty were at least partially "written by" Weiner. It became enough of an industry inside joke that it was the subject of a sight gag on *30 Rock*.

Talking about the policy, Weiner was defensive but steadfast. "For me, it's just a matter of the well-being of my daily interaction with the people I work with," he said. "For me to watch somebody go up and get an award for something I had written every word of . . . I couldn't live with it. I'm not Cyrano de Bergerac."

Despite Weiner's assertion that "there's no residuals in basic cable. I'm not fighting for money," the arrangement included a financial component. Half credit on a script indeed meant half the residuals on reruns, foreign broadcasts, and so on for the other credited writer. (Giving Weiner the benefit of the doubt, he may have been suggesting that the residuals for *Mad Men* were so negligible as to be nonexistent; still, one imagines a writer preferring to make that judgment on his or her own.)

The debate was charged enough to itself end up in an episode of *Mad Men*—which, after all, is in part about creative people working together in a collaborative atmosphere where, nevertheless, some members are more equal than others. In "The Suitcase," Peggy complains to Don about his not giving her sufficient credit for her ideas. The fight gets heated.

Don: That's the way it works. I give you money, you give me ideas.

Peggy: You never say "thank you!"

Don: That's what the money is for!

"I don't know how it ever got to be the other way," Weiner said of the tradition of a sole writer getting credit, no matter what the circumstances. "It's like, 'You know what you wrote and I know what I wrote. You *really* want everyone to think you wrote all of it? You can really sit there and not have a problem with that?' I mean, it's one thing for me to pretend I didn't write something. But for someone to pretend that they *did*? That's hard to stomach."

Other showrunners, if they didn't adopt Weiner's policy, certainly sympathized with him, even admired his abandoning of traditional niceties. All had at least one stomach-wrenching experience of watching someone take credit for their work.

"I'm impressed," *Breaking Bad*'s Vince Gilligan said. "I recall times when I would rewrite other people's scripts and my name wouldn't go on the rewrite and, more than missing out on some money, I would have the feeling of 'The world's not going to know the work I did here.' It would gall me. Maybe tradition is something to fight against."

Gilligan was speaking in a roundtable that also included Weiner and David Milch. "Ego suppression," Milch agreed, "can be an act of unhealthy ostentation."

"Well," said Weiner, "I'm very healthy."

. . .

Certainly it was not a unique question in the history of the arts: how some-one capable of seeming insensitive and out of emotional touch in the real world could also produce work of exquisite emotional intelligence and empathy. And *Mad Men*, in its best moments, was just that.

It was the first major show of the Third Golden Age to forgo any instantly recognizable genre; it didn't arrive in the guise of a cop show, a Mob show, a western, or even a soapy family drama. It was, however, as much of a Trojan horse as any of its predecessors, with the costumes, the smoking, the drinking, and the nostalgia standing in for *The Sopranos'* blood, guns, goombah jokes, and strippers. Article after article described Weiner's fetish for period detail; a pocket Internet industry popped up to catalog and explicate each episode's references, no matter how oblique or even imaginary. With no apparent irony, Banana Republic launched a *Mad Men* marketing campaign and line of clothes; Bloomingdale's devoted its entire Third Avenue window display to the show.

Beneath that, though, it is in many ways a story as brutal and ruthless in its view of human nature as its predecessor. Don may be a searcher, but he is a blinkered, often selfish, sometimes ridiculous one. Weiner never lets us forget how frequently Don is on the wrong side of history: he sides with Nixon over entitled, glib Kennedy; he doesn't get the Beatles. Emotionally, like Tony Soprano, he makes, at best, halting progress—forcing the audience to re-examine its affection for and loyalty to him at every turn. That people act nearly always on their worst impulses, whether they're aware of it or not, was an item of bedrock faith for Weiner; anyone who felt differently was fooling himself.

"He has absolutely a conviction not only that his characters think the way they do, but that *all* people think the way that his characters think," said Bedard.

Male-female relations—in both the personal and the historical contexts—are the most obvious subject of *Mad Men*. In many ways, the series is as much about the journey of Peggy Olson as it is about Don's. Weiner copped to having a special affection for Peggy, perversely most evident in his granting her foibles (ego, irritability, bad judgment, coldness about her abandoned baby) that mirrored those of her boss and mentor. (Weiner was guilty, it seemed, of loving the show's other great female character, Joan, too much: alternating between sanctifying her as office Madonna and punishing her with grotesque plot twists.)

But the show was as much about male combat—its infinite variations and the constant, exhausting toll it takes. This, more than alcoholism, the effects of smoking, or any other bad results of ancient mores, was the dark side of unequivocally running the world. It was also vital to Weiner's worldview, a fact that explained, as much as anything, the rougher edges of his personality.

"I'm constantly putting on my armor," he said. "It's all about what you think you're entitled to, what your ambition is, what's in your way. I'm not somebody who tries to destroy people, but I am very conscious of these things. It *is* combat: Do *you* ever want to give up feeling sexually viable? I don't. Do you ever want to give up feeling powerful? Do you want to look at a twenty-year-old kid and say, 'He can beat the shit out of me'? It's all combat."

Above all, *Mad Men* may have been the purest use of the new form of serialized TV. Weiner understood innately the rhythms of thirteen one-hour episodes, the ways in which they could be made to serve an overarching narrative while simultaneously acting as discrete hour-long weekly "movies." An episode was closer to a feature film than it might at first appear, he pointed out, since a two-hour movie often required as much as an hour of setup, exposition, and characterization. At the start of any given hour of *Mad Men*, that work was already done, by the two, or three, or sixty-five hours before it.

And *Mad Men* used the ongoing, open-ended format to approach a kind of radical realism that went way beyond whether, say, the refrigerator in the Draper home was the perfect shade of 1962 olive green. The show, in a wildly un-TV-like way, insisted on portraying how the passage of life *feels*.

"The first season of *The Sopranos*, you literally felt like you were being dropped out of an airplane every episode," Weiner said. "You constantly had the sensation that you missed an episode: 'Everybody in this story seems to know that guy. Do *I* know that guy? Was he on last week?' No, they act like they know that guy because they have a life without you."

This ethic came to the fore, especially, at the outset of *Mad Men*'s season three, when all the initial mysteries that animated the first two seasons had been resolved—Don's true identity, the fate of his and Betty's marriage, what Peggy would do about her baby—and the show became more about life simply *happening*, much the way it actually does, tough truths included: First wives become small, distant chapters of a person's life. People leave to take new jobs. Hurts are forgotten or else harbored much longer than necessary. Sometimes there are both a Bert and a Burt in an office (just as New Jersey had a Big and Little Pussy); sometimes a man named Don winds up with a secretary named Dawn. What other show would have thought to devote an entire season—its fifth—to the problems of having a *happy* marriage?

The ethos extended perhaps most of all to the insight into what it means to live through momentous periods in history—when it's not clear which side is the right side or which events will later be important. "If you're in the middle of a divorce, and there is the Cuban Missile Crisis," Weiner said, "your problem is bigger."

Mad Men is about a transitional generation—caught between the upheavals of World War II and the youthquake of the 1960s—written by another such generation, one growing up under the shadow of the baby boomers' self-mythologizing, but too near to claim something new as their own. As much as it is an act of obsession with the 1960s, the show is also a thrilling Oedipal demystification of The Sixties and what it meant to live through them. What it meant, Weiner seemed to be saying, was waking up every day struggling with the exact same things, making the same mistakes, and missing the same big pictures as any generation before or after.

If much of *Mad Men* feels like a child's rapt view of his parents' glamorous, mysterious doings ("I'm often in the role of Sally," Weiner said, referring to the Drapers' daughter), it is because that insight applies as much to the personal sphere as to the public. To imagine your parents as real people—to truly investigate the question "How are they like me?"—is an act of empathy, adoration, and also murder.

It is such truths that become the chief pleasure of watching *Mad Men*, more than the specific twists and turns of what can at times feel like contrived "action." (Though the occasional foot being cut off by a lawn mower doesn't hurt.)

"I always thought it would be the experience of a human life," Weiner said. For that goal, serialized television turned out to be the perfect, if accidental, instrument—and its perfect artist a man who could say with total confidence, "I've always assumed that people have the same feelings as me. And I'm usually right. They just won't admit it."

Thirteen

The Happiest Room
in Hollywood

I t was an all-time record hot day in the San Fernando Valley. On West Burbank Boulevard, lined with offices and strip malls, the air shimmered; people took pictures of their cars' temperature displays: 110, 112, 116. In an anonymous building across from an AutoZone, the lobby directory showed the offices of a private eye, a dental supply company, a handful of financial companies, and, in suite 206, something blandly mysterious and vaguely sinister called Delphi Information Sciences Corporation. The plastic nameplate on the suite's door did little to illuminate the nature of what such a corporation might do. Certainly it offered no clue that behind the door, under the dropped ceilings, the fluorescent lights, and the hum of air-conditioning of the onetime data services office, was the most coveted workplace in Hollywood: the *Breaking Bad* writers' room.

It was so not only because *Breaking Bad* was arguably the best show on TV, in many ways the culmination of everything the Third Golden Age had made possible, but because its creator and showrunner, Vince Gilligan, was known as a good man to work for—someone who managed to balance the vision and microscopic control of the most autocratic showrunner with the open and supportive spirit of the most relaxed. He was a firm believer in collaboration.

"The worst thing ever the French gave us is the auteur theory," he said flatly. "It's a load of horseshit. You don't make a movie by yourself, you certainly don't make a TV show by yourself. You invest people in their work. You make people feel comfortable in their jobs; you keep people talking."

In his room, he said, all writers were equal, an approach that he insisted had less to do with being a Pollyanna than with pure, selfish practicality. "There's nothing more powerful to a showrunner than a truly invested writer," he said. "That writer will fight the good fight."

On this day, a Monday, he sat at the head of a conference table as his writers gathered for work after the weekend, chattering about the heat. Forty-three years old, he wore light jeans, an orange T-shirt, and silver sneakers; his face, with its goatee and glasses, was poised at a precise fulcrum between relaxed southern gentleman—a young Colonel Sanders, maybe—and eager fantasy geek. You could easily see a shadow of the young Gilligan who had showed up in Washington Square to be an NYU undergraduate film student.

Gilligan, surprisingly, was the only major showrunner of the Third Golden Age to have started his path to TV with a semisuccessful, if frustrating, career in feature films. On the strength of a script he completed at NYU— which would much later become the movie *Home Fries*—he spent five years writing screenplays back home in Virginia. One, *Wilder Napalm,* a romantic comedy about pyrokinetic brothers vying for the same woman (sort of *The Fabulous Baker Boys* bred with *Firestarter*), actually got made, starring Dennis Quaid and Debra Winger, in 1993.

That was also the year that *The X-Files*, Chris Carter's latter-day incarnation of *Kolchak: The Night Stalker*, debuted on Fox. Gilligan was an immediate fan and arranged to meet Carter, who then offered him a freelance episode. The experience turned out to be satisfying and fun enough to lure him across the country to relocate in L.A. By the end of *The X-Files'* run in 2002, Gilligan had risen to executive producer and penned some thirty episodes.

The X-Files was about two FBI agents, Fox Mulder and Dana Scully, he a true believer in the supernatural, she a skeptic, assigned to investigate paranormal activity. It was a notable waypoint in the evolution of quality TV. Faced with the network necessity of seasons in excess of twenty episodes, Carter made an ingenious adaptation: half of the series consisted of tightly wrought, often funny stand-alone episodes, while the other half was an ever more recondite "mythology" of aliens, secret agencies, and other conspiracy theories.

Ironically, given that he would become a master of serialized TV, Gilligan's specialty on *The X-Files* was the stand-alone episodes. One of his most memorable was called "Drive." In it, Mulder ends up trapped in a car with an ugly, anti-Semitic character who is afflicted with a condition whereby he must keep driving west or his head will explode. It was a difficult role to cast. "You needed an actor who could play this guy who is an asshole, an unpleasant redneck creep, and yet at the end of the hour, you need to feel bad when this guy dies," Gilligan said. "Casting bad guys is easy. Casting a bad guy you feel sympathy for is much trickier." The actor he found, Bryan Cranston, would eventually perform the same tightrope act as Walter White, the antihero of *Breaking Bad*.

Near the end of *The X-Files*, Gilligan spent one season on a spin-off, *The Lone Gunmen*. It was a project so patently doomed that Gilligan said the fellow Fox show *King of the Hill* featured a character wearing a "Bring Back *The Lone Gunmen*" T-shirt that was scripted before the spin-off ever aired. He then spent four years becoming reacquainted with the frustrations and snail's pace of feature-film making, working on *Hancock*, a movie about a surly, alcoholic superhero. "There's a weird kind of hang-fire misery involved in living a life in which you get paid a lot of money, you can go write in the south of France if you want, instead of a crappy little stiflingly hot office in Burbank, but there's a very good chance that what you're working on may never get made," he said. "In television, at least, you write something, and a week or two later it's being produced."

In the midst of the endless rewrites, in 2005, Gilligan was on the phone with an old friend and fellow *X-Files* writer Thomas Schnauz. The two were complaining about the state of the movie business and wondering what they might be qualified to do instead.

"Maybe we can be greeters at Walmart," Gilligan said.

"Maybe we can buy an RV and put a meth lab in the back," said Schnauz.

"As he said that, an image popped into my head of a character doing exactly that: an Everyman character who decides to 'break bad' and become a criminal," Gilligan recalled. It was a powerful enough image that he got off the phone and began jotting down notes. The heart of the show came together in a hurry. The main character, Walter White, is a mild and beaten-down high school chemistry teacher who finds himself diagnosed with lung cancer. Inadequately insured, with a baby on the way, he is desperate to provide for his family when he's gone and hits on the idea of going into the crystal meth business with a junkie ex-student named Jesse Pinkman, played by Aaron Paul. Thanks to White's chemistry expertise and relative (by the standard of meth dealers) discipline and devotion to quality, Walt and Jesse's product becomes much in demand. Legal, familial, and moral complications ensue.

The underlying project Gilligan had in mind, though, was something deeper—a radical extension of the antihero trend that had by then become the signature of the decade's TV. The idea was to convincingly transform a milquetoast into a monster or, as Gilligan often put it, "Mr. Chips into Scarface." As the series progressed, he would take away Walt's justifications for his criminal behavior one by one—starting with the cancer, which quickly went into remission. At the same time, Gilligan, more than any other showrunner except maybe David Simon in *The Wire*, gave Walt adversaries the viewer actually cared for—foremost his own brother-in-law, Hank, a DEA agent with whom Walt ends up locked in a zero-sum game. This was not *The Shield*; it was not at all clear whom to root for. The series became a study in empowered masculinity run horribly amok, without even the compensatory wish fulfillment granted Tony Soprano or Don Draper. This made the challenge even more direct: Why *did* we still want Walt to win? Effectively, it was a five-season-long "College" episode.

Walt's journey to darkness was not the only way in which *Breaking Bad* would come to seem like both an echo of and an answer to *The Sopranos*, *The Wire*, and other shows that had ushered in the Third Golden Age. Walter's wife, Skyler, played by Anna Gunn, would end up as a distant sister-wife to Carmela Soprano, grappling with her husband's crimes and their implications, especially for her children, to a degree that her predecessor never did. More

important, whereas the antiheroes of those earlier series were at least arguably the victims of their circumstances—family, society, addiction, and so on—
Walter White was insistently, unambiguously, an agent with free will. His
journey became a grotesque magnification of the American ethos of self-
actualization, Oprah Winfrey's exhortation that all must find and "live your
best life." What if, *Breaking Bad* asked, one's best life happened to be as a
ruthless drug lord?

O ne of the first things you do, when you have an idea like this, is ask yourself, 'Is it a TV show or a movie?'" Gilligan said. Twenty years earlier,
there would have been no question that it was a movie. In 2005, though, he
quickly decided that cable TV was his only hope.

Which didn't mean that, about halfway through his pitch to executives at
Sony Television, he didn't hear himself talking and think, "Gee, this is crazy."
Against the odds, Sony bought the idea and arranged a pitch meeting at TNT.
It was, Gilligan remembered, the best meeting of his life. The TNT execs were
at the edge of their seats, asking what happened next, laughing at all the right
places. When Gilligan was done, they looked at one another, crestfallen. "We
don't want to be stereotypical philistine executives," one finally said, "but
does it have to be meth? We love this, but if we buy it, we'll be fired."

Still, Gilligan remembered the meeting fondly. "I give them great credit
for not leaving me hanging," he said. "The best meeting of all is when they buy
your story in the room. A close second is when they turn you down quickly.
And the third way is you do your song and dance and go away and never hear
from anybody again."

That was the meeting he had with Carolyn Strauss at HBO. "I couldn't tell
whether she was loving it or hating it or even listening. We got to the end, and
she stood up and said, 'Well, thanks for coming in.' I said to my agent, 'Oh boy.
I guess this isn't going to be an HBO show.'" Indeed, HBO never gave them an
answer of any kind.

At the next meeting, with FX, another potential obstacle presented itself.
John Landgraf listened to the pitch and said, "Sounds a little like *Weeds*," the

recently debuted Showtime series about a suburban mom who becomes a pot dealer. Gilligan, who didn't have Showtime, felt his stomach fall into his crotch. "What is *Weeds*?" he asked.

In the end, Landgraf judged *Breaking Bad* different enough to order a pilot. But by the time, two months later, that Gilligan handed it in, there was yet another problem. The network was committed to making only one new series that year, and it had come down to *Breaking Bad* and *Dirt,* starring Courteney Cox, fresh off the juggernaut run of *Friends*, as the editor of a tabloid gossip magazine.

"Nobody had a crystal ball, but at the time it made perfect sense to go with *Dirt*," Gilligan said, though the show would be canceled after two seasons. "I think they were trying to expand their female viewership, and *Dirt* came with a bona fide television star. I don't blame them a bit." *Breaking Bad*, however, he assumed was "dead as a doornail."

So gracious was Gilligan about these and most other matters that one had to remind oneself he was the author of some of the most harrowing, grisly, gleefully sanguine scenes ever to appear on television of any kind: a human body dissolved by acid in a bathtub, for instance, the acid subsequently burning through both tub and floor, so that the entire pink, swollen mess came crashing down in a magnificent *sploosh*. In case that somehow slipped your mind, the writers' room was peppered with further reminders—most strikingly, a clay model of a tortoise on whose back rested a decapitated, mustachioed head. It was a reproduction of an indelible image from season two.

Yet even in the midst of great violence, a certain gentlemanliness reigned. In the script for one of the tensest episodes of the series, in which Jesse and Walt are being held captive in a desert hideout by a psychotic dealer named Tuco, a stage direction contained a parenthetical that would be hard to imagine in a *Sopranos* or *Mad Men* script: "Tuco lunges at Jesse, grabs him by the collar (or hair, if we can make that work without hurting Aaron)."

Gilligan had been justified in assuming, when FX passed on producing *Breaking Bad*'s pilot, that none of this would ever see the light of day. FX owned the show outright, and networks were generally disinclined to see shows they had developed become hits on other channels. That was what had happened to a pilot Gilligan had shot for CBS. "They said, 'We're not going to let you make it. We bought it and now we're going to keep it in a file cabinet somewhere,'" Gilligan said. "At a corporate level I understand those kinds of decisions, but they're hard to justify in any moral way."

In any event, the question was moot. HBO, Showtime, TNT, and now FX had passed on *Breaking Bad*. "There was no place left in the known universe," Gilligan said. With a TV veteran's stoicism, he stopped thinking about the show and turned to yet another rewrite of *Hancock*.

By that time, however, Jeremy Elice, who while working at FX had watched the show's development process excitedly and then disappointedly, had landed at AMC. He certainly remembered it when ICM agent Mark Gordon called to say it might still be available. He and Christina Wayne set up a meeting with Gilligan at the L'Ermitage Beverly Hills hotel. Gilligan was dubious but agreed.

"I figured I'll go to the meeting, get flattered for a half hour, drink a $14 Scotch, and that's all fine with me. Just another jerk-off meeting."

Wayne and Elice laid out what was going on at AMC, where the pilot for *Mad Men* had just been shot. Gilligan, in turn, impressed them by sketching out a multiseason, detailed arc for the show. "Christina and I were getting more and more excited," said Elice. "We're like, 'He's really going to have cancer! Not like *Beverly Hills, 90210* cancer. *Real* cancer!'"

As for Gilligan, "I liked what I heard. I never thought they were bullshitting. But I have to confess that I also left thinking, 'Man, this is never going to happen.'"

Back in New York, the script stalled on Rob Sorcher's desk. "I didn't want to read it," he admitted cheerfully. "I didn't want to read the fucking script about the meth dealer with cancer." For two weeks, Elice and Wayne urged him to pick it up. "This is fucking great," he said, once he finally did. "Why didn't you tell me?"

It still remained to cut a deal with FX and with Sony. Nine months of negotiations passed, during which Elice and Gordon, the agent, spoke nearly every day. In the end, only one hurdle remained: a $5,000-per-episode royalty on "new media"—a term that was beginning to mean more and more—that

Sony was demanding. Sorcher used the company helicopter to fly out to Cablevision's Long Island headquarters and made the request personally. Finally, the deal was done and *Breaking Bad* became the property of AMC.

To Sorcher, this was the defining decision of his time at AMC—even more consequential, and requiring more nerve, than green-lighting and taking on the expense of the *Mad Men* pilot. At least that show and *Broken Trail* were of a piece with some existing elements of the network's brand; they could be packaged with *The Apartment* or *El Dorado* or other films from AMC's well-established inventory. *Breaking Bad* fit no discernible genre at all—except quality. "'If we do this,' I thought, 'we're going all the way out on this limb,'" Sorcher said. "We had had success with *Mad Men*. And once you've had that cookie, it tastes *good*. You want another one. The decision to go a different way, believe me, it was fucking terrifying. But once you did, once you chose quality over everything else . . . you could do *anything*."

By now, the staff in the office of "Delphi Information Sciences Corporation" had assembled and dispensed with the first and most important task of the day: ordering lunch. To Gilligan's left, wearing a green San Diego Zoo T-shirt, sat Tom Schnauz, whose joke had inspired the show and who was now supervising producer. The fifth episode of the fourth season, 405, which was currently on the table, was his to write. Elsewhere around the table were Gennifer Hutchison, Moira Walley-Beckett, Sam Catlin, and Peter Gould. One more writer, George Mastras, was out of the office, writing an episode. At the far end, across the long expanse from Gilligan, the writers' assistant and script coordinator, Kate Powers, sat feverishly transcribing everything said. She wore black carpal-tunnel sleeves over both wrists.

On the wall behind Gilligan was a large corkboard. Across the top were pinned thirteen index cards representing the thirteen episodes of the season. In rows beneath them, more neatly printed cards (Schnauz, who had the best handwriting on staff, was the deputized card writer) contained detailed story points. The cards looked like a pile of leaves that had faced a stiff, left-blowing wind, clustered deep under the early episodes but gradually thinning as the as-yet-unwritten season progressed. Under 413, the final episode of the season, there was only one single, fluttering card. It read in bold, matter-of-fact Magic Marker, "BOOM."

On the other walls were maps of New Mexico and Albuquerque and a detailed schematic, with photos, of Walt's fictional meth superlab located underneath an industrial laundry. Gilligan had originally set the show in Southern California's Inland Empire, the area east of Los Angeles. Thanks to tax incentives, though, production had been moved to Albuquerque, New Mexico. It proved to be a fortuitous change; the tone of the show became inseparable from the Southwest's gaping empty deserts and parking lots, its cul-de-sac communities and domes of vast blue sky. The show was as rooted in its geography as *The Sopranos* was in New Jersey.

Like *The Sopranos*, too, it uncannily anticipated a national mood soon to be intensified by current events—in this case the great economic unsettlement of the late aughts, which would leave many previously secure middle-class Americans suddenly feeling like desperate outlaws in their own suburbs. At the same time, the real-world meth epidemic and, across the border, the increasing violence of the Mexican cartels provided a dramatic new backdrop and a whole world into which to expand.

Behind Schnauz was another corkboard, representing episode 405. As the room worked through the episode, each beat or scene would be written on a card and pinned to the board. The last card was always pinned with a little ceremony that meant the episode was locked down. At that point, Gilligan said, it would be so fully imagined and outlined in such detail that, in theory, at least, any of the writers in the room would be able to take over and supervise production.

Right now, the 405 board was blank.

Nearly every discussion in every writers' room, Gilligan explained, boils down to one of two questions: "Where's a character's head at?" and "What happens next?" Ideas vs. action. Text vs. subtext. This, it happened, was a "What happens next?" day, in which the details of a relatively banal plot point need to be worked out.

"Some days you need to build the blocks," he said.

To borrow a handy acronym, the question was this: WWJD? What will Jesse do? At this point in the series, the two protagonists, Jesse and Walt, had become dangerously, inextricably tied up with Mexican drug cartels and are under the sway of an ice-cold, manipulative kingpin named Gus Fring, who poses as the upstanding head of a fried chicken franchise. Jesse, distraught from having killed a man for the first time at the end of season three, has been falling apart, hosting a meth-fueled house party that lasts the span of the three previous episodes. This is simultaneously a threat to Gus, who needs both men, and an opportunity to gain the upper hand.

As Gilligan recapped, "If Walt is dead, Gus has nothing, because Jesse can't cook like Walt. If Jesse's dead, Walt goes berserk and doesn't cook and Gus has nothing. But if he keeps Jesse alive and yet divides Jesse's loyalties in his Machiavellian fashion, then he's really accomplished something."

To accomplish that, Gus instructs his fixer, a flinty, aging hit man named Mike, to take Jesse on as a partner for the day and give him a task that will raise his self-esteem in a way working for Walt doesn't. That still left a bevy of questions. Mainly: "What would that task be?" But also: "How much does Mike know about the plan?" "Is it something meaningless or something for which Jesse is uniquely qualified?" "Is there *anything* for which Jesse is uniquely qualified?" And so on.

"This is one of those moments where we know in theory what happens, but we need the specifics. We had a lot of good stuff Friday, but none of it really stuck with me over the weekend," Gilligan said. "Part of me thinks it should be supersimple."

"What I like is that Mike doesn't want him there," one of the writers said. "This is the last guy he wants in his fucking car."

"I like that, too," said Gilligan.

"I don't think Mike would tell him jack. I think it's nice for us to just wonder, 'What's going on here?'"

"There's never any harm in that," said Gilligan. "It's okay to be mysterious. It's not good to be confusing, but mysterious is good."

"Are we skipping over the cliff-hanger from 404?" Walley-Beckett wondered. "Of whether Jesse's about to get whacked?"

"I agree, we need to see that moment. But that moment can string out. Say, just for argument, the first scene, Mike pulls his piece-of-shit Buick onto some side street, pulls up to a curb, stops, turns off the engine. Jesse's sitting there, waiting to see what the play is. Mike says, 'All right, here's the deal. See that house there? You walk in there, you buy an eight ball. You got any money on you? Here, buy an eight ball.' He's like, 'I'm going to go in there and have an accident, is that what this is about?' 'Not if you don't fuck up. Today's not the day you die, unless you fuck things up. Which is very possible.' Obviously this is the worst dialogue ever, but there's a way we can take it completely off the table for the audience in the first scene."

"I don't believe it, though," somebody said.

Gilligan sighed. "Yeah, why do that?" he said, answering himself. "Why take away the drama?" He sighed again.

With lunchtime approaching, there was a marked increase in shifting in the writers' office chairs. In the center of the table, there were three categories of items. In ascending order of importance: things to play with (magnets, puzzles, paper clips, a lump of clay) things to write with (stacks of legal pads and index cards, a pretzel jar filled with pens and Sharpies), things to eat (candy and snacks of every description). Catlin was diligently involved in manufacturing miniature Mark Rothko reproductions using highlighters and index cards. There were more and more bathroom breaks and a brief conversational detour into quotes from *The Big Lebowski*. A small faction of the writers took a quick trip downstairs to see how extreme the temperature had gotten. The patter became slightly punch-drunk, as in an exchange about a scene, ultimately discarded, in which a character walks across the desert, dragging a dripping roller bag.

"What's in the suitcase, that you'd bother dragging across the scorching hot desert?"

"Dope."

"Money."

"Organs on ice."

"*Orchids?*"

"Yes, orchids. Rare orchids."

"Tulips. He's doing business with the Dutch and they demand payment in tulips."

Throughout it all, Gilligan kept up a stream of talk about the problem at hand, sometimes as if to himself. "Fuck," he finally said, spinning around in his chair. "Why is this so *hard*?"

Many options had already been explored: Jesse would be sent into a drug house to buy meth. He'd be sent to *sell* meth. It would be as simple as getting something out of the trunk of Mike's car or as complicated as becoming Gus's informant. Should it be two missions—one a failure, the other successful? *Three* missions?

Inevitably, the line between "What happens next?" and "Where's a character's head at?" began to blur. "By the end of the season, it should be that Jesse is torn between two friends, or masters . . . ," Gilligan said, groping toward a breakthrough.

"Just say 'lovers,'" said one of the writers.

"No, it's a custody battle! 'I don't know whether I want to live with Mom or Dad!'" Gilligan nearly shouted, grinning.

This instantly rang true. Jesse's relationship with Walt had always been that of a dysfunctional father and son. And the room's energy was suddenly refocused.

"Walt is like, 'He's trying to turn you against me, don't you see?'"

"His house is bigger than mine. Is that the problem?"

Gilligan was laughing: "'He's got a PlayStation. All I have is Sega.'"

The insight did little to overcome the immediate hurdle, but it added yet another thread to the dense psychological warp and weft of the series. One thing notably missing from the conversation was discussion of dialogue. In part, this was because that would fall under the purview of Schnauz when he took a finished outline and began to write his script. More than that, though, it spoke to Gilligan's approach to television.

"Historically, this has been a medium in which you say more than you show. You just didn't have the budgets and scheduling largesse that movies had, so you had to have two people in a room, talking it through," he said. As television budgets increased—along with the size and quality of televisions themselves—that had changed, and Gilligan was intent on taking advantage of the shift. *Breaking Bad* is by far the most visually stylized show of the Third Golden Age. It employs and empties the entire filmic bag of tricks—from high-speed time-lapse montages to wide-open landscapes that are more John Ford than anything a revisionist western like *Deadwood* could ever allow itself.

The signature shot, used at least once per episode, is a fish-eye view up from under or inside some improbable place—a table, a toilet, a bag, a massive chemical boiler. Seen once, it is a cool effect; twice through ten times, a self-conscious gimmick; sixty-five times, something approaching a guiding ethic.

At the same time, as behooves a story with chemistry at its heart, the show is obsessed with the concrete and literal. The camera lingers with intense curiosity on significant objects—a broken pair of glasses, a box cutter, the missing eye of a stuffed animal—and on processes, How Things Work: Walt shaving his head; an insistent finger of chemical pushing its way through a tube; the somber disassembly of a motorbike for disposal, after its young owner has stumbled, fatally, upon Walt and company robbing a train. A jaunty montage of Gus's meth distribution network, tucked into vats of fried chicken batter, played like a factory tour on 1970s *Sesame Street*.

All of this adds up to a commitment to visual storytelling that makes *Breaking Bad* a perfect complement to its hyperverbal network mate, *Mad Men*. Midway through season three, Gilligan said, Peter Gould had come up to him, beaming. "Look at my script that we're about to start shooting," Gould said. "I've counted and there's five uninterrupted pages where not a word of dialogue is spoken!"

"I was so proud of him," Gilligan said. "I was like, 'Yeah, man, that's something to be excited about! That excites me, too!'"

. . .

This afternoon, it seemed, little storytelling would be taking place—visual, verbal, or otherwise. Lunch came and went, with no answer to the Jesse question. "It's the kind of thing where we'll know it when we hear it," Gilligan said with genial resignation. "I just haven't heard it yet." Finally, the staff broke for the day. The discussion would take up another three days before being settled: Jesse would be explicitly instructed to guard the radio knobs in Mike's car while Mike ran errands—not *touch* the knobs, merely guard them. The detail was duly recorded on an index card and pinned to the bulletin board. At the end of the day, it would be included in a fifteen-page, single-spaced digest of daily notes. Then it was enshrined in an outline, to be fleshed out in Schnauz's script. That, in turn, was passed around for notes from each of the other writers and Gilligan himself, before being sent back for a revision. Eventually, it would make its way into the crisp white pages of a production draft.

Then the story moved onward: to the tone meeting, the production meeting, the table read. It was pored over by line producers, prop masters, location scouts, production designers, scenic designers, costume designers, directors, assistant directors, second assistant directors, and second second assistant directors—at each step becoming more real, as if slowly emerging from the shimmer of some distant desert horizon. Finally, it was off to New Mexico to be set, forever, on film.

And then it came to us: By fiber-optic cable, by the Internet, by digitally imprinted disk; into our homes, our bedrooms, the phones in our pockets; and we absorbed it, discussed it, argued about it, recapped it, pressed it on our friends. It became one more holy object in the communal sacrament that, thanks to the gods of business, technology, and creativity, TV had become in the early twenty-first century.

Somewhere along the line, the knobs were dropped. The task ended up as nothing more complicated than riding shotgun while picking up hidden packages of money in a series of remote locations. Unfolding as a montage, it took up eighty-two seconds of screen time.

Epilogue

Endings are the hardest part.

VINCE GILLIGAN

In the new world of television, now nearly fifteen years old, there may be nothing more unnatural than an ending. After all, the whole financial model of the medium depends on longevity, the long run, the gaudy number of seasons. In a perfect TV world, no door shuts forever, no show ever dies. As the song goes, "The movie never ends, it goes on and on and on and on. . . ."

It was the happy accident of the Third Golden Age that precisely that impulse, in the right hands, helped transform TV into not only a serious art form, but the dominant art form of the era. No endings came to mean no *crappy* endings, no cheap catharsis—new kinds of stories free to wend their way through an approximation of real life.

At the same time, we know that all shows have a natural life span, a period after which the intersection of overfamiliarity and overcontrivance starts producing diminishing returns. Rare is the show—thanks to commercial pressure and the myopia that comes from being too close to the action—that recognizes its organic expiration date until after it's passed. Remember what David Milch said: "There are some series that end halfway through and just don't know it."

Certainly the revolution in how we watch, where we watch, and what we watch goes on beyond the span of this book, just as it flowed out of events before it. Let's, then, honor the approach to endings taken by *The Wire*, which closed every season, including the last, with a montage of its characters and institutions, forever in motion, sailing into the future.

David Simon continued to work at HBO, moving toward the conclusion of *Treme*, his and Eric Overmyer's love letter to post–Hurricane Katrina New Orleans, rendered in both *The Wire*–like documentary detail and a deeply romantic blush. It was, he said, a kind of rejoinder to *The Wire*, a celebration of what the urban experiment does well, why it is necessary, in a city that nearly disappeared.

"You go into a bar in Kathmandu or Budapest and some form of African American music with a flatted third and a flatted seventh note has triumphed as almost the dominant musical form of the species. That could only happen and did only happen in an eight-square-block area of New Orleans. And it only happened because of a variety of things that are uniquely American. It's the greatest American export. This is what the city is capable of. This is what the city can give you," he said.

Simon had also increasingly become a kind of pundit laureate, a ranter in chief, particularly on the subjects of urban policy and the future of newspapers. He tacitly embraced the role by starting a blog titled *The Audacity of Despair*—as if his output were not already sufficiently prodigious or, for that matter, audacious and despairing. Oddly, for such a dedicated newsman, he explained the move to the Web in part as a way to circumvent traditional media, which, he said, often misinterpreted him.

In any event, it gave us the gift of an anecdote, from a family summer vacation in Italy: Simon and his teenage son were in Pisa, regarding the Leaning Tower. "I'm supposed to be the pessimist," he wrote. "I'm the guy who is reputedly drawn to a constant parsing of human failure. The Leaning Tower should be pretty much in my philosophical wheelhouse, right?"

Instead, he began thinking of other towers around the world— Seattle's Space Needle, the Shot Tower at home in Baltimore—and how they *didn't* lean.

I'm thinking to myself, "It's a Homeric fucking triumph that every other one doesn't just tilt on over. It's a victory for all of humanity that this one Italian edifice is world famous for doing what other structures just don't seem to do.

"Maybe there's cause for hope."

S imon's partner, spiritual twin, and worthy adversary, Ed Burns, left Baltimore. After *The Wire* and *Generation Kill*, he and his wife, Anna, moved to the rural panhandle of West Virginia, to a big house overlooking a hill up which deer come to nibble at the landscaping.

Burns did not work on *Treme*. "Ed recognizes two songs: One is by Van Morrison, and the other one isn't," Simon said. "He didn't dig this show." After a decade the men also needed a break from each other. But the newly bucolic surroundings did nothing to diminish Burns's energy—every third or fourth sentence seemed to be about a new project, a possible collaboration, an amazing new book he'd read. The small city nearest his house was both a victim of the recession and a stop on the drug pipeline east toward Washington and Baltimore. Burns was busy spearheading an ambitious educational reform program there, based on the philosophy of Harlem's Geoffrey Canada. An intrepid development executive, one who managed to find West Virginia on a map, could rent a truck, head up the dirt road, scratch Burns's bemused surface, and watch ideas flow like sap from a maple. One hopes that Simon is the one who does it instead.

As for *The Wire* actors, they suffered the fate of all actors: the need to work, even if, in some cases, they'd already done the best work of their lives. Some rode the prestige of the show to fine second acts: Idris Elba as cop and classic difficult man in the BBC series *Luther*, as well as in softer roles, like a guest stretch on *The Office*; Wendell Pierce and Clarke Peters in *Treme*. Others popped up in awkward places—commercials, network sci-fi and teen dramas—causing severe cognitive dissonance. Given the still limited range and number of roles for African American actors, many members didn't pop up at all.

. . .

*T*he *Sopranos* alumni likewise ended up spread across the new TV landscape. Terence Winter and Matt Weiner assumed showrunner status. Robin Green and Mitchell Burgess moved back to working successfully on more conventional network and basic cable shows. Todd Kessler was beginning a new post-*Damages* project.

Edie Falco slid over to Showtime, to star in *Nurse Jackie*, where she was finally the top antihero: an addicted, adulterous, morally compromised nurse, though still only in a half-hour format. And James Gandolfini, the man on whose broad, burdened shoulders the Third Golden Age was borne into our lives, was blessedly allowed to leave Tony Soprano behind. He acted on Broadway and in movies, produced two HBO documentaries about the effects of post-traumatic stress disorder on returning soldiers, was involved in a long-gestating biopic of Ernest Hemingway and a pilot for a new HBO series, co-written by Richard Price, with the most un-HBO-sounding name, *Criminal Justice*. In 2009, he bought a big house with a long driveway, deep in the New Jersey suburbs. News reports said it was invisible from the street.

*C*hris Albrecht's post-HBO time in the wilderness was brief. By the end of 2007, he had accepted a position as the head of the talent management titan IMG Global Media and a partnership in its parent company, Forstmann Little & Co. In December 2009, he became the president of Starz, another pay movie channel hoping for a transformation through the magic of original programming. Carolyn Strauss moved deftly from the buyer's side of the table at HBO to the seller's, executive-producing three of the network's highest-profile series: *Treme*, David Milch's *Luck*, and the fantasy adaptation *Game of Thrones*.

It was a list that pretty much summed up the range of dramatic programming on HBO thirteen years after *The Sopranos* debuted. *True Blood*, kept from pure pulpdom by Alan Ball's hand and a patina of racial and sexual allegory, was the network's biggest hit since Tony left the scene. The show posited

northern Louisiana as a menagerie of beautiful, horny half-humans of seemingly infinite variety.

This was one end of the new HBO spectrum: big, splashy productions that
wore their budgets on their sleeves. Here was where genre pieces had settled:
the vampire soap opera, the 1920s gangster saga (Terence Winter's *Boardwalk
Empire*), the fantasy epic (*Game of Thrones*). It was also, in the spirit of HBO's
earliest days, where you found almost comically gratuitous sex, often in the
background during otherwise boring but necessary scenes. The critic Myles
McNutt coined a term for it: "sexposition." The basic cable barbarians may
have eaten away at chunks of HBO's brand, but, now and forever, there would
always be boobs.

On the other end of the spectrum, there was space seemingly reserved for
showrunners emeriti to explore their private obsessions outside the confines
of genre or even traditional drama. For Simon, it was New Orleans; for Milch,
the world of the racetrack. After *Deadwood*, *John from Cincinnati*, and an
abortive pilot set in 1970s New York, Milch came to *Luck* under a set of new
rules. To executive-produce, HBO brought in Michael Mann—a film director
accustomed to the power and primacy writers usually enjoyed on TV shows.
Milch was barred from visiting the set and the editing room. It was, he admitted, an adjustment.

"It's been absolutely different, but it hasn't been awful. It's a different discipline, a different experience," he said midway through the first season.
"Learning to live with the given is the great humbling educational process of
life. And I've had a sufficiency of education this past year." As it turned out, the
education was not complete; *Luck* suffered the same fate as its predecessors.
After three horses broke down and needed to be euthanized during production of the first two seasons, HBO abruptly suspended filming. A day later, the
network canceled the show outright. Despite the woes, it appeared that the
charm Milch exerted over network executives remained undiminished. With
his daughter, he was already involved in developing a project for HBO based
on the novels of William Faulkner. As the network's Sue Naegle said, "You
want to help him achieve his vision. It's transcendent."

The most notable change at HBO, as the Bush years faded in memory and the Obama era proceeded, was that its programs no longer seemed as intent on challenging its viewers with characters from the other side of the sociopolitical spectrum. When the final polygamous Mormon of the underrated *Big Love* left the screen, we were left with the liberated pansexuals of *True Blood*, the spoiled Brooklyn strivers of *Girls*, the twee Brooklynites of *Bored to Death*, the bloviating, middlebrow liberal superheroes of Aaron Sorkin's *The Newsroom*. Watching HBO, it seemed, was now less about discovering new worlds and hearing new viewpoints and more about seeing oneself.

O f the men who brought the Third Golden Age to basic cable, Peter Liguori was the most peripatetic since leaving FX, logging time as the chairman of entertainment at Fox Broadcasting, the COO and senior vice president of Discovery Communications, a consultant at the Carlyle Group, and, finally, CEO of the troubled Tribune Co. Kevin Reilly, after a stay at NBC—where he developed the fine, cablelike *Friday Night Lights*, among others, landed back at Fox Broadcasting, as chairman of entertainment. He had several big hits but complained that he couldn't get A-list actors to come work for the network. They wanted to act only on cable.

Chic Eglee, the writer on *The Shield* who had worked in television going back to the MTM days, said that Shawn Ryan was the showrunner who most reminded him of Steven Bochco—a man with the creative nimbleness and strength of ambition to be the builder of a TV empire. For a little while, it did seem that all of Fox Studios ran through Ryan's office. Moving back and forth between cable and broadcast, Ryan said, didn't faze him.

"I can write a poem in free verse and enjoy writing that poem," he said. "But now if someone says, 'Write a haiku,' I'm not going to bitch about the restrictions. I'm going to say, 'What's the best poem I can write by haiku rules?'"

None of Ryan's shows, though, approached the success of *The Shield*. Two in a row, *Terriers* for FX and *The Chicago Code* for Fox, were canceled after one season. Eventually he left Fox for ABC, where he debuted *Last Resort,* a big, splashy, very network show about a nuclear submarine gone rogue. That show, too, ended after only thirteen episodes.

In the years after *The Shield* and *Rescue Me* and *Damages*, FX had turned the testosterone dial even further up on its dramatic series—most notably in *Sons of Anarchy* and *Justified*, a neo-western adapted from the work of Elmore Leonard. The subversive, boundary-pushing, devil-may-care spirit of the network's early shows was funneled more into comedies—a gleefully profane string of them, from the cerebral shocks of *Louie* and *Wilfred* to the raucous vulgarity of *It's Always Sunny in Philadelphia* and *The League*. Louis C.K.'s *Louie*, which the comedian wrote, directed, edited, and starred in, suggested yet another model of auteurship, in which creative freedom was granted in exchange for tiny budgets. The approach was not without its risks, as *BrandX with Russell Brand*, also on FX, proved.

By 2013, the small group of executives who had brought *Mad Men* and *Breaking Bad* to AMC had all moved on, largely because of friction with new management. Rob Sorcher ran the Cartoon Network; Jeremy Elice and Christina Wayne were both on the producing side of the development table. The network would retreat into brandable genres and have by far its biggest ratings hit with *The Walking Dead*, a zombie horror show created by Frank Darabont, based on a comic book, and later run by *The Shield* alum Glen Mazzara. Despite the show's overwhelming success, Mazzara, too, would leave after two seasons, the network citing "a difference of opinion about where the show should go moving forward." Combined with the ouster of the creator of one of its other original series, *Hell on Wheels*, about the building of the transcontinental railroad, and its very public contract battles with Matthew Weiner, the network that had given the world *Mad Men* and *Breaking Bad* had developed a reputation for, of all things, having trouble playing well with showrunners.

And what of their revolution? In 2012, no Emmy nominee for Outstanding Drama Series was from a traditional broadcast network. (Except for PBS's *Downton Abbey,* all appeared on cable.) Nobody evinced much surprise at this development. Where once the broadcast networks had reserved a spot on their schedules for prestige, quality drama, even if just as award bait, they had long since ceded that niche to cable. Even when acting with the best of intentions—trying to keep alive a show like *Friday Night Lights*, whose only crime was not having been a cable show—the networks proved time and again that, when it came to one-hour drama, they were simply out of the quality business.

To judge by the torrent of film people lining up to work in television, the same was true of the movie business. There might have been no more emblematic moment than when Martin Scorsese, hero of the seventies New Cinema, signed on to be an executive producer of *Boardwalk Empire* and to direct its pilot. Soon afterward, Dustin Hoffman was starring in *Luck*. Steven Soderbergh, a Scorsese of the indie film movement, was right behind them. After directing thirty-three movies, large and small, he told the Associated Press, he was giving up and switching to television. "American movie audiences now just don't seem to be very interested in any kind of ambiguity or any kind of real complexity of character or narrative," he said. "I think those qualities are now being seen on television and that people who want to see stories that have those kinds of qualities are watching television."

So, could we pull the *Six Feet Under* trick from *its* finale and slide forward— see where we'll all be in two, five, ten years' time?

The artistic triumphs of the Third Golden Age were the product of creative opportunism in the face of dislocation, confusion, and low stakes. The men and women who took advantage of the moment were working below the radar, without a map, and with all the incentive in the world to take wild risks. Of course, the very things those circumstances allow—success and innovation—are the very things all but guaranteed to change them. Thus we've seen the locus of TV's best work hopscotch across the dial: from HBO to FX to AMC to wherever it lands next. All had brilliant first acts in the Third Golden Age, and although they certainly produced quality work afterward, none was equal to its first, thrilling wave. By the evidence, this is a structural problem, perhaps never to be overcome.

The good news is that there is seemingly no end to the number of places for quality to alight next. By 2012, the drive toward original programming was ubiquitous, not only among cable networks but with all the other ever-multiplying, ever more fragmented platforms and systems used to deliver media. There was a new profusion of innovative deals from entities not previously thought of as content producers. Netflix had original programming. So did Hulu. DirecTV believed it was in its best interest to get involved directly with the resuscitation of shows no longer considered viable on either cable (*Damages*) or network (*Friday Night Lights*). It had become clear, in a landscape of infinite choice, that content was the only identity any "channel" could claim.

The other, related, cause for hope was the new economic reality that "success" no longer requires a huge, or even very large, audience. As long as there is no true consensus audience for anything—or at least as long as the chase for one is relegated to the broadcast networks and the multiplexes—quality storytelling, fresh voices, challenging ideas, all the hallmarks of the Third Golden Age, may be able to remain another brand, a niche, right alongside home improvement, cute puppies, and weather disasters.

Shawn Ryan, surprisingly, had the bleakest view of what might be to come. He looked at the bland, populist, nominally "quirky" shows on more family-friendly cable networks and imagined executives getting spoiled by their relative success. He invoked the blockbuster films of the late seventies that Peter Biskind, in his seminal *Easy Rider* and *Raging Bull*, blamed for the downfall of the New Hollywood. "I'm saying USA shows are the equivalent of *Jaws* and *Star Wars*," he said.

David Milch had a different take. "I think we're in such a state of fluidity in terms of the changing of the market and form that in five years this conversation is gonna seem childish," he said. "I couldn't tell you for the life of me what the new paradigm is gonna be, but something absolutely different is gonna be going on."

A s for David Chase: He would not have approved of this exercise. He had already made his views on endings perfectly clear.

The final scene of *The Sopranos* had begun to take shape two years before it was written, when Albrecht approached Chase, asking him to start thinking of a way to end the series. "He wanted us to write toward something, have a definitive ending, so that the last episode was like the end of a movie or a book," Chase said. He had never considered the luxury of constructing an ending to be a foregone conclusion. Shows, most of them, just disappeared one day, resolution or not. And it was both in Chase's temperament and crucial to his ongoing creativity to assume that the same would be true of *The Sopranos*, regardless of how successful it had been. Nevertheless, he said, "Chris asked, 'Are you up for that?' I thought about it, and I was."

The notion of an ending presented a problem, however. Mob story convention suggested a limited number of options for a boss: Tony in jail, Tony becoming a rat and going into hiding, Tony killed. None felt right to Chase.

"The object of all these shows in the past had always been, the protagonist pays for his sins. Crime doesn't pay. Well, that's false. Crime *does* pay. Having done the show for all that time, I knew that crime paid," he said.

For five and a half seasons, the show had been distinguished and animated by a worldview and storytelling philosophy that rejected easy endings, dismissed cheap catharsis, insisted that life was more complicated than that. If this insistence sometimes drove the audience crazy—what the *hell* ever happened to the Russian whom Christopher and Paulie shot in "Pine Barrens"?—it was also inseparable from what had made the series great.

As Chase described it, the answer came impressionistically. One early idea was that Tony would be last seen heading off into Manhattan for a meeting with New York boss Johnny Sack (who would have been left alive, rather than felled by cancer). As the Rolling Stones' "The Last Time" played, Tony would descend into the same Lincoln Tunnel from which we had seen him emerge at the very beginning, on his way to who-knew-what fate.

Soon afterward, though, other images began coming to Chase. "I saw this diner. Actually, the diner I pictured was a diner across from the Santa Monica Airport. Why it would be there, I don't know. But the spark was *Nighthawks*, the Edward Hopper painting. Like everybody else, I've always been taken with that painting. I always thought it would have made a good series, about those four people in the diner."

The painting had been the subject of an argument between Chase and his wife. Denise, like many, saw it as the embodiment of loneliness. "But I don't

see it that way," he said. "Because it's in the light. In the middle of all this darkness, they're in the light. And they're talking to each other. There's a little
community in there. If you were walking along that street at night, and you
saw that place, you'd want to go in."

This had been a recurring image in *The Sopranos*, ever since the family
(small "f") had gathered at Vesuvio during a storm in the final scene of season
one. "What does the ending mean?" Chase said. "I don't know if it means this,
but a lot of it had to do with people huddled against the cold. It was a repeat of
that scene: there's a storm outside and they're in a place where there's food,
and light, and warmth, and human companionship."

Now, though, as the family gathered over onion rings at a Jersey diner
called Holsten's, there was also something else: menace, in the person of a
mysterious "Man in Members Only Jacket." Though perhaps the point was
that it was always there, lurking on the periphery. In any event, the answer
was not forthcoming. Instead—to the strains of Journey's "Don't Stop Be-
lievin'"—we got one last look at Tony's quizzical face, no closer to an answer
than he had been when we first met, and then . . . darkness. Ten long seconds of
it. Millions across the country believed their cable systems had gone out at the
worst possible moment.

Chase remembered telling Carolyn Strauss about the plan, which was
originally to sustain the black screen throughout the entire length of what
would have been the credits. (That was scratched after the Directors Guild objected.) "I think she was like, 'Oookaaay . . . ,'" he said. "I don't remember if she
asked, 'What does it mean?' But what I would have said was, 'It's not what you
think. It's what you *feel*.' That's what I was always trying to go for."

At the cast's final table read, the last page of the script was met with
stunned silence. "Nobody moved. It was like none of us wanted to leave,"
Chase said. Then Falco began to cry softly. Chase looked at Gandolfini, to
gauge his reaction. It was the same as it had been at eighty-five previous such
readings: He closed his script. He stared into space for several long moments.
And then he pushed his chair back and got up from the table.

Three days after the final episode aired, Chase was in France while a
small maelstrom over the finale raged at home. Talking by phone, he came as

close as he ever would to saying that Tony Soprano met his end in that diner booth. "Everything that pertains to that episode was in that episode. And it was in the episode before that and the one before that and seasons before this one and so on," he said. "There had been indications of what the end is like. That's the way things happen: it's already going on by the time you even notice it."

"Are you saying . . . ?" came the question.

"I'm not saying anything," he said. "And I'm not trying to be coy. It's just that I think that to explain it would diminish it."

Which was not to say that, for all his dim view of human nature and the course of history, he did not believe in happy endings—or at least progress:

> People have said that the Soprano family's whole life goes in the toilet in the last episode. That the parents' whole twisted lifestyle is visited on the children. And that's true—to a certain extent. But look at it: A.J.'s not going to become a citizen-soldier or join the Peace Corps to try to help the world; he'll probably be a low-level movie producer. But he's not going to be a killer like his father, is he? Meadow may not become a pediatrician or even a lawyer, but she's not going to be a housewife-whore like her mother. She'll learn to operate in the world in a way that Carmela never did. It's not ideal. It's not what the parents dreamed of. But it's better than it was. Tiny, little bits of progress—that's how it works.

"Go look at Albert Camus's *Myth of Sisyphus*," the supposed misanthrope went on. "Life seems to have no purpose, but we have to go on behaving as though it does. We have to go on behaving toward each other like people who would try to love."

Half a decade later, now sixty-seven, he sat in the study of his huge apartment in a historic building on the Upper East Side. He had just, finally, completed his first feature film—a music-filled New Jersey coming-of-age story, originally called *Twylight Zones*. As with *The Sopranos*, there had been pressure to change the title; this time, however, Chase had agreed to the change. The film, which would open the 2012 New York Film Festival, would do so under the name *Not Fade Away*.

It had been a difficult experience—physically exhausting and, he said, artistically challenging. After years of working on *The Sopranos*, he had grown used to a certain way of telling stories. "I had gotten used to the idea that things could be taken back and fixed. Or that we could go take a little excursion, check out Patsy Parisi's wife or something. I thought I had cut all that out, but I really hadn't. The script was too discursive. So we had a lot of film that had to be cut," he said.

The voices of *The Sopranos* characters rarely popped into his head anymore, he said. Occasionally, he or Denise would quote a line to each other: "Oh, poor you," or, "You go about in pity for yourself." The much-speculated-on idea of a *Sopranos* movie, picking up where the series had left off, was a nonstarter—the end was the end—but the idea of a prequel, or expanding a tangential story, had occurred to him. "Maybe Johnny Boy"—Tony's father—"and that period. That's interesting to me. Or something you saw hints of during *The Sopranos*. Like, 'What was production like on *Cleaver* [Christopher's fictional pulp mobster/horror movie]?'"

Despite the rigors of *Not Fade Away*, and the fact that he was writing a miniseries about the history of Hollywood for HBO, he was still insistent on focusing on feature films: "Someone once said that movies are a cathedral, and I still do feel that. A cathedral is big. It's epic. It's intense."

And another series wasn't in the cards. "The chances of me doing it as well again are almost nil. Plus, I'm not a kid anymore, I don't have that much time to keep fucking around, giving five years to a TV series," he said. Then he added, "But it's not because movies are a more creative place. Not at all."

As concessions went, it was the equivalent of his view of progress—incremental, but not insignificant. And it would have to do—paired, perhaps, with something he had said in an optimistic moment toward the end of *The Sopranos*: "Look, I can't argue with destiny. This is what happened. And I'm very lucky that as I lie on my deathbed I won't have to say, 'I accomplished nothing.' I did something, you know?"

Acknowledgments

Thanks, first and foremost, are due to the people who so generously shared with me their time and stories. That includes, with few exceptions, all the major players in this story as well as dozens of other writers, producers, directors, executives, actors, cinematographers, assistants, and so on. All did as much to create the Third Golden Age as they did to animate these pages. To the many who are not explicitly mentioned—or who preferred to go nameless—please know that I nevertheless relied on, and valued, your wisdom, insights, and perspectives.

Three significant interviewees did not live to see the project's end. I am especially grateful for having had the chance to meet and learn from Henry Bromell, David Mills, and Stephen J. Cannell and to include their voices here.

At The Penguin Press, I will forever be grateful to Eamon Dolan for his early faith in me and this project; to Colin Dickerman for patiently and expertly shaping the result; and to Laura Stickney for a pleasant, if too brief, assist. Likewise to my agent, Daniel Greenberg, for his support and guidance, and to his colleague, Lindsay Edgecombe. I thank Jim Nelson and my other colleagues at *GQ* for their inspiration, indulgence, and friendship: Mark Lotto, Devin Friedman, Dan Fierman, Amy Wallace, Mary Kaye Schilling, and Alex Pappademas, among them. For close, perceptive, and immeasurably helpful reads and feedback, thank you to both Michael Oates Palmer and my old *Time Out New York* cubicle mate, Jason Zinoman. William Bostwick began this project nominally as my "assistant" but has since grown into a valued colleague; I fully expect to be working for him someday.

For aid—logistical, spiritual, and otherwise—along the way, I'd also like to thank the following: Diego Aldana, Theano Apostolou, Leslee Dart, John Solberg, Tobe Becker, Nancy Lesser, and Chuck Slocum; Adam Mazmanian, Jenny Ewing Allen, Brett Anderson, Nathalie Jordi, Pableaux Johnson, Rien Fertel, J Dagney, Chris Hannah, Adam Blank, and David Hirmes. It remains true that this could not have been done without the skill, good company, and forbearance of Jennifer Fistere.

To my parents, who once bribed me with a suction-cup bow-and-arrow set to watch no television for a month, I forgive you. To Scott Martin, who fortified and distracted me with yaka mein and companionship in the final stages of writing, I welcome you to our family's new city. And to Kira Henehan, my indispensable, beloved gumshoe and partner, I hope my gratitude is evident every day.

Notes on Sources

Except where noted below and in the text, the material in this book is derived from original reporting and author interviewing.

Prologue

On Victorian serialized novels, I consulted David Payne's *The Re-Enchantment of Nineteenth-Century Fiction: Dickens, Thackeray, George Eliot and Serialization* (Basingstoke and New York: Palgrave Macmillan, 2005); *Author and Printer in Victorian England* by Allan C. Dooley (Charlottesville: University of Virginia Press, 1992); and, in particular, "No Time to Be Idle: The Serial Novel and Popular Imagination," an essay by Shawn Crawford (*World & I* 13 [November 1998]: 323–32). Here and elsewhere, I also draw on my own *The Sopranos: The Book,* produced for HBO in 2007 by Melcher Media and accompanied by an episode guide assembled by Mimi O'Connor.

Chapter One: In This Maligned Medium

On MTM Enterprises and the Second Golden Age, I found two books to be invaluable: *Television's Second Golden Age: From* Hill Street Blues *to* ER, by Robert J. Thompson (New York: Continuum Publishing, 1996); and *MTM "Quality Television,"* edited by Jane Feuer, Paul Kerr, and Tise Vahimagi (London: British Film Institute Publishing, 1985). Also helpful for context was "Television's Real A-Team" by David Freeman (*Esquire* magazine, January 1985) and "How I'd Fix Network TV" by Steven Bochco (*Los Angeles Times*, August 16, 1992).

Chapter Two: Which Films?

The 2007 *Vanity Fair* profile to which David Chase refers is "An American Family" by Peter Biskind (April 2007). Stephen J. Cannell was interviewed extensively for the Archive of American Television, which is a deep and wonderful resource for anyone interested in how TV gets made.

Chapter Three: A Great Notion

On the early history and economics of HBO, I relied heavily on *Inside HBO: The Billion Dollar War Between HBO, Hollywood and the Home Video Revolution* by George Mair (New York: Dodd, Mead & Co., 1988).

Chapter Five: Difficult Men

Some of the analysis in this chapter was aided and abetted by Susan Faludi's *Stiffed: The Betrayal of the American Man* (New York: William Morrow & Co., 1999), which I'm grateful to have been pointed toward by Todd Kessler. Also useful, for Scott Sassa's unfortunate quote about cable vs. network, among other details about Alan Ball and *Six Feet Under*, was "The Next Big Bet" by Tad Friend (*The New Yorker*, May 15, 2001). The economics of basic cable bundling were summarized nicely in a National Public Radio report, "'Where's My AMC?' DISH Network Dispute Drags On," by Lauren Silverman, aired September 13, 2012.

Chapter Six: The Arguer

Both *Homicide: A Year on the Killing Streets* and *The Corner: A Year in the Life of an Inner-City Neighborhood* are essential reading. Some of David Simon's account of his year spent at BPD's Homicide Unit, as well as his disillusionment with and divorce from the *Baltimore Sun*, comes from his afterword to the 2006 Holt Paperbacks reprint of *Homicide*. The tension between Simon and Charles Dutton on the set of HBO's *The Corner* was the subject of "Who Gets to Tell a Black Story?" by Janny Scott (*New York Times*, June 11, 2000).

Chapter Seven: The Magic Hubig's

David Simon's letter to Carolyn Strauss was reprinted in *The Wire: Truth Be Told* by Rafael Alvarez (Edinburgh: Canongate Books, 2009) and also quoted in "Stealing Life" by Margaret Talbot (*The New Yorker*, October 22, 2007). Simon's account of "Little" Melvin Williams's drug empire and its downfall ran in the *Baltimore Sun* from January 11–15,1987. Several quotes from the novelists who worked on *The Wire* come from "Baltimore's Finest" by Alex Pappademas (*GQ*, December 2008).

Chapter Eight: Being the Boss

The account of David Chase's appearance at New York's Museum of Modern Art was informed, among other sources, by "Leaving the Family" (*Newark Star-Ledger*, February 14, 2001).

Chapter Nine: A Big Piece of Equipment

The documentary *Without a Net: Creating NYPD Blue* (later subtitled *David Milch's Creative Process*), directed by Marc Ostrick, is everything its two subtitles promise: a candid, fly-on-the-wall record of Milch's final year at *NYPD Blue* and a vivid portrait of his unusual methods. Also very useful was "The Misfit" by Mark Singer (*The New Yorker*, February 14, 2005); the essay "Robert Penn Warren, David Milch and the Literary Contexts of *Deadwood*" by Joseph Millichap, collected in *Reading Deadwood: A Western to Swear By*, edited by David Lavery (London: I. B. Tauris, 2006); and *Deadwood: Stories of the Black Hills* by David Milch, interviews by David Samuels, produced by Melcher Media (New York: Bloomsbury USA, 2006), a veritable bonanza of Milchiana from which several of the on-set anecdotes are drawn.

Chapter Ten: Have a Take. Try Not to Suck

David Simon's charges against star *Sun* reporter Jim Haner were laid out in "Favorite Son" by Abigail Pogrebin (*Brill's Content*, October 2000). Other details are from "Stealing Life" by Margaret Talbot, referenced above.

Chapter Eleven: Shooting the Dog

Amy Wallace's profile of Chris Albrecht, "Violence, Nudity, Adult Content," appeared in the November 2010 issue of *GQ*. On *Rescue Me*, I drew from the preface by Denis Leary and Peter Tolan in *Rescue Me Uncensored: The Official Companion* (New York: Newmarket Press, 2007).

Chapter Twelve: See You at the Emmys

Alone among the major showrunners covered here, Matthew Weiner declined, politely, to sit for interviews specific to this book. I was, however, able to draw on our multiple conversations in other contexts and on the truly heroic amount of talking he's done on behalf of *Mad Men* elsewhere. Chief among those sources were an hour-long interview conducted by Weiner's sister Allison Hope Weiner for her video podcast *Media Mayhem* and "'Mad Men' Has Its Moment" by Alex Witchel (*New York Times Magazine*, June 22, 2008). Some quotes here come from my own articles: "Breakout: Jon Hamm" (*GQ*, December 2008) and "The Men Behind the Curtain: A *GQ* TV Roundtable" (*GQ*, June 2012). The latter is also the source of David Milch and Vince Gilligan quotes elsewhere.

Index

ABC, 45, 97, 175, 228
advertisers and advertising
    act-outs preceding commercial breaks, 224
    influence on content, 85–87
    sensibilities of, 217, 220, 221
African American actors and audience, 51,
    130–31, 140, 152
Albert, Lisa, 252
Albrecht, Chris
    arrest and dismissal from HBO, 236
    background in entertainment, 55–56
    on cancellation of *Deadwood,* 232–33
    on *The Corner,* 131
    on Gandolfini as Tony Soprano character,
        67–68
    on HBO's failures, 231
    on HBO's successful formula, 212
    on hospitable environment for artists at HBO,
        229–30
    on *John from Cincinnati,* 235
    on *Lucky Louie,* 230, 231
    positions at HBO, 55–56, 229, 236
    on Simon's pitch style, 200–201
    on *The Sopranos* "College" episode, 92–93
    on *The Sopranos* pilot, 65–66, 69
    successful series produced, 57–58, 229
    work after dismissal from HBO, 281
    working relationship with Strauss, 55, 57, 237
Almost Grown, 45, 69, 73, 75
Alvarez, Rafael, 113, 115–16, 125, 144–45

AMC. See also *Breaking Bad; Mad Men*
    Broken Trail, 247, 271
    Emmy awards, 247
    internal problems, 284
    original-programming strategy, 246–47
    transformation from commercial-free
        network, 245–46
    The Walking Dead, 284
American Beauty (film), 95, 107
antihero principle, 4–6, 87–88, 175, 222,
    267–68

Ball, Alan
    American Beauty (film), 95, 107
    on antiheroes, 106
    approach by HBO with funeral home concept,
        95, 96–97
    Oh, Grow Up, 97–98
    post-traumatic stress, 97–98
    praise for *The Sopranos,* 94–95
    Six Feet Under, 4, 60, 98–104, 107
    supportive showrunner style, 102–3
    True Blood, 107, 281–82
basic cable. *See* cable dramas
Bedard, Bridget, 252–53, 255, 260
Bewkes, Jeff, 55, 56, 229, 237
Bianchi, Ed, 184
Biskind, Peter, 160, 286
black actors and audience, 51, 130–31, 140, 152
Boardwalk Empire, 5, 232, 282, 285

Bochco, Steven
    approach by MTM for police drama, 27–28
    autocratic showrunner style, 30
    creative autonomy, 28, 29
    on creativity in television writing, 32
    dismissal from MTM, 32
    on disparagement of television, 23
    failures, 174
    Hill Street Blues, 28–32, 172–74
    NYPD Blue, 174–78
    on working with Milch, 172–74, 177
Bradbury, Ray, 23
Brand, Joshua, 51–55, 156
Braun, Lloyd, 58, 65
Brazil, Scott, 218
Breaking Bad
    acquisition by AMC, 270–71
    antihero protagonist, 267–68
    concept for, 266–68
    female character, 5, 267
    New Mexico production location, 272
    pilot, 269
    pitches for, 268–70
    references to current events, 272
    visual storytelling, 276
    writers' room, 264–65, 271–77
Broken Trail, 247, 271
Bromell, Henry
    on Chase as showrunner, 161
    on Chase's writing, 45, 52–53
    on new approach at HBO, 231
    on pressure of showrunning, 9
    sketch of television history, 24
Bronchtein, Henry, 243–44
Burgess, Mitchell
    Almost Grown, 45
    on Chase's ambition, 78
    Emmy award, 168
    Northern Exposure, 75
    on quality of *The Sopranos,* 70
    The Sopranos, 74–75, 159, 162, 169, 243
    work after *The Sopranos,* 281
Burns, Ed
    background and learning experiences,
        120–22
    as Baltimore police officer, 109–10, 122–25,
        136–38
    book collaboration with Simon, 125–27
    exclusion from *The Corner* writing staff,
        130–31
    Generation Kill, 119, 207
    responsibilities after Colesberry's death, 199
    on *The Shield,* 223–24
    The Wire as social activism for, 135
    The Wire pilot script, 136–38
    in *The Wire* writers' room, 143–46, 192–96,
        199–200, 207–8

    work after *The Wire* and *Generation Kill,*
        208, 280

cable dramas
    actors' job insecurity, 196
    antihero principle, 4–6, 87–88, 175, 222,
        267–68
    bond between viewer and show, 16–17
    in cable operator packages, 86, 212
    as distinct and dominant art form, 11, 278
    female characters, 5, 13, 227
    literary storytelling structure, 6–7, 60
    male-focused programming, 13–14
    male inner struggle, 84, 104–6, 189–90, 228
    opening credits, 15–16
    pilots, 59–61
    powerful showrunners, 8–9, 72–73, 148
    producers' responsibilities, 25n
    quality of, 14, 285–86
    season length, 6, 204–5
    technologies affecting audience, 14–16, 31, 32,
        85, 155, 203, 277
    timeline, x–xi
    traditional genres, 84, 260
    unresolved endings, 120, 278
    writers' rooms, 70–73
Cablevision. *See* AMC
Cahill, Jason, 76
Cannell, Stephen J., 25–26, 41–42, 86
Carnivàle, 230
Carter, Chris, 265–66
Castleman, Dan, 75
Catlin, Sam, 271, 274
CBS, 45, 64, 169, 215
Chase, David. *See also Sopranos, The*
    Almost Grown, 45, 69, 73
    as director, 65–66
    disdain for television, 8, 34–35, 45
    Emmy awards, 44, 168
    experiences inspiring *The Sopranos,* 35–36,
        38, 62–63
    failed pilots, 61–62
    fame, 156
    I'll Fly Away, 52–54, 65, 75
    interest in filmmaking, 37–39, 44–45, 69,
        289–90
    Kolchak: The Night Stalker, 39–40
    negative temperament, 35, 52, 53–54,
        64, 105
    Northern Exposure, 53–55, 73, 75
    Off the Minnesota Strip, 43–44, 62–63
    power and autonomy as showrunner, 8, 159,
        161–62, 252, 258
    primitive impulses, 88–89
    The Rockford Files, 42–43, 73
    on showrunning, 73–74
    and Simon, compared, 111–12

start of television career, 39–40
worry and stress, 156, 160–61
Chernin, Peter, 213, 220
Chiklis, Michael, 218–19, 223
C.K., Louis, 230, 284
Cleveland, Rick, 101
Close, Glenn, 227
Colesberry, Bob, 131, 140–41, 191, 198
Collins, Chris, 143–44
Corner, The: A Year in the Life of an Inner-City
    Neighborhood (Burns and Simon), 126–27
Corner, The (miniseries), 130–32
Corrado, Regina, 186–87, 189
Coulter, Allen, 90
Curry, Jack, 49

Damages, 12, 13, 166–67, 227
Deadwood
    cancellation, 232–34
    as classic American narrative, 181
    female characters, 5
    Milch's work process and style, 183–87
    repurposed pitch for, 178–81
    themes and characters, 4, 181–83
Def Comedy Jam, 51, 130
Dexter, 6, 12
Dirt, 269
Dolan, Charles, 47, 48
Doman, John, 150
"Doug & Dad," 55
Dunham, Lena, 211–12
Dutton, Charles "Roc," 131, 132

Eglee, Charles "Chic," 218, 283
Elba, Idris, 140, 197–98, 280
Elice, Jeremy, 220–21, 247, 254–55, 270, 284

Falco, Edie
    as actress, 1
    audition for The Sopranos, 68–69
    Emmy awards, 96, 168
    at final episode of The Sopranos, 288
    work after The Sopranos, 281
Falsey, John, 46, 51–52, 54
Fin-Syn Rules (Financial Interest and
    Syndication Rules), 26, 32
Fitzgerald, Susie, 56, 61, 67, 79
Fogel, Alexa, 139–40
Fontana, Tom, 57, 127–28
Four Arguments for the Elimination of Television
    (Mander), 23–24
Free Fire Zone (Rebeck), 176
Frolov, Diane, 54, 158
Fuchs, Michael, 48, 55, 56
FX. See also Shield, The
    Breaking Bad ownership and sale, 269–71
    Damages, 12, 13, 166–67, 227

Dirt, 269
Justified, 284
Louie, 230, 284
Nip/Tuck, 227
offices, 214–15
original programming and brand identity, 86,
    212–14, 228–29
profane and violent programming, 214,
    226, 284
Rescue Me, 4, 105–6, 227–28
Sons of Anarchy, 226, 284

Game of Thrones, 235, 281, 282
Gandolfini, James
    casting of, 67–68, 69
    Emmy award, 168
    erratic behavior, 1–3, 17, 157
    work after The Sopranos, 281
Generation Kill, 119, 207
Gilliam, Seth, 57, 149, 150–51, 152, 194
Gilligan, Vince. See also Breaking Bad
    on credit for script writing, 259
    on difficulty of television production, 11
    feature films, 265, 266
    supportive showrunner style, 264–65
    visual approach to storytelling, 275–76
    The X-Files, 265–66
Girls, 211
Glazer, Mitch, 241
Gould, Peter, 271, 276
Green, Robin
    Almost Grown, 45
    Emmy award, 168
    on Milch's erratic behavior, 174
    Northern Exposure, 51, 75
    The Sopranos, 74–75, 78, 162, 168–70, 243
    work after The Sopranos, 281
    on working with Weiner, 244
Greenblatt, Bob, 64, 99
Grey, Brad, 25n, 65
Griffiths, Rachel, 100, 103
Gyllenhaal, Stephen, 128

Hall, Barbara, 14, 51, 52, 70
Hamm, Jon, 249–51
HBO. See also Deadwood; Sopranos, The;
    Wire, The
    adult themes and gratuitous sex, 50, 214,
        231, 282
    African American actors and audience, 51,
        130–31, 140, 152
    Boardwalk Empire, 5, 232, 282, 285
    Carnivàle, 230
    The Corner, 130–32
    Def Comedy Jam, 51, 130
    failures, 230–31
    Game of Thrones, 235, 281, 282

HBO (*cont.*)
   Generation Kill, 119, 207
   inception as cable subscription service, 47–48
   independence from advertisers, 85
   internal problems, 229, 231–32, 234, 236–38
   John from Cincinnati, 235–36
   The Larry Sanders Show, 50–51, 230
   Luck, 187, 233, 281, 282, 285
   Lucky Louie, 230, 231
   on-demand service, 203–4
   original-programming mission, 4, 12, 49–51,
      58, 229–30
   Oz, 57–58, 68
   personnel changes, 55–56, 229, 236–38, 281
   programming spectrum, 48–50, 281–83
   Sex and the City, 12, 58, 229
   Six Feet Under, 4, 60, 98–104, 107
   successful formula and signature attributes,
      96, 204–5, 212, 228–29
   successful runs, 14, 95–96, 229
   Tell Me You Love Me, 231
   Treme, 132, 142–43, 207–8, 279, 281
   True Blood, 107, 281–82
Hill, Walter, 181, 247
Hill Street Blues, 27–32, 171, 172–74
Homicide: A Year on the Killing Streets (Simon),
   117–20
Homicide: Life on the Street (television series),
   127–30, 175
Huggins, Roy, 39
Hutchison, Gennifer, 271

I'll Fly Away, 52–54, 65, 75

Jacquemetton, Andre and Maria, 252
James, Caryn, 154
Job, The, 228
John from Cincinnati, 235
Johnson, Clark, 129–30, 138–39, 141, 218, 223
Justified, 284

Kael, Pauline, 13–14
Kaplan, Bruce Eric, 101
Kecken, Joy Lusco, 136, 144
Kessler, Todd
   on Chase's primitive impulses, 88–89
   Damages, 12, 13, 166–67, 227
   The Sopranos, 164–66
Kolchak: The Night Stalker, 39–40
Kozoll, Michael, 27–28, 30
Krause, Peter, 100, 103–4

Landgraf, John, 86, 227, 268–69
Landress, Ilene, 25n, 69
Landsman, Jay, 110, 118, 120, 123
Larry Sanders Show, The, 50–51, 230
Leary, Denis, 228

Lehane, Dennis, 148
Levin, Jerry, 48
Levinson, Barry, 127, 128
Lewis, Jeffrey, 30, 172
Liguori, Peter
   on casting for *Rampart* (later *The Shield*), 219
   on debut of *The Shield,* 222–23
   decision to produce risky program, 217–18
   on male-focused programming, 13
   mission to transform FX, 213–15
   plea to advertisers for *The Shield,* 221
   on Tony Soprano character, 85
   work after departure from FX, 283
Liss, Ira, 248
Lombardo, Michael, 201, 230, 231, 232, 237
Lombardozzi, Domenick, 149, 150–51, 152,
   194–95
Long, Rob, 48
Luck, 187, 233, 281, 282, 285
Lucky Louie, 230, 231

Mad Men
   artistry and emotional intelligence, 260–63
   casting, 140, 249–51
   female characters, 5
   Golden Globe Award, 257
   HBO's rejection of, 239, 244
   pilot, 248–49, 252
   promotion strategy, 256
   story line, 59, 249
   writers' room, 252–56, 258–59
Mander, Jerry, 23–24
Mann, Michael, 282
Manos, James, Jr., 60–61, 72, 76, 93–94, 225
Mastras, George, 271
Mazzara, Glen, 225, 226, 284
McLarney, Terrence, 110, 118, 120, 123–24
McNutt, Myles, 282
Milch, David. *See also Deadwood*
   on cancellation of *Deadwood,* 233–34
   creative process, 176–77, 187–89
   on decline in influence of advertisers, 86–87
   early successes, 171
   Emmy awards, 171, 173
   failures, 174
   on future of original programming, 286
   health problems, 172, 177
   Hill Street Blues, 27–32, 171, 172–74
   John from Cincinnati, 235
   Luck, 187, 233, 281, 282, 285
   NYPD Blue, 171, 174–78
   on standard season length, 204–5
   unpredictability, 172, 173–74, 176
   on work at MTM, 32
   on writers' collaboration, 72–73
Mills, David, 113, 128–29, 175–76, 200
Minow, Newton, 22

MTM Enterprises
  creation of, 24
  creative freedom for writers, 26–27
  Hill Street Blues, 27–32, 171, 172–74
  influential dramas, 27
  St. Elsewhere, 31–32, 51

Naegle, Sue, 27, 237, 282
Nash Bridges, 215
NBC, 27–29, 30–31
Nevins, Sheila, 49
Nip/Tuck, 227
Noble, Nina K., 141, 199, 201–2
Northern Exposure, 51–52, 53–55, 73, 75
NYPD Blue, 171, 174–78

O'Connor, John J., 44
Off the Minnesota Strip, 43–44, 62–63
Oh, Grow Up, 97–98
Oliver, Nancy, 101
Overmyer, Eric, 127, 142, 144
Oz, 57–58, 68

Palmer, Tom, 252
Paltrow, Bruce, 31, 51
Patterson, John, 37–38, 39
PBS, 54, 284
Pelecanos, George
  on failure of *The Wire* season five, 204, 207
  on relationship between Simon and Burns, 144, 207
  on Simon's antiauthoritarianism, 138
  The Wire, 147–49, 193, 194, 195–96, 197–98, 207
Peranio, Vince, 142
Peters, Clarke, 150, 280
Pierce, Wendell, 150, 151, 280
pilots, functions and challenges of, 59–61
Playdon, Paul, 39–40
Plepler, Richard, 51, 231, 237
Polcsa, Juliet, 243
Poniewozik, James, 203
Post, Mike, 25–26, 43
Poul, Alan, 99, 100, 101, 103
Powers, Kate, 271
Price, Richard, 148–49, 281
Provenzano, Chris, 73, 252, 253, 255

Rampart. See *Shield, The*
Rebeck, Theresa, 176, 185–86
Reilly, Kevin
  on Albrecht's response to *The Sopranos* pilot, 69
  on Chase's ideas and views, 62, 64
  on Chernin's response to *The Shield* pilot, 220
  on HBO ratings in early years, 51
  mission to transform FX, 213–15

on reaction of advertisers to *The Shield,* 221
on risk in producing *Rampart* (later *The Shield*), 217–18
on *The Shield*'s Emmy prospects, 223
on unsuitability of *The Sopranos* for network television, 64
work after departure from FX, 283
Renzulli, Frank, 76–78, 91, 162–64
Rescue Me, 4, 105–6, 227–28
Rockford Files, The, 42–43, 73
Rosenbaum, Scott, 225
Royo, Andre, 150–52, 153, 196–97, 200
Ryan, Shawn. See also *Shield, The*
  early work, 215–16
  on future of original programming, 286
  Nash Bridges, 215
  on television as commercial venture, 224–25
  work after *The Shield,* 283

Sapan, Josh, 245–46
Saraceni, Mark, 76
Sassa, Scott, 96
Schnauz, Thomas, 266, 271, 275
Schneider, Andrew, 4, 32, 54, 158
Sex and the City, 12, 58, 229
Shield, The
  act-outs preceding commercial breaks, 224–25
  advertisers, 217, 220, 221
  antihero protagonist, 217, 226
  casting, 218–20, 227
  comparison with *The Wire,* 223–24
  debut following September 11 terrorist attacks, 221–23
  Emmy award, 223
  one-line story summary, 60
  pilot's risky ending, 217–18
  references to current events, 216–17, 226
  run-and-gun production style, 218
  writers' room, 225–26
showrunners
  institutionalized autocratic role, 30, 252
  power of, 8–9, 72–73, 148
  primitive impulses, 88
  script rewriting and writer credit, 258–59
Showtime
  Dexter, 6, 12
  Nurse Jackie, 281
  Weeds, 13, 268–69
Silverman, Fred, 27, 30–31
Simon, David. See also *Wire, The*
  antiauthoritarianism, 138
  argument as creative process for, 112–13, 133, 145
  blog, *The Audacity of Despair,* 279–80
  and Chase, compared, 111–12
  The Corner (book), 126–27

Simon, David (*cont.*)
　The Corner (miniseries), 130–32
　divorce and unhappiness, 136, 138
　Homicide (book), 117–20
　Homicide (television series), 127–30, 175
　as journalist, 111, 113–17, 124–25, 129, 205
　persuasive writing, 133–34, 200–201
　Treme, 132, 142–43, 207–8, 279, 281
　year-in-the-life book proposal, 192
Sirico, Tony, 68, 160
Six Feet Under, 4, 60, 98–104, 107
Solberg, John, 220–21
Soloway, Jill, 101–2
Sons of Anarchy, 226, 284
Sopranos, The
　antihero protagonist, 84–85, 89, 92–93
　characters foreshadowed in Chase's earlier
　　works, 43–44
　Chase's intention to end series, 157, 167–68
　"College" episode, 90–94
　cultural climate at debut of show, 87
　as cultural event, 154–57
　Emmy awards, 93–94, 96, 168
　Falco as Carmela character, 1, 68–69, 96,
　　168, 288
　final episode, 286–89
　Gandolfini as Tony character, 1–3, 17, 67–68,
　　69, 157, 288
　inspirations for characters, 35–36, 38,
　　62–63
　minimovie-like episodes, 90–91
　music, 83–84
　New Jersey setting, 15, 62, 65, 78, 90, 157
　opening credits, 15
　pilot, 64–70
　premiere, 78–79
　production costs, 158–59
　studio set and crew, 3–4
　title, 92
　writers' room, 27, 70, 74–78, 162–66, 168–70,
　　243–45
Sorcher, Rob, 245–48, 254, 270–71, 284
St. Elsewhere, 31–32, 51
Sterling, John, 120, 125, 192
Strauss, Carolyn
　approach to Ball with funeral home idea, 95,
　　96, 99
　on concept of antihero protagonist, 65
　disengaged executive manner, 232, 237, 268
　dismissal from HBO, 237–38
　move to executive-producer position, 281
　on viability of *The Wire,* 201
　on working environment at HBO, 58
　working relationship with Albrecht, 55,
　　57, 237
Sutter, Kurt, 225–26, 232
Sydnor, Marvin, 110, 123

Tartikoff, Brandon, 27–28
television. *See also* cable dramas
　advertisers' influence on content, 85–87
　cable transmission, 47
　Fin-Syn (Financial Interest and Syndication
　　Rules), 26, 32
　limitations of early technology, 21–22
　microwave-receiving dish, 47, 56
　movie actors working in, 227, 229, 285
　one-hour dramas on broadcast networks,
　　284–85
　reality programming, 32
　as reviled medium, 22–24
　subscription service, 4, 48
Tell Me You Love Me, 231
Third Golden Age of television. *See* cable
　dramas
Thorson, Karen, 198
Tinker, Grant, 24–27, 32, 230
Tinker, Mark, 176–77, 178, 185, 235
TNT, 268
Tolan, Peter, 228
Toll, John, 15–16
Treme, 132, 142–43, 207–8, 279, 281
True Blood, 107, 281–82

Van Patten, Tim, 156, 232
Van Zandt, Steven, 66–67

Wagner, Michael, 30
Walking Dead, The, 284
Walley-Beckett, Moira, 271, 273
Wayne, Christina, 246–48, 257, 270, 284
Weeds, 13, 268–69
Weiner, Matthew. See also *Mad Men*
　abrasive personality, 243–44
　autocratic showrunner style, 252,
　　254–55
　background and early work, 239–42
　credit for script rewriting, 258
　egoism and competitiveness, 256–59
　on pressure of showrunning, 160
　The Sopranos, 25n, 72–73, 159, 243–45
　working relationship with Chase, 244–45
Welles, Orson, 23
West, Dominic, 139, 150–51, 202
White, E. B., 23
White Shadow, The, 27
Williams, Michael K., 152–53
Winter, Terence
　Boardwalk Empire, 5, 232, 282, 285
　on Chase's authoritarianism, 162, 166
　on Chase's discontent, 167–68
　concern for Gandolfini, 17
　friendship with Renzulli, 162, 164
　on HBO's unreceptiveness to new ideas, 232
　on popularity of *The Sopranos,* 155

The Sopranos, 3, 25n, 162, 243
  on working with Weiner, 244–45
Wire, The
  basis in real-life Baltimore, 110–11, 126–27,
    136–38, 149–50
  camaraderie among actors, 150–51
  casting, 138–40
  after Colesberry's death, 199
  comparison with *The Shield,* 223–24
  DVD release of first three seasons, 203
  emotional toll on actors, 151–53, 196–97
  failure of season five, 205–8
  as Greek tragedy, 145–46
  media as seasonal theme, 200, 205–6
  on-demand previews, 203–4
  pitch for, 133–34, 200–201
  politics and drugs as seasonal themes,
    193–96
  production team and locations, 140–42
  public school system as seasonal theme,
    199–200
  reviews, 203–4, 206–7
  shortened season five, 204–5

  as social activism and entertainment, 134–35
  story outline, 59, 136–37
  theme changes each season, 192–94
  writers' room, 143–49, 193–94, 206, 207
Wolynetz, Vlad, 247
Wright, Craig, 88, 101, 102
writers
  creative freedom, 26–27, 284
  credit for scripts, 258–59
  deference to showrunner, 72–73, 148
  displacement by reality programming, 32
  disrespect for, 25–26
  praise for other writers, 94
  spec scripts, 101
  writers' rooms, 70–73
writer-showrunners. *See* showrunners

X-Files, The, 265–66

Yoshimura, James, 127, 129, 130

Zappa, Frank, 23
Zorzi, William, 110, 115–16, 143, 191